EVENING FOOD

Cafe Beaujolais

Christopher Kump

with

Margaret Fox

and

Marina Bear

photography by Faith Echtermeyer

TEN SPEED PRESS

Berkeley, California

photo by John Aquino

Dedicated to the memory of Peter Kump
my father, teacher, and inspiration

Ten Speed Press
P.O. Box 7123
Berkeley, California 94707
www.tenspeed.com

Distributed in Australia by Simon and Schuster Australia,
in Canada by Ten Speed Press Canada, in New Zealand by
Tandem Press, in South Africa by Real Books, in Southeast
Asia by Berkeley Books, and in the United Kingdom and
Europe by Airlift Books.

Cover and interior design by Fifth Street Design, Berkeley CA

Photography by Faith Echtermeyer, St. Helena CA

Library of Congress Cataloging-in-Publication Data
on file with the publisher

ISBN 0-89815-848-6

First printing, 1998

Printed in the United States of America

2 3 4 5 6 7 8 9 10 — 01 00 99 98

• C O N T E N T S •

Preface

by Margaret Fox

When Chris Kump came to Cafe Beaujolais to interview for the dinner chef position in the spring of 1984, I had no idea that hiring him would be, as they say, the beginning of a beautiful relationship. We traveled to Europe together that fall, bought a house in the midst of an antique fruit orchard in Mendocino the next year, acquired a total of four Labrador retrievers, got married, started a bed and breakfast in a twelfth-century Austrian castle, and adopted our baby daughter, Celeste. All in all, the fourteen years that have passed since our first meeting have gone by amazingly quickly.

Over the years, with the exhausting demands of the restaurant business and our personal lives, the one constant has been Chris's delicious food. I don't think he has ever made anything that tastes bad or even mediocre. When he's tired and hungry, he'll still take the time to assemble a satisfying meal. Me, I'll just sigh, eat a crunchy apple while reading a cookbook, and go to bed. I watch him carefully slicing a chicken breast and chiffonnading basil and realize that I would be haphazard, if not downright sloppy, in the interest of just getting the job done. His meticulous approach earns my respect and amazement every time. Readers of my books know that I tend to be spontaneous with my cooking. I wander into the walk-in and, if something looks good, I add it to my preparation. Chris is more thoughtful and consequently his food has an elegance I admire. His French training steers him in this direction while I careen, occasionally crossing over the culinary double line. The push and pull of our differing styles keeps the interest level up.

Throughout this book, I'll be adding my two cent's worth in the sidebars, sometimes an elaboration of Chris's explanation, sometimes a suggestion of how to simplify the recipe. It's what I do every day in the kitchen at Cafe Beaujolais to collaborate with Chris's approach, and I hope it helps you to cook your way through this collection of our favorite evening food dishes.

The staff at Cafe Beaujolais

Acknowledgments

So many people influence the development of a palate, the education of a chef, and the fruition of a cookbook, that my expressions of gratitude to all the sources of inspiration, support, and collaboration who helped me reach this point could fill its own volume. However, in the interest of publication in this millennium, my editor implored me to limit my effusions to the following list. These are the professional mentors, dedicated coworkers, dear friends, and family in my past and present life to whom I extend heartfelt thanks:

My boss, Margaret Fox, who hired me as a green young chef to head my first kitchen, and had the patience to remain supportive and encouraging, sticking with me during my first season as I struggled to learn the difference between cooking a good meal and successfully running a professional kitchen.

My wife, Margaret Fox (yes, the same one!), who has stood by my side professionally and personally, for fourteen crazy years of restaurateurship, sharing all the highs and lows one encounters in this business, juggling it all and more, and all the while maintaining a glass-is-half-full confident optimism that continually amazes and inspires me.

Our adorable baby daughter Celeste Isabella, the new goddess in my life.

Our lovable Labrador pack, Sanxi, Nini, Rhoni (& Willi in absentia), with whom I've shared countless walks in the woods and on the beach, where I inevitably come up with my best new menu ideas.

The food mentors I've known since childhood, especially Diana Kennedy and the late Simca Beck, dear friends of my dad's and mine, whom I admire as the two most wonderful cooks with the sharpest palates I've ever had the great pleasure to cook with personally.

My mom, Carolyn Davis MacKinnon, her husband Barry MacKinnon, my sister Amanda Jarque, my brother Cameron Burr, my stepfather Bob Burr, and all the rest of the extended Davis family, who served as enthusiastic tasters of my early forays in the kitchen when I would bring back ideas from my father's and my food trips in Europe.

The Wargnies-Touzés, my adoptive French family, with whom I lived during my apprenticeship in Paris, and who were so nurturing during that formative education in French language and cuisine.

Jacques Cagna and the chefs at his eponymous Parisian restaurant, where I apprenticed in the spring and summers of 1980 and 1981, especially saucier Taira Kurihara and poissonier "Monsieur Maigda," who taught me so much about fine restaurant cooking.

Chef Joël Robuchon and his sous chef Benoît Guichard, with whom I worked for an extremely intensive week—my second apprenticeship—at the Robert Mondavi Winery Great Chefs Program in the spring of 1988, and whose profound focus and uncompromising perfectionism were inspirational and remain unequaled in my experience since. They taught me that in the pursuit of great cuisine, there are no details—every aspect of a meal demands your full scrutiny.

Gary Jenanyan, coordinating chef at the Great Chefs Program and friend who, along with the rest of the program's staff, made my memorable time there possible.

Patricia Priano, longtime manager and wine buyer, and Gina Salamone, equally veteran bookkeeper at the restaurant, who I value as much for their steadfast friendship as for their help holding together the aspects of the business that Margaret and I simply can't.

John and Jill Stroup, our invaluable sous chef and pastry chef, a seemingly indefatigable couple who joined our management team just when Margaret's and my life seemed to become untenably complicated. Their industry and dedication have allowed us to start a bed and breakfast business in our recently-inherited Austrian castle, to enrich our personal lives with our daughter Celeste, and to finally complete this book project, all the while maintaining the quality of our food, a dedication that we hold dear.

Howard Knight, our equally tireless and committed dining room manager, whose consummate professionalism, genuine warmth, patience, and upbeat attitude in such a challenging job I am in awe of.

The rest of the wonderful staff of the restaurant and Brickery, past and present, too numerous to credit individually, yet who feel like extended family to me, who have put up with my own sometimes overly demanding style, and whose dedication has made possible the creation and success of our evening cuisine.

Sally-Jean Shepard, our good friend and publicist, who works assiduously to keep us on the map.

Anne, Harold, and Emily Fox, the most caring and supportive in-laws I could ever have hoped for.

Alice Waters, whom I admire endlessly for her outspoken, trailblazing commitment to full-flavored, healthful food through small-scale, sustainable agricultural and animal husbandry. Her inspiration has made our espousal of those same goals at Cafe Beaujolais that much easier to realize, and our customers that much more appreciative.

Our local organic farmers, especially Charles and Catharine Martin, Beth and Alan Spring, Homer and Lilian Drinkwater, Big River Nursery, and Bob and Marialice Canclini, without whose beautiful produce our food wouldn't be the same.

Bill Niman of Niman-Schell Ranch, whose high standards as a cattle rancher and pioneering move to serve as a meat packer and distributor for small family pork and lamb ranchers of equal integrity has enriched our menu.

Alan Scott, who designed and led a workshop to build our Brickery's bread oven, and Bill Brown and Darren Wilton, who helped enormously with the building and documentation of that project.

Nick Malgieri, head pastry instructor at Peter Kump's New York Cooking School, who rushed to my aid when I was struggling with sourdoughs in the Brickery, and the rest of the faculty at my dad's school, who enthusiastically taught several Beaujolais recipes at the school, and who were incredibly helpful to Margaret and me when we twice traveled to New York City to cook Cafe Beaujolais fare for the James Beard Foundation.

Hannes Sigwart, the gifted Austrian baker who generously shared his multiseed and grain bread recipe with us, a loaf that quickly became our Brickery's most popular bread.

Jake Zahavi and Sallie McConnell, whose capable stewardship (in our absence) of our fledgling castle bed and breakfast business has allowed us to keep the restaurant open and complete this book without losing that Tyrolean dream.

Kim Badenhop, Cyrus Kroninger, Julie Schreiber, and Jocelyn Sugrue, dinner chef alumni and meticulous recipe testers for all the recipes included in this book and those that are destined for its underground sequel (see Daughter of Evening Food, at the back of this book). They painstakingly verified that our restaurant-scale recipes, even the more complex specimens, could be and were in fact accurately transcribed for reproduction in a home kitchen.

The Bear family, John, Marina, and Mariah, who collaborated with me in the trenches, doggedly achieving the formidable task of transforming an unwieldy pile of many multipage recipes and multihour tapes of commentary into its current svelte form.

Introduction

This book has been several years in the making. We first saw it as a companion to *Morning Food*, whose 1990 publication it was supposed to follow shortly. Between that initial conception and today, much has happened at Cafe Beaujolais and in Margaret's and my life. At the restaurant, we made the reluctant decision in the fall of 1995 to stop serving breakfast and lunch, after eighteen years. Aficionados will be happy to know that Margaret's two cookbooks, *Cafe Beaujolais* and *Morning Food*, are still in print and provide lots of favorite recipes from our daytime menus during that period. With great humor, they also reveal the struggles of entrepreneurship in a difficult business and a remote area. Closing for these two meals, a necessity due to a changing market, was an especially hard decision for Margaret, a morning lark whose love of a good breakfast had been shared with dozens of employees and thousands of fans for nearly two decades. But it was her decision, and by making it, painful as it was, she showed the business acumen that helped her survive those eighteen years on the rollercoaster that is the restaurant business. And, we are still around to celebrate the twenty-first year of her ownership. So, if anything can console our disappointed breakfast and lunch customers, hopefully it is this explanation, together with the confession that we miss those meals dearly as well.

On a personal level, since the initial phase of considering, testing, and organizing recipes for this book, my father, Peter Kump, died. His picture is the frontispiece of this book. Without my father's influence and support, I quite likely never would have learned to cook, nor would I have learned to appreciate good food to such a degree. As he was fond of saying, eating is the second greatest sensual pleasure in life, and the one you will spend the most time doing over the course of your lifetime, so why not make the most of all those meals! Why not indeed? He introduced me to most of my food mentors, whether through their restaurants (Jacques Cagna, Michel Guérard, Joël Robuchon), their books (LeNôtre, Paula Wolfert), or their cooking in person (Simca Beck, James Beard, Diana Kennedy). When I was still in high school he arranged for my first cooking apprenticeships in Paris and jobs in Manhattan. He gave me my first knives, cookbooks, pasta machine, copper bowl, and whisk and taught me cooking techniques, how to plan a menu, and how to shop. But above all, he shared with me and instilled in me his passion for food.

When I'm asked how and why I became a chef, I answer that it grew out of a love of good food that I learned at a young age. All the rest followed naturally. This book is dedicated to my father's memory, and to the memory of the many, many joyous meals we shared together as I was growing up, from those served on elegant silver and linen-clad tables of Michelin-starred restaurants, to French scrambled eggs cooking on a rickety stove while camping on a rocky Corsican beach.

The recipes in this book are all dishes that have appeared on the dinner menu or at our nightly staff meal at the restaurant some time in the past thirteen years since I have been the dinner chef. A few have been on the menu almost continuously, such as the Toasted Goat Cheese Salad. Many have reappeared frequently, sometimes evolving in composition and/or presentation with each new appearance, and some, specifically some of the recipes from our New Year's Eve menus, have been served infrequently at the restaurant, or even just once. Such "shooting star" dishes were too costly to make or too labor-intensive to be kept on the menu for long.

Fortunately, the slow birth of this volume has coincided with ethnic ingredients becoming more readily available in markets than they were when we first tested these recipes. So don't be intimidated by those calling for huitlacoche, achiote, or galangal if these foods are new to you. With a few trips to specialty and ethnic markets, you can easily stock your pantry with everything needed for the dishes in this book.

My approach to cooking, reflected in our evening food at Cafe Beaujolais, was also shaped over many years of meals and conversations with my father. Here are some thoughts I would like to share.

As a responsible cook, you can never taste your own food enough. A good cook is above all else a good eater, a gourmand passionate about discovering, indulging, and celebrating the sensuality of the palate. If you don't feel this way about the food you eat, you won't about the food you prepare for others, and if the two don't overlap, you're wasting your time in the kitchen.

When planning a menu, keep in mind the rule that first and last impressions in a meal often overshadow whatever comes in between. I've had many a decent meal marred by a lousy dessert. And a spectacular appetizer will make me more magnanimous towards a plainer entrée. Consequently, when I prepare a menu, I devote extra energy and attention to its opening and closing dishes.

When thinking about food combinations and plate presentations, remember that flavor is king! I never conceive a new dish solely because of how it will look when presented, let alone how it will sound on the menu. Still, for an important meal, I will sketch the plate presentations of each dish ahead of time for our cooks to review; that way, the presentation is not a hurried last-minute decision, slowing down service. The look and description of a dish are always exercises to be performed only once the flavors are established. When you go out to dinner and the plates look beautiful, but the food isn't properly seasoned, or the taste and texture combinations are unsuccessful, you'll be disappointed. If, by contrast, the flavors are wonderful but the presentation is a bit plain, you'll still be content. Of course, if the meal succeeds in both look and taste, you'll be jubilant. The palate should never be neglected while the eye is being seduced.

Stylistically, I vacillate between the stick-to-the-ribs nurturing experience on the one hand and the religious dining experience on the other. In the former mode, I try to woo with comfort and nostalgia; in the latter, I want to wow with an intense symphony of flavor. I like to cook in both styles because they reflect how I think most of us like to eat: a lifetime of comfort food punctuated by great moments of intoxicatingly sublime food. For food enthusiasts, always eating in one mode to the exclusion of the other would be spiritually and aesthetically incomplete, a gastronomic yang missing its yin. In fact, I find the combination of these styles a font of inspiration and I develop many dishes by blending elements of homey and haute.

Since our offerings evolve and change with the seasons and with our evolution as eaters and chefs, we develop new recipes all the time. In a surprising turn of events, I recently inherited a twelfth-century country castle in the Austrian Tyrol, and it has become a second business as well as a second home. In the course of establishing the castle as a bed-and-breakfast inn, we have developed a fondness for the region's rustic cuisine and ethereal breads and pastries. Many Austrian specialties have appeared on the menu in the past few years, and the country's culinary inspiration will surely continue to add to our ever-expanding recipe box. We hope this cookbook captures the experience of eating with us. We also invite you to dine with us in person at Cafe Beaujolais on the beautiful Northern California coast.

APPETIZERS

• APPETIZERS •

Seared Sea Scallops with Black Chanterelles,
Coconut Milk, and Chervil / 4

Fire-Roasted Stuffed Poblano Chile
with Achiote Sauce / 6

Sautéed Duck Foie Gras with Garlic Confit Purée
and either Gooseberry–Red Currant Sauce
or Huckleberry Sauce / 9

Marinated and Sautéed Prawns with Pumpkin Seed
and Chipotle Sauces (à la Diana Kennedy) / 12

Rosemary Sea Scallop Skewers with a Fig,
Fried Polenta, and Shredded Radicchio / 15

Salmon Cooked on the Plate
with Mustard, Horseradish, and Dill / 18

Sea Scallop Ceviche / 19

Roasted Eggplant Tapenade Tart / 20

Oysters on the Half Shell
with Two Dipping Sauces / 23

Spicy Lamb Brochettes with Red Lentil Sauce
and Cucumber Raita / 25

Chicken and Goat Cheese Ravioli / 28

Rabbit, Chanterelle, and Leek Risotto / 31

Kale Spaetzle / 34

Crab and Shrimp Ravioli
in Hot and Sour Broth / 36

We often include on
the menu the name of
the ranch that our
meat comes from,
because we want peo-
ple to know we're tak-
ing the time to find the
best-quality ingredients
possible—the ones that
are the freshest and
the least adulterated.
Day-boat scallops are
that kind of product.
New England fishermen
go out on their boats in
the morning and col-
lect as many scallops as
they can in one day,
returning that night
with their catch. The
scallops are flown cross-
country to San
Francisco and we get
them trucked up to us
at Cafe Beaujolais the
next day. Scallops har-
vested and distributed
with this commitment
to freshness are also
referred to as "dry-
pack" because they are
packed and shipped
dry—that is, without
any additives to mask
off odors and flavors
associated with aging.
The more common way
to commercially harvest
and distribute scallops
in this country is for
boats to go out for a
week or so at a time,
with refrigeration or
freezing facilities
onboard. There the
scallops are washed
with a chlorine-based
solution to preserve
them and packed in a
(continued on page 5)

Seared Sea Scallops
with Black Chanterelles, Coconut Milk, and Chervil

Makes 4 to 6 servings

Sauce

Several large sprigs chervil

3 to 4 tablespoons dried black chanterelles
(or 1 to 1½ cups fresh, if available)

2 cups canned coconut milk

Scallops

1 pound medium sea scallops, preferably day-boat
caught and dry-packed (cut in half horizontally, if large)
trimmed of small, tough side muscle

Fine sea salt and freshly ground pepper to taste

Reserved chanterelles with minced chervil

1½ to 2 cups reserved coconut mushroom sauce

1 to 2 tablespoons unsalted butter (optional)

Fish sauce to taste (see Glossary)

Reserved chervil leaves, for garnish

To make the sauce, separate the chervil leaves from the stems and reserve both leaves and stems. Combine the mushrooms, coconut milk, and chervil stems in a small saucepan. Bring the mixture to a simmer, cover, remove from the heat, and infuse for 15 minutes. Strain through a fine-mesh sieve, pushing down hard on mushrooms with a small ladle to extract all of the juice. Discard the chervil stems. Strain the milk through a piece of damp cheesecloth and set aside.

Remove the mushrooms from the sieve and wash them thoroughly in sever-al changes of water to remove the coconut milk and any grit. Pick them over to remove any twigs, needles, or leaves, and tear any large mushrooms into small-er pieces. Place the mushrooms in a medium bowl.

Pick through the chervil leaves and set aside 1 nice leaf for every scallop (or half of a scallop if they are large). Place the leaves in an airtight container and set aside. Mince the remaining chervil leaves (you should have about 1 to 2 tablespoons) and toss with the cleaned mushrooms. Set aside with the chervil leaves and coconut sauce.

To make the scallops, heat a large nonstick sauté pan until it is just smok-ing. Meanwhile, rinse and thoroughly dry the scallops and season them lightly on both sides with salt and pepper. Place the scallops, flat-side down, in the smoking-hot pan. Allow them to sear for 60 to 90 seconds, or until they are a rich caramel brown color on the bottom. When they are nicely browned, turn off the heat, add the chanterelles with minced chervil and coconut mushroom sauce, and immediately cover, shaking the pan to loosen the scallops. Steam the scallops for 30 to 60 seconds. Remove the lid and transfer the scallops to a warm bowl while you finish the sauce.

Add the butter to the pan with the sauce, swirling the pan until the butter is incorporated. Season the sauce with a little fish sauce (be careful, it's very salty!), then divide the sauce and mushrooms evenly among warm, clean scallop shells or shallow soup bowls. Nestle the reserved scallops attractively among the mushrooms in the shells or bowls with their browned side facing up. Garnish each scallop with a whole chervil leaf and serve immediately.

Note: To get more use out of the mushrooms, they can be infused a second time before cleaning to make more sauce; keep in mind, however, that any extra sauce or extra coconut milk will last only 2 to 3 days refrigerated before turning sour. To keep opened coconut milk or sauce longer, you can freeze it. After thawing, it needs to be reboiled and blended in a blender (or with a handheld immersion blender) before using.

saline solution to plump them. The resulting scallops look white and juicy and remain odorless (actually they have a mild "chlorinated" smell) for two weeks or longer. Unfortunately, they also taste bland and watery. If you make the effort to shop for day-boat, dry-pack sea scallops instead, you will be rewarded with the true taste of scallops, which is deliciously sweet and briny.

The poblano chile is the traditional fresh pepper used in chile rellenos and many other Mexican dishes. In California and Baja California, it is often sold under the name pasilla pepper, which can be confusing because the true pasilla chile is the dried form of a different pepper altogether. Poblano chiles vary in size: they can be as large or occasionally larger than a typical bell pepper, but usually they are slightly smaller. They are distinguished by their dark green, shiny skin, thin flesh, and pointed tip. Their spiciness can vary considerably, so be careful when cleaning them, or you may find your fingers—and any other parts of your body that you touch with those fingers—burning for some time afterward. When we have many chiles to prepare at the restaurant, we wear rubber gloves to protect against such afterburn. While cooked poblanos are less spicy than serrano or jalapeño chiles, they can still be quite hot. If you or your guests don't enjoy spicy foods, substitute bell or Anaheim peppers in this dish. When shopping for poblano chiles to roast and stuff,

(continued on page 7)

Fire-Roasted Stuffed Poblano Chiles
with Achiote Sauce

Makes 6 servings

6 medium-large poblano chiles

4 cups (about 5 potatoes) roughly chunked yellow new potatoes, such as yellow Finn

1 tablespoon plus ¾ teaspoon fine sea salt

½ cup finely chopped white onion

1 tablespoon canola oil

1 tablespoon finely chopped fresh epazote

2 cups (8 ounces) crumbled feta or fresh goat cheese or grated Cheddar, Muenster, or Monterey jack

1½ cups Achiote Sauce (recipe follows)

3 tablespoons coarsely chopped cilantro, for garnish

To roast the chiles, put them directly in or on top of the flame of a gas stove burner or in the fire of a barbecue. (If you don't have any live flame available, roast the chiles as close to the broiler as possible or directly on top of an electric burner.) Leave the peppers in the fire just long enough to char their skins black all over; charring about 75 to 80 percent of the skin is usually sufficient since the steam will help loosen the rest. Turn the peppers with metal tongs to expose all sides to the heat source. Try not to leave the peppers too long on any side or their thin flesh will overcook. It usually takes only a few minutes to sufficiently char the chiles' skins for easy peeling; however, the exact time will depend on the intensity of your heat source and the size and shape of your peppers. (If the blackened skin turns white, it is becoming over-roasted.) Immediately transfer the hot, charred chiles to any container that can be closed—a paper bag, plastic container, or plastic bag, or even a large glass jar—to trap the chiles' steam for at least 5 to 10 minutes. Allow chiles to steam until they have cooled enough to handle before attempting to peel them.

While the chiles are steaming and cooling, make the filling and the Achiote Sauce. Put the potatoes in a saucepan filled with 1 quart of water (to cover) and 1 tablespoon of the salt. Bring to a boil, then reduce heat and simmer until tender, about 10 to 15 minutes. Drain the potatoes in a colander and allow them to cool slightly. Meanwhile, sauté the onions in the oil with the remaining ¾ teaspoon salt and the epazote for 2 minutes to soften them slightly. Remove the pan from heat and set aside.

Coarsely chop the potatoes and then place them in a medium bowl. Add the onion mixture and the cheese and mix together. Taste and correct seasoning with more salt if needed.

Wearing rubber gloves, remove the charred chile skins by rubbing them gently under running water or while dipping the peppers in a bowl of water. Next, remove the seeds from the chiles by slitting them along one side with a small knife from "shoulder" to tip, leaving the stem intact, and pulling the seeds out from the side with the small knife and your gloved fingers. (If you do this without gloves on, be very careful not to touch your eyes, nose, or mouth with your fingers for several hours or you will be very sorry.) When most of the seeds are removed from the peppers, stuff each of them with about $1/3$ to $1/2$ cup of the filling, depending on their size. The chiles may be prepared ahead to this point and kept refrigerated for 2 to 3 days.

When ready to serve, preheat the oven to 425° (a toaster oven works well for this) and warm serving plates. Warm the Achiote Sauce gently on low heat in a pan. Put the chiles in a metal pan and bake for 5 minutes, or until the filling is hot and the cheese is slightly melted. Ladle 3 to 4 tablespoons of the sauce onto each warm plate. Remove the chiles from the oven and transfer them to the plates. Sprinkle with cilantro and serve.

select ones that are not too contorted; their skins will char more evenly and they will be easier to peel and stuff.

Achiote Sauce

Makes 1½ cups

1 tablespoon achiote paste (see Glossary)
¼ cup Seville Orange Juice (recipe follows)
1¼ cups Roasted Tomato Sauce (recipe follows)
¼ teaspoon fine sea salt, or to taste

To make the sauce, whisk the achiote paste into the orange juice in a small saucepan. Add the tomato sauce. Bring to a simmer, whisking constantly. Pass through a fine-mesh sieve to make sure all of the achiote paste is dissolved and the sauce is smooth. Add salt.

Seville Orange Juice

Makes 1⅓ cups

⅓ cup freshly squeezed lime juice
½ cup freshly squeezed grapefruit juice
½ cup freshly squeezed orange juice
2½ teaspoons grated grapefruit zest

Seville oranges are native to the Yucatán. This is chef Diana Kennedy's formula for approximating their very acidic, slightly bitter taste; to make it, just mix all of the ingredients together and refrigerate until needed.

Roasted Tomato Sauce

Makes approximately 4 cups

2¼ pounds (about 6 to 8 medium) red, ripe tomatoes (as
  soft and squishy as you can find)
Fine sea salt to taste

Wash the tomatoes. Place them in a large roasting pan in a single layer. Place
the pan under the broiler or in a very hot oven—500° to 550°—and broil for 10
to 20 minutes, until lightly charred on top. If by the time they char, the tomatoes are not very soft and have not exuded much juice, put the pan in the oven
on a lower shelf and cook until they reach this point. (This will only be necessary if you have an exceptionally hot broiler.)

 Remove the tomatoes from the broiler or oven and allow them to cool slightly. Place the tomatoes in a blender and purée, adding their exuded juice as needed for a fairly smooth, thick purée. (If the tomatoes are still at all warm during
this procedure, remove the center disc in the blender lid to allow steam to
escape. Hold the lid tightly with a kitchen towel or oven mitt, and start the
blender on a low speed. Flicking the switch on and off quickly several times at
first will help prevent steam pressure from building up.) Stir in salt. If the skins
are still noticeably present, blend the sauce a little longer and/or pass it through
a sieve. If the sauce is watery, reduce it in a pan on top of the stove to thicken
it slightly, stirring continuously to prevent scorching. Store in the refrigerator
for up to 5 days, or freeze for up to 2 to 3 months.

Sautéed Duck Foie Gras with Garlic Confit Purée
and either Gooseberry–Red Currant Sauce or Huckleberry Sauce

Makes 4 to 6 servings

1 fresh duck foie gras, A or B grade, approximately 1 to
  1¼ pounds

Fine sea salt and freshly ground pepper to taste

Freshly grated nutmeg

½ to ⅔ cup Garlic Confit Purée (recipe follows)

¾ to 1 cup Gooseberry–Red Currant Sauce or
  Huckleberry Sauce (recipes follow)

4 to 6 fresh basil leaves or chervil sprigs, for garnish

1 to 1½ cups mixed gooseberries and red currants, or
  huckleberries (depending on sauce), for garnish

Trim the foie gras of any green blemishes and cut ½- to ⅝-inch-thick scallops diagonally from each lobe with a thin, sharp knife dipped in warm water. Pair a slice from the large lobe with a slice or two from the small lobe to create each serving, which weighs 2½ to 3 ounces (or more if you can afford it!). Season foie gras scallops on both sides with the sea salt, pepper, and a pinch of the nutmeg. Refrigerate, covered, until ready to cook.

Make the Garlic Confit Purée and the sauce. In a saucepan, warm ½ cup to ⅔ cup of the Garlic Confit Purée and ¾ cup to 1 cup of the sauce, separately, over low heat. Set aside, covered, to keep warm while sautéing the foie gras.

When you are ready to serve, heat a nonstick frying pan to medium-hot (not smoking-hot, but the foie gras should sizzle when it hits the pan). Add the foie gras to the pan and cook for 1 to 2 minutes on each side, depending on the thickness and pan temperature, until the slices are lightly browned on both sides and just soft when pressed with a fork. Do not overcook the slices or they will shrink to nothing! Meanwhile, spread the garlic purée on the centers of warmed appetizer plates with the back of a soup spoon to form a circular bed for the foie gras. Carefully ladle or spoon some of the warm sauce around the garlic purée. As soon as the foie gras scallops are cooked, immediately remove them from the pan to paper towels to absorb any excess fat, then place one larger piece and one smaller piece on the center of each plate. Garnish the foie gras with a small basil leaf or chervil sprig. Decorate with gooseberries and red currants or huckleberries, sprinkling them in an attractive pattern around the sauce and on top of the foie gras. Serve immediately.

Foie gras, because of its price and richness, is meant for special occasions. But when the time is right, there's nothing else quite like it. Until about fifteen or twenty years ago, few people outside of southwestern France had tasted foie gras served any way other than cold in a terrine or pâté. In fact, most Americans I've talked to who aren't cooks still identify foie gras as pâté, if they've heard of it at all. Fortunately, with the relatively recent establishment of foie gras farms in upstate New York and Northern California, foie gras is no longer uncommon on upscale American restaurant menus, though its price remains high. And with its widespread availability has come widespread experimentation with cooking technique and presentation. It is now more common to be served duck foie gras sautéed and served warm, the preferred technique in southwestern France, than it is to see goose foie gras baked in a terrine and served cold, the classic technique of haute cuisine. Not that a good terrine of foie gras is anything short of heaven, but a warm sauté is unquestionably less labor-intensive.

(continued on page 10)

This recipe, with Gooseberry–Red Currant Sauce, is adapted from two warm foie gras dishes published by André Daguin, chef and proprietor of the Michelin two-star Hôtel de France, in Auch, in the heart of French foie gras country. The Huckleberry Sauce version is my own Mendocino-esque variation.

Look for fresh gooseberries and red currants in specialty produce markets and farmers' markets in June; huckleberries in August and September. The gooseberry is an intriguingly tart-sweet old-fashioned berry about the size and color of a green grape. They have long been popular in France and especially so in England. Though they had fallen out of fashion for a while in this country, they are slowly becoming available again. If you cannot find any, substitute tart green grapes, preferably seedless ones.

Garlic Confit Purée

1 cup garlic cloves, unpeeled (approximately 4 heads)
1 cup water
½ teaspoon sea salt
¼ teaspoon sugar
1 cup duck fat (or substitute light olive oil to cover)
2 whole cloves or allspice berries
Several sprigs of thyme
1 bay leaf
6 to 8 tablespoons milk
Freshly ground white pepper to taste (optional)

Combine the garlic, water, salt, and sugar in a small saucepan, bring to a boil, and then reduce heat and simmer for 10 minutes. Drain the garlic cloves and peel, then return them to the saucepan. Add the duck fat to cover along with the cloves, thyme, and bay leaf. Cook very slowly until very tender, but not browned, about 10 to 15 minutes. Drain the liquid from the pan, remove and discard the herbs, and purée the garlic in a food processor (the duck fat may be refrigerated and reused). Pass the garlic purée through a sieve and return it to the saucepan. Add the milk and pepper and bring to a simmer, reducing the liquid slightly to the desired consistency over low heat. Whisk occasionally to avoid scorching.

Gooseberry–Red Currant Sauce

½ cup (about 12) gooseberries
¼ cup fresh red currants
1 tablespoon confectioners' sugar
4 teaspoons sherry vinegar, good red wine vinegar,
  or 2 tablespoons verjus (see Glossary)
½ cup late-harvest Gewürztraminer, Riesling,
  or Sauternes
1 cup reduced poultry stock (preferably duck)

Combine the gooseberries, currants, and sugar in a small saucepan over medium heat, stirring until the sugar caramelizes on the berries. Deglaze with the vinegar and reduce until very syrupy and almost dry, scraping to dissolve any caramelized sugar bits. Add the wine and reduce by three quarters, or until sauce is a syrupy consistency. Add the stock and reduce by one third to one half, or until the sauce is thick enough to lightly coat a spoon. Strain the grapes and currants through a chinois or fine-mesh sieve, pushing the fruit down hard to extract all of the juices. Set the sauce aside until ready to serve.

(If you like, after sautéing the foie gras scallops, you can pour off the fat in the pan, wipe out any blackened residue with a paper towel, and deglaze the pan with a dash of late-harvest Gewürztraminer and then the sauce.)

Huckleberry Sauce

2 tablespoons sugar

1 generous cup (5 ounces) huckleberries, fresh or frozen
and thawed

1½ teaspoons cassis

½ teaspoon sherry vinegar

1 tablespoon ruby port

2 cups reduced duck stock (preferably with good body
from the inclusion of pig's feet and/or other gelatinous
bones; if only regular chicken stock is available, reduce
3 quarts to 2 cups)

Fine sea salt and freshly ground pepper to taste

1 to 2 teaspoons cornstarch dissolved in 1 tablespoon
cold water, if needed

In a small saucepan, caramelize the sugar over medium heat, stirring constantly. When it is rich golden brown, add the huckleberries, cassis, vinegar, and port. Cover, remove from heat, and infuse for 5 minutes. Return the pan to the heat, stirring to dissolve any hard caramel. When all hard bits are dissolved, simmer for 2 minutes, and then add the stock. Simmer gently for 1 hour, skimming as needed.

Pass the sauce through a fine chinois or sieve, pressing down hard on the berries with a small ladle or firm spatula to extract all the liquid. Return the sauce to a small saucepan and reduce to 1 cup, or until the desired flavor and consistency are reached. Season with salt and pepper (it may not need salt if stock is very reduced). Test for thickness by pouring a little on a plate and tilting the plate. If it is thin and runny, thicken it by whisking in a little cornstarch dissolved in water while the sauce is boiling, until it acquires enough body to give it a slightly syrupy consistency (it should move slowly around the plate like warm maple syrup). Set the sauce aside until ready to use.

Marinated and Sautéed Prawns
with Pumpkin Seed and Chipotle Sauces (à la Diana Kennedy)

Makes 6 servings

24 or 30 medium-large prawns (16 to 20 per pound), fresh or frozen and thawed

1¾ cups water

½ teaspoon sea salt

1½ to 2 cups Chipotle Sauce (recipe follows)

1¼ cups Pumpkin Seed Sauce (recipe follows)

½ cup sour cream, for garnish

6 sprigs cilantro, for garnish

Shell the prawns, reserving the shells and leaving the tails intact. Devein the prawns if necessary, and partially butterfly them to allow the marinade and sauce to penetrate. Set aside. To make shrimp stock for the Pumpkin Seed Sauce, combine the shells with the water to cover and salt and simmer for 15 minutes. Strain through a fine-mesh sieve, pressing down on the shells with a small ladle or firm spatula to extract all of the liquid. Remove and discard the shells and reduce the liquid to 1¼ cups. Remove the pan from the heat and set aside.

Prepare the Chipotle Sauce and the Pumpkin Seed Sauce.

Put the shrimp in a large bowl and toss with all but about ½ cup of the Chipotle Sauce. Cover and allow to marinate for several hours at room temperature or refrigerated overnight.

Purée the remaining Chipotle Sauce in a blender until smooth. If you have a couple of small plastic squirt bottles, like the ones ketchup and mustard come in at diners, fill one with the puréed Chipotle Sauce and one with the sour cream (thinned with a little bit of heavy cream or water to make it squirtable). Pour 2 to 3 tablespoons of the warm Pumpkin Seed Sauce onto the center of each plate and tilt the plate to coat it evenly with the sauce. With the sour cream-filled squirt bottle, make a zigzag or other attractive design around the border of the Pumpkin Seed Sauce, interspersed with red Chipotle Sauce accent dots. If you're not feeling artistic or lack squirt bottles, spoon a dollop of sour cream in the center of each plate and drizzle the Chipotle Sauce lightly over it. When the plates are decorated, put them in a low (200°) oven to warm while you cook the shrimp.

Cook the shrimp gently for a couple of minutes in their marinade in a covered nonstick sauté pan over medium heat, thinning the sauce with a little water or white wine if it seems too thick. As soon as they are barely cooked, transfer the shrimp to the warmed, decorated plates with all of the tails facing the same direction. If serving 4 shrimp per person, try standing one of them upright in the center of the plate. Garnish with a sprig of cilantro in the center of each plate and serve immediately.

Chipotle Sauce

Makes 2 to 2½ cups

3 tablespoons canola oil
1 cup chopped white onion
¼ teaspoon fine sea salt, or to taste
2 teaspoons minced garlic (2 medium cloves)
⅓ cup dry white wine
½ teaspoon dried oregano (preferably Mexican), toasted
1 small canned chipotle chile
1½ cups Roasted Tomato Sauce (page 8)

Heat the oil in a small saucepan over medium heat. Add the onions and salt and cook until soft, 3 to 5 minutes. Add the garlic and cook for another minute, stirring, until fragrant but not browned. Add the white wine and oregano, bring to a boil, and simmer for 1 minute. Purée the chile and tomato sauce in a blender until smooth. Add the purée to the pan and return the mixture to a boil. Remove the pan from the heat and allow the sauce to cool before using. Keep refrigerated for up to 3 days, or freeze for up to a month.

Chipotle chiles, the smoked version of the jalapeño pepper, are usually sold cooked and canned in adobo sauce and are available in Mexican markets and most supermarkets.

Pumpkin Seed Sauce

Makes about 1¹/₂ cups

½ cup (2 ounces) hulled pumpkin seeds (see Note)

1¼ cups reserved shrimp stock

6 to 8 sprigs cilantro (stems and leaves)

1 large serrano chile or 1 small jalapeño pepper

⅓ cup coarsely chopped white onion

6 tablespoons canned coconut milk, crème fraîche,
  or heavy whipping cream

¼ teaspoon fine sea salt, or to taste

Toast the pumpkin seeds very lightly in a heavy, dry skillet, stirring until they begin to swell and pop. Do not let them brown. Allow the seeds to cool completely, then grind them finely in two or three batches in an electric spice mill.

Purée the ground pumpkin seeds with the shrimp stock, cilantro, chile, and onion in a blender. When the mixture is smooth, pass it through a fine-mesh sieve and reblend anything strained out. When the mixture is completely smooth, cook in a saucepan for 5 to 10 minutes over medium heat, whisking frequently until thickened. Stop just short of boiling. Add the coconut milk and salt, and heat again, whisking constantly until thickened. If the sauce becomes grainy, blend it again in a blender or with a handheld immersion mixer. Allow the sauce to cool slightly, and then pour it onto plates while it is still slightly warm—it will be much easier to cover the plate evenly. The sauce keeps for several days refrigerated, and it may be frozen successfully, but it may have to be reheated to return it to pourable consistency. If frozen (or overheated), it may need to be reblended to make it smooth.

Note: Hulled pumpkin seeds are available in Mexican markets and some health food stores. Be sure to get the green, hulled seeds, not the white, unhulled version.

Rosemary Sea Scallop Skewers
with a Fig, Fried Polenta, and Shredded Radicchio

Makes 4 servings

Fried Polenta

3 cups water

1 teaspoon fine sea salt

1 teaspoon grated orange zest

¾ plus ⅓ cup polenta

1½ tablespoons unsalted butter

Cornmeal for dredging

Dressing

4 ounces pancetta, cut into ¼-inch lardons

¼ cup balsamic vinegar

¼ teaspoon fine sea salt

1½ teaspoons minced garlic (1 large or 2 small cloves)

½ cup fruity olive oil

Freshly ground pepper to taste

16 medium sea scallops (about 1 pound), preferably day-boat caught and dry-packed, trimmed of small, tough side muscle

Eight 3- to 3½-inch-long rosemary sprigs (pick sprigs with about 2 inches of woody older stem before the softer new growth tip)

Fine sea salt and freshly ground pepper to taste

4 large, ripe, fresh figs, such as the green-skinned Calimyrna variety

1 small head radicchio

1 tablespoon chopped fresh flat-leaf parsley

To prepare the polenta: Bring the water, salt, and orange zest to a boil in a small saucepan. Add the polenta and cook over medium heat, stirring occasionally, for about 10 minutes, until the polenta is cooked through and is the consistency of thick porridge.

Meanwhile, lightly butter or oil the bottom of a 9-inch loaf pan. Stir the unsalted butter into the warm polenta, and then pour it into the loaf pan. It should be about 1 inch deep. Smooth the surface and place in the refrigerator to cool.

There's a French tradition that we've done from time to time, of giving everyone a little taste of something at the very start of the meal. It's a nice touch. It's elegant. It's a way of saying that we consider you a guest, not just a customer. Restaurants in the two- and three-star category in France have been doing this for a while. The French call them *amuse gueules* or *amuse bouches*, which basically translates as palate ticklers. They're offered just as you're given the menu or sometimes even before. It's usually a little tart-let or a small cheese puff or something like that. A touch of class.

We were eating a meal at La Folie, a very elegant French restaurant in San Francisco, and the chef sent out a complimentary taste teaser at the start of the meal. It was scallops skewered on a rosemary sprig. I thought, "Ah, that's a very clever idea." It worked perfectly—the scallop picked up the rosemary flavor and the rosemary provided a fun little handle, the perfect finger food. We took that idea home and played around with it, and now we're doing a version of it as part of this appetizer.

To prepare the dressing: In a dry skillet over medium heat, cook the pancetta lardons slowly to render their fat and brown them. Stir them often enough to keep them from burning. When they are richly browned but not too dark, pour the contents of the skillet through a sieve into a small bowl, reserving both the lardons and the rendered fat. (Don't bother washing out the skillet—you will be using it soon to fry the polenta.) Combine the lardons in a small saucepan with the vinegar, salt, garlic, oil, and 1 teaspoon of the rendered fat. Taste for seasoning, adding pepper as desired, and set aside.

When the polenta is cool and set, run a knife around its edge and bang the loaf pan upside down on the counter to unmold it. Cut eight $\frac{1}{4}$-inch-wide strips from the polenta loaf, cutting crosswise so each piece is about 4 inches long. Cut these strips in half to yield sixteen $\frac{1}{4}$-inch-thick rectangles that are 1 inch wide by 2 inches long. Dredge the slices in cornmeal and pat off any excess. Heat half of the remaining rendered pancetta fat in the skillet and fry the polenta pieces over medium heat until they are golden brown and crisp on both sides. Drain the fried polenta on paper towels and set aside.

To prepare the skewers: Strip the needles off the bottom 2 inches of the rosemary sprigs (the woody ends), reserving the needles. Skewer the scallops horizontally on the sprigs, using two per sprig, so their flat sides are exposed. Season the scallops lightly with salt and pepper and set aside.

Cut the tips (stem ends) off the figs, stand them upright, and cut them in thirds vertically, tip to tail, about three quarters of the way through. Don't cut through to the base! Set aside.

Cut the head of radicchio lengthwise into quarters. Remove the core from each quarter and discard. Shred the radicchio thinly crosswise, as cabbage is cut for coleslaw. Place $1\frac{1}{3}$ cups of the radicchio in a bowl, cover and refrigerate until you are ready to assemble plates. Any leftover radicchio can be saved for another use.

Finely mince enough of the reserved rosemary needles to yield a scant teaspoon. Mix with the chopped parsley and set aside. The recipe may be prepared in advance to this point.

When you are ready to cook the scallops, rewarm the dressing slightly on the stove and heat the polenta rectangles for a few minutes on a metal pan in the oven until they begin to sizzle (a toaster oven or convection oven works well for this).

Heat the remaining pancetta fat in a skillet until it is almost smoking. Have a lid that fits the skillet on hand. Sear the scallops, flat side down, for 60 to 90 seconds over high heat until well browned on their bottom side. Remove the skillet from the heat, add about a half cup of water to the pan, and immediately cover to finish cooking the scallops with steam. Keep covered for only 30 to 45 seconds. The scallops are done when they are white and slightly springy to the touch but still a little soft at the center. Uncover the pan as soon as the scallops are done or they will overcook and become rubbery.

Place $\frac{1}{3}$ cup of shredded radicchio in a mound at the top half of each of 4 plates. Below the radicchio on each plate, assemble a diamond-shaped platform out of 4 warm polenta rectangles, overlapping their ends like the flaps of a cardboard box. Set a fig atop each polenta platform, gently opening it up to resemble a flower or starfish. Transfer 2 scallop skewers to each plate, browned side up, resting them in a V shape on top of the radicchio with the tips of the rosemary sprigs meeting at the center of the plate to form the point of the V. Whisk the warm dressing well to blend and ladle it over everything, trying to apportion the pancetta lardons evenly. Sprinkle with the chopped parsley-rosemary mixture and serve.

Note: This recipe uses one quarter to one third of the polenta loaf. You can cut and fry the extra pieces to snack on, or use the loaf for another purpose. It will keep for 4 to 5 days refrigerated, or it can be frozen for up to 2 months. For a quick, no-frills meal, try serving the leftover polenta warmed, with Roasted Tomato Sauce (page 8).

Salmon Cooked on the Plate
with Mustard, Horseradish, and Dill

Makes 4 servings

12 to 14 ounces fresh salmon fillet, skinned and boned
¼ cup fruity olive oil or melted unsalted butter
Salt and freshly ground white pepper to taste
3 tablespoons dry white wine
2 tablespoons whole-grain mustard
4 to 5 teaspoons grated fresh horseradish
⅓ cup loosely packed small dill sprigs

With a very sharp, thin knife, slice the salmon diagonally in 1/4-inch-thick slices. You should be able to cut enough slices to cover 4 medium-sized oven-proof plates. (If you haven't been able to cut the salmon as thinly as you wanted, lay it between two pieces of lightly oiled plastic wrap, parchment, or waxed paper, and tap gently with a rolling pin to spread them thinner.) Liberally paint the plates with the oil and sprinkle them with salt and pepper. Place the salmon pieces on the plates, spreading and trimming with a small knife to fit the pieces without gaps.

Mix the wine with the mustard in a small bowl. With a pastry brush or small (clean!) paintbrush, coat the salmon all over with the mixture. Dot the salmon liberally with the horseradish. The plates may be prepared ahead to this point and refrigerated.

Twenty to thirty minutes before serving, remove the plates from the refrigerator and preheat the oven to 450°. Five minutes before serving, strew the fresh dill leaves generously over the salmon. Season boldly, as the strength of the salmon flavor demands a strong accompaniment. Cook the plates of salmon in the hot oven for 2 minutes, or until the salmon is just barely cooked (it should be opaque). It is best to pull the salmon out slightly underdone, since it will continue to cook and set with the residual heat of the plates. If the slices look at all dried out, spritz them with wine or water using a plastic mister. Serve immediately.

Sea Scallop Ceviche

Makes 4 servings

- 8 ounces fresh sea scallops (about 12), preferably day-boat caught and dry-packed, rinsed, drained, and trimmed of small, tough side muscle
- 1 teaspoon pink or white peppercorns
- 1 teaspoon coriander seeds
- ¼ teaspoon toasted cumin seeds
- ⅓ cup freshly squeezed lime juice (about 3 limes)
- 1½ teaspoons fine sea salt, or to taste
- 2 tablespoons fruity, extra virgin olive oil
- 1 ripe Haas avocado, halved, peeled, pit removed
- 1 ripe tomato, halved, seeded, and diced (about ½ cup) or, if out of season, substitute diced roasted red bell pepper (see page 8 for roasting instructions)
- 2 tablespoons coarsely chopped cilantro, for garnish

Slice the scallops horizontally using a thin, sharp knife into 3 or 4 rounds each, approximately ⅛ inch thick. In an electric spice mill or with a mortar and pestle, grind the peppercorns with the coriander and cumin seeds to a powder. Toss the scallop slices in a shallow bowl with the lime juice, ¾ teaspoon of the salt, and the spice mixture. Put the scallops in the refrigerator and marinate for 30 to 45 minutes, tossing from time to time until the scallops are evenly white.

Drain the marinade into a small bowl and set aside. Toss the scallops in a bowl with 1½ tablespoons of the oil and arrange them in a single layer on 4 small, chilled plates, forming a 4-inch circle of scallop slices on each plate.

Cut the avocado halves crosswise into ⅛-inch-thick slices. Gently toss the slices in the bowl with the reserved marinade and the remaining ½ tablespoon oil and ¾ teaspoon salt. Surround the scallops on each plate with a ring of dressed avocado slices. Toss the diced tomatoes in the remaining dressing and scatter them over the scallops. Refrigerate until ready to serve (but don't prepare more than an hour or two in advance). Just before serving, sprinkle with the cilantro.

Margaret: It's important to me that people realize it's okay to read a foreign word and not be afraid of it or believe that it means something complex. I've overheard people talking at the restaurant and have been completely flabbergasted by the level of anxiety people experience reading foreign words. All over the world, especially in other Western cultures, people eat foods very similar to what we eat here, they just call it by their language's name. On behalf of that large number of people, I offer this: "We call it blah-blah, but what it really is, is just marinated seafood."

Tapenade is a Provençal
black olive spread that
usually includes
anchovies and capers. A
few years ago, when we
were regularly roasting
eggplant slices for pizzas
in our brick oven, we
tried adding some
chopped roasted egg-
plant to our tapenade
and found we loved the
combination. (See varia-
tion on page 22.) We
often spread our tape-
nade on baguette crou-
tons and send it out to
everyone at the begin-
ning of their meal. In
this form, it would be a
good addition to an
hors d'oeuvre buffet,
simply served in a bowl
with croutons on the
side. However, my
favorite version of this
flavor combination
takes the form of the
following tart, which we
developed at the restau-
rant by merely rework-
ing how some of the
ingredients are com-
bined. It's a good illus-
tration of how our
recipes often evolve.
Our method of roasting
eggplant is a technique I
much prefer to the com-
mon frying approach.
The eggplant doesn't
come out too greasy or
soggy because you can
use much less oil; it
browns nicely, and on
parchment paper,
there's no problem of it
sticking to the pan.
Served with

(continued on page 21)

Roasted Eggplant Tapenade Tart

Makes 6 to 8 servings

1 globe eggplant, or 2 Japanese eggplant
  (about 12 ounces)

2 small heads garlic

Fruity olive oil for drizzling

Fine sea salt and freshly ground pepper to taste

1 large egg, lightly beaten

½ cup milk

¼ cup heavy whipping cream (or substitute milk
  for a lighter custard)

Pinch of ground allspice

1 tablespoon freshly chopped flat-leaf parsley

1 cup (4 ounces) good-quality brined olives, pitted
  (black, green, or mixed)

2 salt-packed or canned anchovy fillets, well rinsed
  and drained

1 tablespoon salt-packed or canned capers, well rinsed
  and drained

½ teaspoon minced fresh thyme leaves

1 tablespoon dark rum or brandy (optional)

One 9-inch tart shell, frozen

Preheat the oven to 350°.

Peel two opposite lengths of the eggplant and cut the eggplant into ¼- to ⅜-inch-thick slices, lengthwise. (This way there won't be any "end pieces" that are all skin on one side.) Break open the heads of garlic and set aside 1 small clove.

Cut a piece of parchment paper to fit a 17 x 10-inch baking sheet. Brush the paper lightly with olive oil. Lay the eggplant slices and the garlic cloves on the oiled paper in a single layer. Brush the tops of the eggplant slices and drizzle the garlic cloves with olive oil and sprinkle lightly with salt. (If using salt-packed anchovies and/or capers, skip the salt here; it can always be added at the end if it's still needed.) Place the pan in the oven and roast until the eggplant and garlic are golden brown and soft, about 20 minutes. If any pieces become too dark before all are done, remove them first. Remove the pan from the oven and allow the eggplant and garlic to cool slightly.

While the roasted garlic is still somewhat warm, squeeze it out of its skin into the bowl of a food processor fitted with the metal blade. Peel the reserved raw clove of garlic, add it to the bowl with the roasted garlic, and purée until smooth. Add the egg, milk, cream, and allspice and blend to incorporate. Pass this batter through a fine-mesh sieve into a bowl to remove any hard bits of garlic ends. Stir in the chopped parsley and a pinch of salt. Taste for seasoning. (It is best to under-salt the custard since it will be combined with the olive tapenade and the salted eggplant.) Set aside.

To make the tapenade: In the bowl of the food processor (which doesn't need to be cleaned from the garlic batter), add the pitted olives, anchovies, capers, thyme, and rum and purée until smooth. Add a little olive oil if the mixture seems too dry.

To assemble the tart, bake the tart shell, removing the foil and weights after the sides are set but not yet brown, and finish baking until the shell is an even, light brown. Brush the bottom of the shell generously with the tapenade, and then arrange a layer of 2 or 3 roasted eggplant slices on top, browned side up. Ladle a thick coating of the garlic custard over the eggplant slices and cover with another layer of eggplant slices, browned side up. Repeat this process until you have 3 layers of eggplant and 3 layers of custard, finishing with a thin coating of custard on the top (you should be able to see the browned surface of the eggplant through the final custard layer). The tart shell should be just full. Bake at 350° for about 30 minutes, or until the custard is set. Remove from the oven and allow to cool in the pan before slicing. Serve at room temperature.

a small green salad, the tart has been a popular appetizer. It would also make a splendid entrée for a light summer lunch. For a completely vegetarian version, you could omit the anchovies.

Roasted Eggplant Tapenade

Makes 2¹/₃ cups

- 1 small eggplant (8 to 10 ounces)
- 1 head garlic
- Fruity olive oil for drizzling
- Fine sea salt to taste
- 2 tablespoons salt-packed or canned capers, well rinsed and drained
- 4 salt-packed or canned anchovy fillets, well rinsed
- 2 cups (8 ounces) good-quality black and/or green olives, pitted
- 1 teaspoon minced fresh thyme leaves
- ¼ cup chopped fresh flat-leaf parsley
- 1 tablespoon dark rum or brandy (optional)

Roast the eggplant and garlic as directed for the Roasted Eggplant Tapenade Tart. Place the roasted garlic on a large cutting board along with the eggplant, capers, anchovies, and pitted olives. Using a large chef's knife, chop everything to a medium-fine texture. Transfer to a bowl with the herbs and rum. Stir to blend evenly and taste for seasoning. Add salt if desired and moisten with more olive oil if it seems dry. Serve at room temperature, spread on croutons. May be stored 1 to 2 weeks in the refrigerator, covered with a thin film of olive oil in a tightly sealed container.

Oysters on the Half Shell
with Two Dipping Sauces

Makes 6 servings

- Dipping sauces (recipes follow)
- 30 to 36 small fresh oysters in their shell
- Crushed ice, seaweed, and/or rock salt for presentation
  (and to keep the oysters from tipping over)

Prepare one or both of the dipping sauces and set aside. Open the oysters and arrange them attractively on the ice or salt and seaweed, serving one or both sauces in small ramekins in the center of each plate for dipping.

Smoked Duck Sauce

Makes about ²/₃ cup

- 8 ounces smoked duck wings and/or necks, coarsely chopped (see Note)
- ¼ cup chopped shallots
- 1⅓ cups dry white wine or vermouth
- ²/₃ cup heavy whipping cream

Combine the smoked duck, shallots, and wine in a small saucepan and bring to a boil. Lower the heat to just simmering and cook, uncovered, skimming periodically, until the meat is falling off the bones, about 1½ to 2 hours. Add water as needed to keep the bones covered with liquid. Pour through a fine-mesh sieve into a bowl, pressing down hard with the back of a ladle or wooden spoon to extract as much liquid as possible before discarding solids. Chill the stock overnight.

The next morning, lift off and discard the solidified fat, or pour the stock into a degreasing pitcher to remove the solid fat floating on top, and discard. Place the stock in a saucepan and reduce to about ¼ cup, skimming off any scum. Add the cream, bring to a boil (don't let it boil over), and then reduce heat to a strong simmer. Reduce the liquid by one quarter to one third, or until thick enough to lightly coat a spoon. Serve warm.

Note: This recipe may be doubled and frozen for later use. After thawing, bring to a boil, stirring to blend, and serve.

We smoke our own duck wings: First, we brine them overnight in a solution of 1½ cups salt and 1½ cups sugar dissolved in a gallon of water. Then we put the wings into a small smoker with fruitwood chips for 6 to 8 hours. If you can't smoke your own duck, try substituting the bones and skin from any smoked fowl (duck, chicken, or turkey), or use smoky slab bacon or ham hocks.

I love oysters on the half shell; nothing tastes more vividly of the sea. As a teenager, I used to visit a local seafood restaurant at happy hour with a fellow aficionado just to take advantage of their twenty-five-cent oysters—we averaged a couple dozen each! Like many purists, I prefer my fresh oysters either unadorned or with just a drop of fresh lemon juice. Nonetheless, these two sauces, along with the popular mignonette sauce (shallots, wine, and vinegar), have won a high ranking on my palate. The first is an idea from André Daguin of the Hôtel de France in Auch, France, and is a great use for duck trimmings such as necks and wing tips if they aren't needed for stock. The second sauce comes from Diana Kennedy, the chef who first introduced me to the delicious acidity of tomatillos.

If you can, select one or more of the oyster varieties from Tomales Bay in California, or Puget Sound in Washington. I especially enjoy Rock Points when they are in season.

Salsa Verde (Tomatillo-Cilantro Sauce)

Makes about 1 cup

8 ounces tomatillos
2 tablespoons coarsely chopped white onion
1 teaspoon coarsely chopped garlic (1 clove)
¼ teaspoon fine sea salt
¼ teaspoon dried oregano
½ cup loosely packed, coarsely chopped cilantro

Remove the husks from the tomatillos and wash and dry them. Put the tomatillos in a small saucepan with water to cover and weight them with a small saucer or lid to keep them submerged while they cook (they are very light and want to float). Simmer gently for about 5 minutes, until drab green all over and soft, but not mushy or falling apart. Set aside, in the cooking water, to cool.

Meanwhile, place ¼ cup of the tomatillo cooking water in a small pan with the onion, garlic, salt, and oregano and cook gently, covered, for 5 minutes, to soften onions and bring out the garlic flavor. (If you prefer the bite of raw onions and garlic, this step may be omitted and the onion and garlic may be added to the blender raw.) Allow to cool. The sauce should be made the day it is served, or it will lose its bright green color. However, the tomatillos may be cooked several days in advance or even prepared and frozen. Just remember to save their cooking water. (The cooking water and tomatillos must be cool before blending so they don't cook the cilantro and darken the sauce right away.)

When the liquid is completely cool, put it into a blender with the cilantro and blend until almost smooth, adding additional cool cooking water from the tomatillos, if necessary. Add the drained, cooled tomatillos and pulse for a few seconds to mix coarsely. The sauce should have a rough texture. Serve cool or at room temperature.

Note: This is not a spicy salsa. If you would like it to be spicy, add a whole serrano chile or jalapeño pepper to the pan with the tomatillos, and cook and blend it along with them.

Spicy Lamb Brochettes
with Red Lentil Sauce and Cucumber Raita

Makes 6 servings

Brochettes and Marinade

½ teaspoon cumin seeds

1 teaspoon fine sea salt

¾ teaspoon ground red chiles or ground cayenne pepper

2 teaspoons minced garlic (2 cloves)

½ cup light olive oil

1¼ to 1½ pounds boneless lamb shoulder, trimmed of excess fat and gristle and cut into ¾-inch cubes (36 pieces)

Several sprigs rosemary and oregano

2 bay leaves

Cucumber Raita

½ English cucumber, halved lengthwise, seeded, and sliced ¼-inch thick (1 cup)

½ teaspoon fine sea salt

1 cup plain yogurt

2 teaspoons freshly squeezed lime juice plus ½ teaspoon grated lime zest (optional)

1 teaspoon garam masala (see Note)

1 tablespoon chopped green onions

2 tablespoons coarsely chopped fresh mint

2 tablespoons coarsely chopped cilantro

Red Lentil Sauce

2 tablespoons light olive oil

⅓ cup chopped yellow onion

2 teaspoons minced garlic (2 cloves)

⅔ cup red lentils, picked over for stones, rinsed, and drained

1¾ cups chicken or lamb stock

1 tablespoon tomato paste

1 teaspoon curry powder

¾ teaspoon fine sea salt

12 (3- to 4-inch) bamboo skewers

6 small lettuce leaves, for serving (optional)

2 to 3 teaspoons chopped fresh oregano, for garnish

Cucumber raita is an Indian relish commonly served with curries as part of a series of dishes in a more elaborate meal. In this recipe, it is a sauce for dipping the bits of lamb. You need to thicken the yogurt a bit by draining out some of the whey. Also, salting the cucumbers in advance and draining them softens them a bit and concentrates their flavor by leaching out excess water.

A day ahead, heat the cumin seeds in a small, dry skillet over medium heat and toast them until they are fragrant. Do not let them burn. Allow the seeds to cool slightly, then grind them in an electric spice mill or in a mortar. Blend the cumin, salt, ground chiles, garlic, and oil in the bowl of a food processor fitted with the metal blade. Put the lamb cubes in a bowl and massage the spiced oil, herb sprigs, and bay leaves into the meat. Cover and marinate, refrigerated, overnight. Put the yogurt for the raita in a sieve lined with a damp cheesecloth or kitchen towel, and drain into a bowl. Refrigerate overnight, or until ⅓ cup of whey is collected. (If you want to prepare this dish in one day, both of these steps can be accomplished in several hours at room temperature.)

The next day, or several hours later if preparing recipe in one day, begin preparations for the Cucumber Raita. Toss the cut cucumber with the salt and drain in a colander for an hour or so while making the lentil sauce.

To make the lentil sauce: In a medium saucepan, heat the oil and sauté the onion in the oil until softened, about 3 to 5 minutes. Add the garlic and cook another minute, stirring over medium heat until fragrant. Add the lentils, stock, tomato paste, curry powder, and salt, and bring to a simmer. Lower the heat and continue to simmer, covered, for 30 minutes, or until lentils are very soft. Remove from the heat and allow to cool to slightly, then purée in a food processor or blender until smooth. Taste for seasoning and set aside.

To make the raita: When the cucumbers and yogurt have drained, put them in a bowl and toss with the lime juice and zest, garam masala, green onions, mint, and cilantro. Refrigerate the raita while cooking the brochettes.

To cook the brochettes: Heat a grill, broiler, or cast-iron skillet. (Soak the bamboo skewers for 15 minutes in water if using an open flame so they don't catch fire or char and fall apart.) Put the lentil sauce in a saucepan over low heat and warm 6 appetizer plates. Put 3 pieces of lamb on each skewer, brush with the marinade oil (or more light olive oil if all of the marinade has been absorbed), and cook until browned on all sides but still medium-rare in the center, about 3 to 8 minutes.

To serve, divide the Cucumber Raita among 6 small ramekins or lettuce leaves and place one of these containers at the top of each plate. Ladle 2 to 3 tablespoons of lentil sauce onto each plate below the raita, and place two skewers in a V shape on top of the sauce with the lettuce leaf or ramekin at the open end of the V. Sprinkle the chopped oregano over the meat and serve immediately.

Note: The cooking time for the brochettes will vary considerably depending on the heat source used. Also, do not expect the surface of the meat to brown significantly if using a standard home broiler. For the best surface browning without overcooking the centers of the pieces of lamb, use either a very hot barbecue or a smoking-hot cast-iron skillet.

Garam masala can be store-bought or homemade. The following recipe will keep a long time in your spice cabinet. Use whole spices, and, when you are ready to use it, grind the amount you need in an electric spice mill.

Garam Masala

Makes ½ cup

2 tablespoons coriander seeds
1 tablespoon cumin seeds
3-inch length cinnamon bark
1 tablespoon mace or nutmeg (preferably freshly grated)
1 tablespoon black peppercorns
1 teaspoon cardamom seeds
1 teaspoon whole cloves

Break up the cinnamon bark, or crush it with the back of a heavy knife. In a small, dry skillet over medium heat, toast the coriander and cumin, swirling the pan until the spices are fragrant. Transfer to a small bowl and allow to cool. Mix together with the remaining ingredients and store in an airtight container until needed.

This is a dish that I created at my mom's house
while just playing
around in the early
spring of 1984, prior to
my job interview at Cafe
Beaujolais. I had read an
article about professional
chefs using won ton
skins in place of pasta
dough for quick ravioli,
so I thought I would
experiment with the
idea for dinner one
night. I think it was this
Asian connection that
led me to try soy sauce in
a classic beurre blanc
sauce and throw fresh
ginger into the ravioli
filling. The minute our
family tasted the ravioli
that night, I knew I had
stumbled upon a special
flavor combination. And
sure enough, as I wit-
nessed when I prepared
them as part of the
Beaujolais's seventh
anniversary meal (which
served as the test to
secure my job as the
restaurant's dinner chef)
people go wild for this
sauce. I put the dish on
the opening menu as an
appetizer, whimsically
dubbing it "Chicken and
Goat Cheese Won Tons
Christopher" and was
overwhelmed at its
reception. It was so pop-
ular that we rarely took
it off the menu during
the next four years. My
father had an equally
enthusiastic response
among his students
when he taught it at his
(continued on page 29)

Chicken and Goat Cheese Ravioli

Makes 4 servings

Filling

½ cup cooked chicken, cut into ¼-inch dice

⅓ cup fairly dry, fresh goat cheese, crumbled

2 tablespoons chopped green onions

1 tablespoon chopped cilantro

1 teaspoon peeled and grated fresh ginger

½ teaspoon freshly ground white pepper

Large pinch of fine sea salt

1 recipe homemade pasta dough (recipe follows), or 6
egg roll wrappers (see Note)

1 egg, lightly beaten with 1 teaspoon water

Soy Beurre Blanc Sauce

2 tablespoons chopped shallots

¼ cup dry vermouth, shao-hsing wine, sake, or white
wine

2 tablespoons soy sauce

2 tablespoons heavy whipping cream

¾ to 1 cup unsalted butter, diced and chilled

Freshly ground white pepper to taste

2 to 3 cups chicken stock

¼ cup diced tofu (¼-inch dice), for garnish

2 tablespoons finely julienned carrot (¹⁄₁₆ inch thick and
1 to 1½ inches long), for garnish

4 cilantro leaves, for garnish

To make the filling: Mix all of the filling ingredients together in a bowl. Adjust the
seasoning as desired, but keep it undersalted to allow for the saltiness of the sauce.

To prepare the ravioli: Place level tablespoonfuls of filling onto a sheet of
pasta or onto egg roll wrappers; leave 1 inch between mounds. (If using egg roll
wrappers, you should be able to fit 4 ravioli on each of three wrappers.) Brush a
second sheet of pasta or wrapper with egg wash or water and place it on top of
the first, pressing well around the edges to remove air bubbles and seal the two
sheets together. Cut excess dough from around the outside edges with a round
cookie cutter or with a glass jar and a small knife, leaving about ¼ inch of dough
around the filling. Put the ravioli on a piece of parchment paper or a dry kitchen
towel and set aside until ready to cook.

To make the sauce: Put the shallots, vermouth, and soy sauce in a small
saucepan over medium heat and reduce to a glaze, about 5 minutes. Add the cream
and reduce by half, about 1 to 2 more minutes. Whisk in the chilled butter pieces,

EVENING FOOD

a few at a time, over medium-low heat. Taste the sauce after you've added ³/₄ cup of the butter—the sauce is done when it has a café au lait color (light brown) and tastes of soy without being too salty. If it is too strong (salty) for your taste, whisk in more butter; if it's too weak, add a dash more soy sauce. Season with finely ground white pepper and set aside in a warm, but not too hot, place, such as the back of the stovetop.

Warm 4 shallow soup or pasta bowls in a 200° oven for 10 to 15 minutes. Heat the chicken stock to a simmer in a broad, shallow saucepan. Poach the ravioli in the simmering stock until the pasta is al dente, about 2 minutes. Remove to a warm plate. Heat the tofu and carrot garnishes for 5 to 10 seconds in a small strainer held in the simmering stock.

Set 3 ravioli in each bowl and blanket them with 3 tablespoons of the sauce. Top each ravioli with a pinch of carrot julienne and spoon a small mound of diced tofu in the center of each bowl between the ravioli. Top the tofu with a cilantro leaf and serve immediately.

Note: Usually sold in packages of twenty, egg roll wrappers freeze well if kept in an airtight container. They are available in the produce section of most supermarkets.

Pasta Dough

Makes 4 to 6 servings (about 1 pound of dough)

2½ cups organic unbleached bread or all-purpose flour
3 large eggs, lightly beaten

Put the flour in a food processor. With the machine running, add the eggs in a steady stream. Stop the machine as soon as all of the liquid has been added. Scrape the contents down from the side of the bowl and pulse a few times while shaking the processor gently, until the mixture is fully blended. The dough texture is perfect when it stays in distinct grains like instant tapioca and is damp enough to hold its shape easily when squeezed in the palm of your hand. (It has been described as having the consistency and texture of wet sand.) If it is too dry—a little powdery to the touch and it crumbles and falls apart as you try to flatten and roll it out—return it to the food processor and blend in more beaten egg or water, a tablespoon at a time, until it feels right. If it begins to ball up in the processor bowl, feels sticky to the touch, or sticks to itself very easily as you begin to roll it out, it is too wet. Again, return it the food processor and blend in more flour by the tablespoon, with the machine running, until it feels right.

New York cooking school. The one change he made was to rename the dish "ravioli" because he felt that Italian cuisine was better known than Asian in New York at that time. But whether you call them ravioli or won tons, whether you use homemade pasta dough or storebought wrappers, try this recipe!

Fresh pasta can of course be made by hand without either a food processor or a pasta machine. However, it has been so long since I have done so that I won't attempt to give instructions here. I believe in faster, less laborious cooking through technology, as long as it doesn't compromise the flavors or textures of a dish. This is the case with any recipe in this book calling for food processors, pasta machines, electric mixers, or spice mills (nothing lost but extra cooking time). If you would prefer to make your pasta completely by hand (or have no choice), I recommend following the instructions in Marcella Hazan's *The Classic Italian Cook Book* or another authentic source.

To roll out the dough using a pasta machine: Divide the dough into 4 balls. Cover all but 1 ball with a damp kitchen towel or with plastic wrap. Flatten the uncovered ball of dough with the palm of your hand into a sheet, ¼ to ⅜ inch thick. Knead this piece through the machine's rollers on the widest setting (position 1), fold it in thirds, and roll it through again. Repeat 2 more times, until the dough is soft and smooth on its surface and sides. Leave the dough sheet flat. Adjust the rollers to the next narrowest (#2) position, roll the dough through, then adjust rollers to the #3 position, roll the dough through, and repeat until you reach the #6 or #7 position and the dough is the thickness you desire. Slightly thicker dough (position 6) is often nice for flat noodles, whereas very thin (position 7) is usually best for ravioli, but use your judgment and personal taste, since pasta machines vary. We once had a machine on which we discovered the perfect setting was position #6½, which meant you had to hold the adjustment knob halfway between the two notched settings while you rolled— a three-handed operation! Cover the sheets with a slightly damp kitchen towel until you are ready to fill, seal, and cut them.

EVENING FOOD

Rabbit, Chanterelle, and Leek Risotto

Makes 8 servings

1 small rabbit, about 2 to 2½ pounds, fresh or frozen and thawed

Fine sea salt and freshly ground black pepper to taste

1 tablespoon vegetable oil

2 quarts plus 1 cup water

6 cups fresh chanterelles, as dry as possible (see Note)

3 leeks, washed thoroughly and white and green parts chopped separately (1½ cups white and 2 cups green)

1 carrot, chopped

1 celery stalk, chopped

Small bunch fresh cilantro, stems and leaves separated

Several sprigs fresh thyme, or ½ teaspoon dried

4 tablespoons plus 2 tablespoons unsalted butter or olive oil

2 cups arborio rice

¾ cup dry white wine

2 tablespoons peeled and finely chopped fresh ginger

2 tablespoons Madeira

2 tablespoons minced green onions, for garnish

At least 4 hours or the night before serving, bone the rabbit and cut the meat into bite-sized pieces. Season lightly with salt and pepper, cover, and refrigerate until ready to cook. Reserve bones.

To make the broth: With a heavy cleaver, chop the rabbit bones into 2-inch lengths. Heat the vegetable oil until almost smoking in a heavy-bottomed 3- to 4-quart pot. Add the rabbit bones and cook over high heat, stirring occasionally, until well browned. Adjust the heat if necessary to prevent scorching. Pour off any excess fat from the pan and add a cup of water. Return the pot to the heat and scrape the bottom with a wooden spatula to deglaze. Add 2 quarts of water to the pot and bring to a simmer.

Meanwhile, prepare the chanterelles. Using a pastry or vegetable brush and a kitchen towel, brush and wipe the mushrooms clean. Be especially careful to brush away all dirt in the gills. Any very embedded grit can be cut away with a paring knife. If the mushrooms are large, cut them into large bite-sized pieces (usually halving, quartering, or thickly slicing lengthwise leaves wild mushrooms most attractive and reminiscent of their original shape); if mushrooms are small, leave them whole.

Risottos appear frequently on our menus at the restaurant because both Margaret and I are wild for them when they are made properly. Unfortunately, it is rare outside of Italy to be served a perfect risotto. I attribute this fact to the finesse it requires to get the texture just right. It's tricky!

There are a couple of things to pay attention to in order to ensure a perfect risotto. The right rice is certainly important, but the broth must be flavorful and well seasoned, since no amount of salt added at the end will properly penetrate the rice and give the same flavor that good broth used from the beginning will. And pay close attention to the texture at all times, for that is what distinguishes risotto from other rice dishes. A true risotto should be creamy, not soupy and not gluey. Whether you prepare it restaurant-style, as directed here, or in the classic home style, as you approach the finish of the dish, add the broth judiciously so that you can stop just at the moment you achieve that perfect combination of al dente (not chalky!) rice grains in a creamy base.

(continued on page 32)

I have omitted
Parmesan here because
I find it clashes with the
fresh ginger, but if you
have some on hand, try
it and be your own
judge.

Add 1 cup of the least attractive mushroom pieces to the broth, along with the chopped leek greens, carrot, celery, cilantro stems, and thyme. Coarsely chop the cilantro leaves and reserve them, along with the chopped leek whites, covered and refrigerated, until needed. Season the stock with salt and pepper, adjust the heat to a slow simmer, and cook for 3 hours. Strain the broth, discarding the bones and vegetables. Measure 2 quarts of stock for the risotto. (If you have less, top off with water.) When you are ready to cook the risotto, return the broth to low heat, taste for seasoning, and heat to just below simmering.

Butter and refrigerate a 17 x 10-inch baking sheet to chill.

To make the risotto: In another 3- to 4-quart heavy-bottomed pot (or larger one), melt 4 tablespoons of butter over medium heat. Add the reserved chopped leek whites and a generous pinch of salt and cook, stirring occasionally, until the leeks are soft and translucent, about 10 minutes. Don't let the leeks brown. Add the rice and cook for another minute, stirring well to coat the rice with the butter and leeks. Add the white wine and bring to a simmer. Cook, stirring, until the wine is absorbed and the rice is creamy. Add ³/₄ cup of the warm rabbit broth and continue stirring until absorbed, about 2 minutes. Add a cup of broth and repeat, making sure that all of the rice is covered by the liquid. (It should be slightly soupy but the rice should not be drowning.) Stir constantly until the rice is still creamy but the bottom of the pot is visible between stirs. After about 16 to 18 minutes of cooking with the liquid additions, there should be only about 3 cups of broth left. As soon as the rice is almost cooked through and the most recent addition of broth is absorbed, empty rice onto the buttered, chilled baking sheet and spread out evenly. When testing rice for near-doneness, bite into several different grains and cut a grain or two in half crosswise—there should be just a touch of white, raw rice in the center of the grain. Allow broth and rice to cool completely and store, covered with plastic wrap, in the refrigerator until ready to serve. (The risotto may be prepared several hours or even a day or two ahead to this point.)

When ready to serve, warm 8 shallow bowls in a 200° oven for 10 to 15 minutes. Remove the rabbit from the refrigerator and pat the meat dry on a kitchen towel. Return the risotto to its cooking pot with 1 cup of the remaining broth. Cover the pot and place on low heat.

Melt the 2 tablespoons of butter in a large (12-inch) sauté pan over high heat. When the foam subsides, add the rabbit meat and chanterelles and sauté quickly over high heat, stirring until the rabbit loses its raw pink color, about 2 minutes. Uncover the risotto pot and give it a stir. Add the ginger to the skillet and cook for another 1 to 2 minutes, stirring, until the rabbit pieces begin to brown and the chanterelles and ginger have softened slightly. Remove the pan from the heat, season lightly with salt and pepper, and add the Madeira. Cover and shake the pan to deglaze and steam. Remove the pan from the heat and set aside.

Give the risotto another stir and taste for doneness. If it is not quite cooked through, add a little more broth, increase the heat, and cook, stirring constantly, until no chalkiness remains but the rice is al dente. (This final cooking should take no more than 3 to 5 minutes.) Divide the risotto among the warm bowls. Spoon some of the sautéed rabbit and chanterelles on top of the risotto. Sprinkle with the minced green onions and reserved chopped cilantro. Serve immediately.

Note: Chanterelles should be dry because wet chanterelles are much harder to clean and tend to have a soggy texture.

The precooking technique used in this recipe is how we cook risotto at Cafe Beaujolais and how risotto is usually prepared in restaurants since it is impractical to cook something to order that requires 20 to 30 minutes of constant attention. It is also a useful technique for the home cook who wants to be able to visit with guests until 6 to 8 minutes before serving. If precooked and refrigerated, however, the final risotto texture will not be quite as perfectly creamy-chewy as it can be if it is cooked straight through. So, if you want the pure, authentic experience and don't mind being tied to the stove for 30 minutes just prior to serving, prepare the risotto without interrupting the cooking process, as described for precooking, and proceed to the finishing instructions.

This recipe interprets a
Tyrolean specialty that
has been a Kump family
favorite for over twenty
years. In the traditional
preparation, tiny spaet-
zle noodles are flavored
with spinach and served
in a lusciously rich cream
sauce studded with
small strips of Speck, a
Tyrolean smoked ham
that is reminiscent of
prosciutto. At the
restaurant, instead of
spinach, we use earthy
kale grown for us by
local organic farmers,
and we've lightened the
sauce for contemporary
palettes by substituting
chicken stock for the
cream. If you are unfa-
miliar with spaetzle and
this recipe intrigues you,
it is worth the effort to
acquire a spaetzle
maker. They are avail-
able at upscale kitchen
supply stores, are not
very expensive, and
make it simple to create
the distinctive spaetzle
noodle shape.

My father and I were
so fond of this Austrian
comfort food that in the
mid 70s he included it in
a class at his then newly-
founded cooking school.
He loved sharing his
Tyrolean discoveries not
only with his students,
but his peers and men-
tors alike. Two of his
closest friends and
teachers, Simone
"Simca" Beck and James
Beard, came to stay with
(continued on page 35)

Kale Spaetzle

Makes 6 servings

Pasta

4 quarts stemmed and loosely packed kale
  or green chard or spinach

3 tablespoons sea salt

2 cups semolina (see Note)

2 cups unbleached all-purpose flour

2 large eggs

1 to 1¼ cups milk

2 tablespoons heavy whipping cream or vegetable oil

2 tablespoons unsalted butter

3 cups chopped yellow onion

¼ teaspoon fine sea salt

6 ounces thinly sliced Speck (Austrian smoked prosciutto)
  or good-quality prosciutto, cut into ¼-inch-wide ribbons

1½ cups chicken stock

Freshly grated nutmeg to taste

Freshly ground pepper to taste

½ cup freshly grated imported Parmesan cheese

1 to 2 tablespoons unsalted butter (optional)

To make the pasta: Wash and trim the stems from the kale. In a 4-quart pot,
bring 3 quarts of water to a rolling boil. Add 3 tablespoons sea salt, return to a
rolling boil, and add kale (in batches if necessary—don't crowd the pot too
much). Blanch, uncovered, until tender, about 3 minutes. Remove the kale from
the pot, reserving the blanching liquid, and refresh in a bowl of ice water for 10
to 15 seconds. Drain the kale and squeeze it as dry as possible. You will need 2
packed cups of kale.

Put the drained kale in the bowl of a food processor fitted with the metal
blade and process for 1 to 2 minutes to purée. Add the semolina and flour,
process to mix, and then add the eggs. With the machine running, add the milk.
Check the texture after adding 1 cup of the milk. It should be wet and elastic,
like thick, rubbery pancake batter. Add the remaining milk if the batter is too
dry. If it is too loose, run the machine a little longer to develop elasticity.

Transfer the spaetzle batter from the processor bowl to a mixing bowl. Bring
the blanching water to a simmer and set a spaetzle maker above it. If you do not
own a spaetzle maker, you can use a heatproof (metal) colander with very coarse
(¼-inch) holes. Transfer the batter to the spaetzle maker (or colander) in several
batches and force it through the holes with a wooden spatula or spoon. (This
will be somewhat slow-going.) The batter will drop into the water in little squig-
gles or blobs. As soon as the pieces all float to the surface, simmer for another

15 to 30 seconds, and then remove the spaetzle to a fine-mesh sieve and refresh briefly in cold water. Transfer the cooked and refreshed spaetzle to a bowl until all of the batter has been used. When all of the batter has been cooked and refreshed, rinse the spaetzle off in hot water to remove excess starch. Drain in a sieve or colander, and then transfer spaetzle to a medium bowl. Toss with the cream or oil and set aside.

Heat the butter in a medium saucepan. Add the chopped onions and the $\frac{1}{4}$ teaspoon salt and cook over high heat, stirring occasionally, for 30 to 40 minutes, until golden brown. Increase the heat and frequency of stirring as the onions soften. Add the julienned Speck or prosciutto, stock, nutmeg, and pepper, and bring to a boil. Remove the pan from the heat, allow the mixture to cool slightly, then add it to the bowl with the spaetzle and toss well to coat. Adjust seasoning as desired.

To serve, preheat the oven to 450° for 10 to 15 minutes. Divide the spaetzle among shallow soup bowls or put it in a buttered casserole or baking dish to hold the spaetzle in a 1- to 1½-inch layer. Sprinkle with the Parmesan and dot with butter. Heat on the top rack of the oven for 5 to 8 minutes, or under a broiler for 2 to 3 minutes, to heat through and brown the top. Serve hot.

Note: Semolina is a highly glutinous flour made from hard winter wheat and used primarily for making dry (extruded) commercial pastas. If unavailable, it may be replaced in this recipe with bread or all-purpose flour.

us at the castle. A hotelier friend in a nearby village arranged for her chef to prepare an array of local specialties. They were both charmed by these treasures of traditional fare: Simca went back to the castle to immediately try her hand at old-fashioned hand-pulled strudel, and James would later draw on the visit for his own culinary inspirations.

Margaret: Spaetzle are quite similar to my other favorite European comfort food, gnocchi. I think of them as miniature free-form dumplings. We've introduced many friends and guests at our Tyrolean castle to these heavenly dropped noodles, and everyone has the same reaction—yum! They are so popular they're always on the menus of our favorite local restaurants, often as an accompaniment to a pork and mushroom sauté, which is presented tableside in a large skillet.

If you're like me, when you go out for Chinese food you frequently find yourself torn between the hot and sour soup and the wonton soup, or end up having both. Here's a dish that satisfies the desire for both in one bowl. This dish can be as simple or as complex as you want to make it. In its first incarnation, we made our own pasta dough flavored with sea lettuce (ulva), a delicate seaweed harvested and sold here in Mendocino. We also clarified the broth with egg whites before the final poaching of the ravioli. The result was very refined and special—and a lot of work. Since I wanted this recipe to be made and not just marveled at, I have omitted the clarifying step. I also recommend egg roll wrappers as an alternative to homemade pasta dough; you will be amazed at what a fine substitute they make. Their texture can be kept perfectly al dente and they're extremely easy to store and to work with. The main labor left in this streamlined version is poaching the crab and picking its meat. Of course, you could always buy cleaned crabmeat and a can of clam juice or fish stock, but you would be sacrificing flavor.

Crab and Shrimp Ravioli
in Hot and Sour Broth

Makes 6 servings

One 2¼- to 2½-pound fresh Dungeness crab, preferably live

3 quarts cold water

1 tablespoon sea salt

6 tablespoons white wine vinegar

3 tablespoons palm or brown sugar

3 small fresh chiles, such as serranos, coarsely chopped

9 medium (16 to 20 per pound) shrimp, fresh or frozen and thawed

⅓ cup minced shallots

¼ cup unsalted butter

2 tablespoons minced fresh sage

Fine sea salt to taste

1 egg, lightly beaten with 1 teaspoon water

1 recipe pasta dough (page 29), or 1 package egg roll wrappers

6 fresh sage leaves

6 tablespoons chopped green onions

1 tablespoon chili oil, or to taste

If using live crab, put it in a 6- to 8-quart stockpot with the water, 1 tablespoon salt, vinegar, sugar, and chiles. Bring to a full simmer (200°), remove from the heat, cover, and let sit for 10 minutes. Remove the crab and allow to cool, reserving the cooking liquid. When the crab is cool, remove the meat from the shell and set aside, adding the shells to the cooking liquid. Double-check the crabmeat to be sure no shell fragments remain. If using precooked crab, add crab shells to a large pot with the water, salt, vinegar, sugar, and chiles.

Shell the shrimp and set aside with the crabmeat. Add shrimp shells to the broth.

Sauté the shallots in the butter until soft. Add the minced sage and cook over high heat for 30 seconds to 1 minute, just to bring out the color and aroma of the sage. Remove the pan from the heat and stir in the crabmeat. Chop 3 shrimp coarsely and stir them into the crab mixture. Adjust seasoning, adding salt if desired. Set the remaining 6 shrimp aside.

To prepare the ravioli: Place rounded teaspoonfuls of filling onto a sheet of fresh pasta, leaving 1 inch between the spoonfuls of filling. (If using egg roll wrappers, you should be able to fit 4 ravioli on each of 9 wrappers.) Brush a second sheet of pasta or wrapper with egg wash and place it on top of the first, pressing well around the edges to remove air bubbles and to seal the two sheets together. Cut out ravioli with a 2-inch round cookie cutter or with a glass jar and a small knife. Set the ravioli aside on parchment paper or on a kitchen towel, covered loosely with a dry kitchen towel, until ready to cook. Repeat this process until you have a total of 36 ravioli, 6 per serving. (If you have extra filling, make extra ravioli in case any burst while cooking and become unservable. If you have leftover pasta, either use for another purpose or discard. Leftover egg roll wrappers may be frozen for future use if wrapped airtight.)

Bring the broth and shells to a boil, and then reduce heat and simmer, skimming occasionally, for 15 minutes. Strain the broth through a chinois or a very fine-mesh sieve. Return the stock to the heat and reduce over medium-high heat to 6 cups. Add the remaining 6 shrimp to the reduced stock and poach in barely simmering broth for 45 to 60 seconds, or until barely opaque. Remove the shrimp with a slotted spoon and set aside. Taste the broth and adjust for salt and vinegar as desired. Return the broth to a very low simmer and poach the ravioli for 2 minutes, or until the pasta is tender yet al dente.

Deep-fry the sage leaves in 375° vegetable oil for 15 to 20 seconds, until crisp but still green, then drain them on a paper towel. Warm 6 shallow soup bowls (in a 200° oven for 10 to 15 minutes) and place 1 tablespoon of the chopped green onions in each bowl. Divide the ravioli evenly among the bowls. Place 1 reserved poached shrimp in the center of each bowl. Add chili oil to the broth and ladle the broth over the ravioli and shrimp in the bowls. Decorate each shrimp with a fried sage leaf and serve immediately.

FROM THE BRICKERY

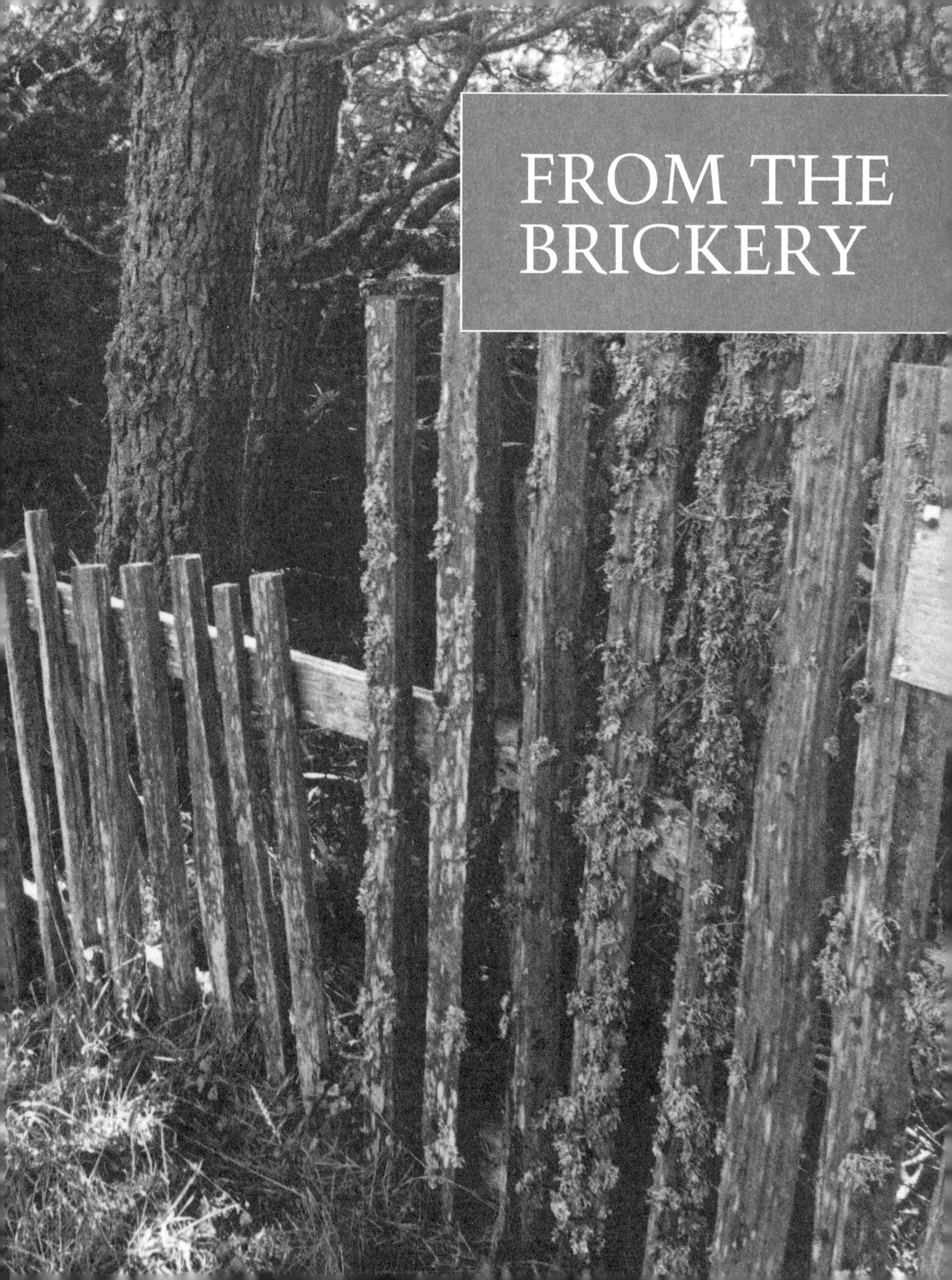

• FROM THE BRICKERY •

Brickery Pizza and Assorted Toppings / 42

Olive Rosemary Fougasse / 46

French Currant Bread / 48

Buckwheat Hazelnut Bread / 50

Potato Walnut Rolls / 52

In the winter of 1989, while Margaret was at home working on *Morning Food*, I traveled to France and Italy with our restaurant manager, Tricia Priano, and two friends. We were at a farmers' market in a small town in Provence and noticed a trail of smoke rising up from the end of a trailer. It was a mobile home, and as we got closer we could see a small wood fire burning away in the middle of the trailer and a sign announcing pizzas for sale. The owner had built a wood-fired brick oven *in* his trailer! That moment was something of an epiphany for me and the genesis of the wood-fired brick oven we would construct later that spring at the restaurant. (We named it the Brickery to avoid confusion with the Cafe Beaujolais Bakery, a mail-order business Margaret started some years ago.) If someone could build such an oven in the back of a mobile home, then we could certainly build and operate one at the restaurant!

The Brickery filled a desire I'd been nursing for quite a while. I had learned what really good bread could be from an early age. My dad had taken me to

(continued on page 43)

Brickery Pizza and Assorted Toppings

Makes 12 individual (6-ounce) pizzas

2 packages active dry yeast

½ cup very warm water

2¼ cups tepid water

¾ cup light olive oil (or fruity oil for a more pronounced olive flavor)

1 tablespoon chopped fresh rosemary or oregano leaves

1 tablespoon finely minced or puréed garlic (3 cloves)

9 cups (2 pounds, 8 ounces) organic unbleached bread or all-purpose flour (12 to 13 percent protein)

Scant ⅔ cup organic barley flour

4 teaspoons fine sea salt

Dissolve the yeast in the warm water in a small bowl. Allow to sit for 5 minutes; it should become slightly puffed and bubbly. Mix the tepid water, oil, rosemary, and garlic together in a large bowl or in the bowl of a heavy-duty electric mixer fitted with the paddle attachment. Add the active yeast mixture to the bowl. Mixing either with a heavy wooden spoon, if proceeding by hand, or with the paddle in the electric mixer, add the white flour gradually until it is all incorporated into a soft, shaggy mass. Knead until the dough is homogenous and elastic yet still quite sticky (about 8 to 10 minutes by hand, or 3 to 5 minutes on medium speed in an electric mixer). Mix the barley flour and salt together in a bowl and add this to the dough. Knead until the dough is smooth and elastic and no longer sticking to the sides of the bowl (another 3 to 5 minutes by hand or 2 to 3 minutes in the mixer). The dough should be soft and slightly sticky. Put the dough in an oiled bowl and let it rise in a warm place until doubled or tripled in volume, about 1 hour.

Punch the dough down and divide it into 6-ounce portions for individual pizzas (or into larger portions for communal pizzas). Using the palms of your hands, roll the dough balls into disks until they are taut and smooth. Set the disks on oiled baking sheets, allowing room for expansion. Brush the tops lightly with olive oil, cover with plastic wrap, and allow to double in volume again, about 45 to 60 minutes, at warm room temperature. Without removing the plastic wrap, flatten the disks and refrigerate. Allow the disks to rest for at least 10 minutes and up to 6 hours in the refrigerator. Flattened pizza dough can be refrigerated overnight, but is best used within 24 hours. We find that the dough is easier to pull out after being chilled.

When ready to bake, pull the disks out to an 8-inch diameter and lay them on a wooden peel (or an inverted flat baking sheet) generously dusted with cornmeal. Quickly cover all but a ½-inch border with your choice of toppings and slide pizzas directly onto a 500° to 600° preheated brick, tile, or other masonry surface, preferably next to a wood fire.

If you are baking in a conventional home gas or electric oven, place a pizza stone or two, or unglazed ceramic tiles such as quarry tiles, on the rack(s) of the oven and preheat it to 500°. Slide the pizzas directly onto this ceramic surface to cook. If you are baking next to a live fire, the pizzas should be rotated from time to time as the side facing the fire browns. Bake for 6 to 10 minutes until the crust border is puffed and evenly browned. Immediately upon removal from the oven, brush the crust border with fruity olive oil and sprinkle the tops of the pizzas with the chopped fresh herbs called for in each topping recipe. Cut each pizza into 4 to 6 slices and serve hot.

Toppings

Each topping recipe is for one individual pizza. If you are making several pizzas, you may multiply the ingredient quantities as needed, or make several toppings for variety. Add the ingredients to the pizzas in the order listed, leaving a $1/2$-inch border for the crust.

Italian

2 tablespoons Roasted Tomato Sauce (page 8), or other
   tomato sauce

$1/3$ cup grated mozzarella cheese

2 tablespoons pancetta lardons

$1\frac{1}{2}$ tablespoons pitted and coarsely chopped brine-cured
   black olives

1 marinated artichoke heart, cut in quarters

1 tablespoon freshly grated imported Parmesan

Chopped fresh parsley and oregano, for garnish

To prepare the pancetta lardons, cut the pancetta into $1/2$-inch slices. Put the pancetta in a small pot filled with cold water to cover and bring to a boil. Drain, place on a baking sheet, and bake in a 325° oven until a light golden brown.

Ham and Roasted Eggplant

2 tablespoons Roasted Tomato Sauce (page 8),
   or other tomato sauce

$1/3$ cup grated mozzarella cheese

2 to 3 slices roasted eggplant

Olive oil and sea salt (for roasting eggplant)

$1\frac{1}{2}$ to 2 slices ham

3 to 4 tablespoons grated fontina cheese

2 to 3 tablespoons thinly sliced red onions

Chopped fresh chervil or parsley, for garnish

Poilâne's, in Paris, which is still considered to be the benchmark of French bakeries. You go down these worn stone steps into a basement, right in the heart of Paris, and there are bakers in shorts, covered with flour—it's all very romantic. I had a book from Poilâne's that gave a model for a wood-fired brick oven and plans for building your own. I'd also heard there was a fellow named Alan Scott down the coast who was building brick ovens, so I wrote to him with my idea. My French is pretty good, but the plans had a lot of technical masonry terms that weren't in my dictionary. Fortunately, Alan knew someone who spoke contractor's French and could help with the translation. As things turned out, we ended up developing our own design, thanks to Alan's expertise, based on our anticipated size and usage needs. It took over a year to get permission to build the thing from the building department and the historical review board. This was at a time when we had enough people working that I wasn't needed on the line anymore and could spend a lot of time

(continued on page 44)

To prepare the eggplant: Preheat the oven to 375°. Cut two to three ¼-inch-thick slices lengthwise from a medium globe eggplant. Brush both sides of the slices with olive oil and place them on parchment paper on a baking sheet. Sprinkle with sea salt and roast at 350° to 375° for 20 to 30 minutes, until golden brown and soft.

Californian

⅓ cup grated mozzarella cheese

2 to 3 slices roasted eggplant (see Ham and Roasted Eggplant topping for recipe, previous page)

2 tablespoons fresh goat cheese, crumbled

¼ to ⅓ cup cherry tomatoes, halved or quartered

1½ to 2 tablespoons roasted garlic

Olive oil and sea salt (for roasting garlic)

Basil chiffonade, for garnish

To roast the garlic: Preheat the oven to 300°. Blanch the cloves in boiling salted water until tender, about 10 to 15 minutes. Peel the cooled cloves, toss with olive oil, and roast in the oven at 300° until golden.

Salami

2 tablespoons Roasted Tomato Sauce (page 8), or other tomato sauce

⅓ cup grated Monterey jack cheese

1½ to 2 ounces thinly sliced salami (enough to cover the pizza's surface)

3 to 4 tablespoons sliced button mushrooms

1 marinated artichoke heart, cut in quarters

3 to 4 tablespoons grated Fontina cheese

Fresh chervil sprigs or chopped fresh parley, for garnish

Neapolitan

2 tablespoons Roasted Tomato Sauce (page 8), or other tomato sauce

⅓ cup grated mozzarella cheese

2 tablespoons pitted and coarsely chopped brine-cured black olives

1 to 2 tablespoons freshly grated imported Parmesan cheese

Chopped fresh parsley and oregano, for garnish

Herculean

¼ cup grated goat or regular mozzarella cheese
2 to 3 slices roasted eggplant (see Ham and Roasted Eggplant topping for recipe, page 43)
⅓ cup spicy ground lamb, divided into marble-sized chunks
1½ tablespoons pitted kalamata olives
2 to 3 tablespoons crumbled feta cheese
¼ to ⅓ cup cherry tomatoes, halved or quartered
Chopped fresh parsley and oregano, for garnish

To make the spicy lamb: Mix together 12 ounces ground lamb, ¼ cup drained capers, 1½ teaspoons paprika, and ¾ teaspoon cayenne.

Mexican

½ cup carnitas (1 pork shoulder, salt, bay leaves, thyme or oregano)
¼ to ⅓ cup plus 2 to 3 tablespoons grated Monterey jack and/or Cheddar cheese
3 to 4 tablespoons salsa, thoroughly drained (see below)
Coarsely chopped cilantro, for garnish

To make the carnitas: Use 1 pork shoulder, cut into ½ x 2-inch strips. Weigh the meat and toss with 1 teapoon of salt for every 1½ pounds. If you don't know the weight of the meat, add salt to taste; you can season them more if needed when they are finished cooking. Place in a heavy-bottomed pan with water to barely cover. Add 2 bay leaves and several sprigs of thyme or oregano. Bring to a strong boil for 60 to 90 minutes, until the pork is tender and browns in its rendered fat. Stir often with a metal spoon and scrape the bottom of the pan to keep the meat from burning. When the meat is well browned, remove the bay leaves and herb sprigs. Drain the meat to remove the fat. Blot remaining grease in the pan with paper towels. Deglaze the pan with water, scraping thoroughly to loosen any browned bits. When the deglazing juices are thick, pour them into a clean bowl. Add the carnitas and mix well.

Salsa

1 ripe tomato, diced
1 teaspoon tomato paste
½ teaspoon fine sea salt
1 jalapeño pepper or serrano chile, stemmed and minced (including seeds)
2 tablespoons white wine vinegar
1 teaspoon dried Mexican oregano or Italian oregano
1 teaspoon minced garlic (1 clove)
⅓ cup chopped red onion
¼ cup chopped green onion
¼ cup coarsely chopped cilantro

To make the salsa, mix all the ingredients together in a large bowl.

We designed our oven to accommodate both breads and pizza (I guess I still had the image of that trailer-oven business in mind) and developed a repertoire of European-style thin-crusted, individual-portion pizzas that we sold out of the Brickery and in the restaurant over the next four years. Sadly, our pizza business finally succumbed to the same economic pressures that led us to retire our breakfast and lunch services, in spite of an enthusiastic following. With these recipes, some of our most popular pizzas will live on.

When the oven was finished, I had to mentally shift gears because I'd been so immersed in the building project, learning about mixing mortar and laying bricks. Suddenly it was done and I had to use it! I had never worked in a bakery, and my French training didn't help me a lot, because there they never bake bread in-house. The European tradition is that you go to the local baker for your bread. So I started reading, but it was frustrating because I just didn't know what I was doing. Finally, the head of the pastry department at my dad's cooking school sent me a very technical bread book in French, written by the master baker and professor of a baking college in France. I laboriously worked my way through it and slowly learned some of the baking science involved in producing good bread, especially good sourdough, which was my chief interest.

Margaret: We would be in bed at night. I would have my murder mystery and Chris would be translating this incredibly technical, scientific French baking text. But even before we knew much about what we were doing,

(continued on page 47)

Olive Rosemary Fougasse

Makes 2 loaves

- 2½ teaspoons (1 package) active dry yeast
- 2 tablespoons very warm water
- 1 cup tepid water
- 2 teaspoons chopped fresh rosemary leaves
- 1 tablespoon finely minced or puréed garlic (3 medium cloves)
- Scant 3¼ cup organic unbleached bread or all-purpose flour (12 to 13 percent protein)
- ⅓ cup coarsely chopped pitted black olives
- 5 tablespoons fruity olive oil
- Scant ½ cup organic barley flour
- 1¼ teaspoons fine sea salt

To make the dough: In the bowl of a heavy-duty electric mixer, dissolve the yeast in the warm water and allow the mixture to sit for 5 to 10 minutes. Add the tepid water, rosemary, garlic, and about 2⅓ cups of the white flour. Using the paddle attachment, knead at medium speed for 6 to 8 minutes, until the dough is smooth and very elastic. Change to the dough hook attachment and allow the dough to rest for 10 minutes.

Scrape down the sides of the bowl, add the olives and 3 tablespoons of the oil, and knead for 1 minute at low speed. In a separate bowl, mix together the barley flour, salt, and remaining white flour and add to the electric mixer bowl all at once. Knead for another 1 to 2 minutes, until all of the flour is absorbed and the dough clings to the hook and pulls away from the sides of the bowl. Turn the dough out onto the countertop and briefly knead by hand until the dough is smooth and elastic. (The dough should be soft but not too sticky; you should be able to touch it with your palm for 5 seconds without it sticking to your hand.) Knead in additional white flour if necessary, but try to keep the dough soft.

Lightly oil the mixer bowl and return the dough to it. Cover the bowl with plastic wrap or with a kitchen towel and allow the dough to rise at room temperature for 1½ to 2 hours, or refrigerate overnight, until doubled to tripled in volume.

Turn the dough out onto a smooth unfloured countertop and divide into two pieces. Roll each piece of dough into a smooth, taut oval, cover, and let rest for 5 to 10 minutes. With a rolling pin, flatten each oval into a rectangle approximately 9 x 6 inches. Cover and let rest for another 5 to 10 minutes.

Preheat the oven to 475°. Using a small sharp knife, cut 6 diagonal slashes about 2 inches long in each dough, cutting all the way through: make 3 parallel cuts on each side of the rectangle, from the upper left to the lower right on the left side, and from the upper right to the lower left on the right side, leaving space between the two sets of lines and along the border of the dough. Lift each dough with your hands and gently pull so the slashes become oval-shaped holes and the dough is stretched to about 10 x 7 inches. Place the dough pieces on an oiled baking sheet that will comfortably hold both doughs, or use two sheets. Cover doughs with a kitchen towel and let them rise at room temperature or in a slightly warmer location until doubled in volume, puffy, soft, and about 1½ inches thick. If the holes have closed up, gently spread them open with floured fingers. Brush the loaves with the remaining 2 tablespoons of oil and bake, preferably on a baking stone or tiles, at 475° for 15 to 20 minutes, until golden brown but still soft (the undersides should also be brown). Remove from the oven, allow to cool slightly, and then remove the loaves from the baking sheet with a metal spatula. Finish cooling on a wire rack.

there was a quality to the crusts that came out of the oven from day one. You knew they came from a brick oven.

This recipe is modeled on a bread I loved at Poilâne's bakery in Paris. It's very dense, with a mixture of white, whole-wheat, and rye flours, and it makes wonderful toast. I came up with the prune and walnut variation for a friend who was teaching a class on the cooking of southwest France and wanted something to go with goat cheese at the end of a meal. This bread is delicious on its own, and it goes very well with warm sautéed chicken or duck livers. It is also the best accompaniment to a terrine of duck foie gras that I've ever tasted.

French Currant Bread

Makes 2 loaves

Sponge

2 teaspoons active dry yeast (1 scant package)

1 teaspoon barley malt syrup or molasses

¼ cup very warm water

Dough

½ cup plus 6 tablespoons tepid water

Scant cup organic rye flour

Scant cup organic unbleached bread or all-purpose flour (12 to 13 percent protein)

2 tablespoons unsalted butter, softened

Scant cup organic whole-wheat flour

1½ teaspoons fine sea salt

2 packed cups organic zante currants or raisins

1 egg, lightly beaten

To prepare the sponge: In a small bowl, whisk the yeast and malt syrup into the warm water. Allow the mixture to sit for 5 minutes to become creamy. To prepare the dough: Put the sponge into the bowl of a heavy-duty electric mixer fitted with the paddle attachment. Add the ½ cup tepid water and rye flour. Blend at low speed for 2 minutes until pasty and slightly elastic. Remove the paddle, cover the bowl with plastic wrap or a kitchen towel and allow to rise at room temperature for 2 to 3 hours, until doubled to tripled in volume.

Return the bowl with the sponge to the mixer fitted with the paddle attachment. Add the 6 tablespoons tepid water and white flour and knead at medium speed for 10 minutes, stopping the machine to scrape down the sides of the bowl once or twice. Add the butter and continue mixing briefly. In a separate bowl, mix the whole-wheat flour with the salt and add it all at once to the mixer, while continuing to mix at low speed. Mix for another 2 minutes, until the dough is homogenous. (Stop the mixer to scrape down the sides of the bowl as necessary.) Turn the dough out onto a lightly floured work surface and, with floured hands, shape dough into a ball (the dough will be sticky). Lightly oil the mixer bowl and place the dough in it. Cover the bowl with plastic wrap or a kitchen towel and allow the dough to rise at room temperature for 1 to 2 hours, or refrigerate overnight, until doubled to tripled in volume and soft enough to easily leave a lasting impression when gently poked with a floured finger.

Preheat the oven to 450°. Return the bowl to the mixer fitted with the paddle attachment, and add the currants, working them into the dough at low speed just long enough to distribute them evenly. Turn the dough out onto a lightly floured work surface, and with floured hands, divide the dough into 2 equal pieces. Shape doughs into rounds or long loaves, cover, and allow to rise on parchment paper or on a greased baking sheet (or in small, greased loaf pans) for 45 to 60 minutes, until doubled in volume and soft. Brush tops with beaten egg and bake on the center rack of the oven for 25 to 30 minutes, until the loaves are well browned and hollow-sounding when tapped. Remove from the oven and let cool on a wire rack.

Prune and Walnut Variation: Substitute 2 packed cups chopped pitted prunes and 1 generous cup whole or coarsely chopped walnuts (both preferably organic) for the currants, adding them as instructed for the currants.

At Cafe Beaujolais, our oven is the type a village baker three or four hundred years ago would have used: There's just one big brick-lined space. You build a wood fire in it, the fire heats up the brick, and then the fire dies down and you scrape out the ashes and swab down the hearth, both to clean it before you put the dough down on it and to introduce some moisture into the oven, which helps develop the crust. You put the loaves in, shut the door, and they bake. What results is a descending heat curve, which is ideal for baking bread. The oven starts out very hot and as the bread bakes the oven slowly cools down and dries out.

To load our sourdoughs into the oven, we invert the cloth-lined baskets in which they've been rising onto the peel (the big wooden paddle). We slide the peel into the oven and then whisk it out quickly so the doughs just plop down onto the brick surface. You have to be pretty precise about where you put each loaf because once you set a loaf down, you can't move it for 10 or 15 minutes. Also, once
(continued on page 51)

Buckwheat Hazelnut Bread

Makes 4 loaves

2½ teaspoons active dry yeast (1 package)

2 teaspoons barley malt syrup or molasses

¼ cup very warm water

1 cup plus 2 tablespoons tepid water

Scant ⅔ cup organic buckwheat flour

Scant 1½ cups organic unbleached bread or all-purpose flour (12 to 13 percent protein)

2 tablespoons unsalted butter, softened

1½ teaspoons fine sea salt

1⅓ cups organic whole-wheat flour

2⅔ cups whole organic hazelnuts

1 egg, lightly beaten

In the bowl of a heavy-duty electric mixer fitted with the paddle attachment, whisk the yeast and malt syrup into the warm water. Allow the mixture to sit for 10 minutes to become creamy. Whisk in the tepid water and buckwheat flour. Add the white flour and beat at medium speed for 8 to 10 minutes, until smooth and very elastic, stopping the machine to scrape down the sides once or twice. Add the butter and continue mixing briefly. Allow the dough to rest for 5 minutes.

Meanwhile, in a separate bowl, mix the salt with the whole-wheat flour. Add it all at once to the mixer bowl, and knead at low speed for 1 to 2 minutes, stopping once to scrape down the sides of the bowl and the paddle. Stop mixing when the dough is homogenous, clinging to the paddle, and pulling away from the sides of the bowl. It should be both sticky and springy to the touch.

Turn the dough out onto a lightly floured work surface and, with floured hands, shape it into a ball. Lightly oil the mixer bowl and place the dough in it. Cover the bowl with plastic wrap or a kitchen towel and allow dough to rise at room temperature for 2 to 3 hours, or refrigerate overnight, until doubled to tripled in volume and puffy and soft enough to leave a lasting impression when gently poked with a floured finger.

If the dough was refrigerated, allow it to come to room temperature for 2 hours before proceeding. Return the bowl to the mixer fitted with the dough hook, and add the hazelnuts to the bowl all at once. Work them into the dough at low speed for less than one minute, just long enough to distribute them evenly. Turn the dough out onto a lightly floured surface and divide it into 4 equal portions (if you are weighing the dough, the portions should be about 9½ ounces each). Roll each portion into a ball, using the outsides of your palms to tuck the sides of the dough underneath and create surface tension. When the rounds are well shaped and springy to the touch, transfer them to 2 oiled or parchment-lined baking sheets, allowing room for them to double in volume. Cover the dough with a kitchen towel and allow to rise in a warm spot for 60 to 90 minutes, until doubled in volume, puffy, and soft (you can use the finger impression test again).

Preheat the oven to 450° for 15 to 20 minutes. Brush the loaves gently with beaten egg. Put the loaves on the center rack of the preheated oven, lower the heat to 400°, and bake for 20 to 30 minutes, until golden brown on all sides (including the bottom) and hollow-sounding when tapped. Remove from the oven and let cool on a wire rack.

you put a loaf in, it begins to bake, and you don't want 10 minutes to go by from the time you put the first loaf in until you load the last one. You have to work quickly. It's really an aerobic job when you're loading up a 6 x 4-foot oven with 32 loaves of bread!

Potato Walnut Rolls

Makes 18 rolls

2½ teaspoons active dry yeast (1 package)

½ cup very warm water

1 tablespoon honey

1¼ cups tepid water

2 cups (1 pound) mashed potatoes, at room temperature

4 cups organic unbleached bread or all-purpose flour (12 to 13 percent protein)

1¾ cups organic oat flour

6 tablespoons organic whole-wheat flour

1 tablespoon fine sea salt

4 cups (1 pound) organic walnuts, whole, coarsely chopped or crumbled

1 egg, lightly beaten with a teaspoon of water

In a small bowl, dissolve the yeast in the warm water. Add the honey and let the mixture stand for 5 minutes. Pour the mixture into the bowl of a heavy-duty electric mixer fitted with the paddle attachment. Add the tepid water and mashed potatoes and mix for 1 minute at low speed. Add the white flour and knead at medium speed for 4 to 6 minutes, until very elastic. In a separate bowl, mix the oat and whole-wheat flours together with the salt and add to the mixing bowl all at once. Continue to knead at low speed for 2 to 3 minutes, stopping once or twice to scrape the sides of the bowl down, until the dough is homogenous and pulling away from the sides of the bowl. Transfer the dough to an oiled bowl or a container large enough to allow the dough to double to triple in volume. Cover the bowl with a kitchen towel and let rise at room temperature for a couple of hours, or refrigerate overnight, until doubled to tripled in volume and puffy and soft to the touch.

If the dough was refrigerated, allow it to come to room temperature before continuing. Deflate the dough by punching it down with your hands and return the bowl to the mixer. Add walnuts all at once and mix at low speed for 1 minute, or just long enough to incorporate them evenly into the dough.

Cut the dough into 18 equal-sized portions. With well-floured hands, flatten the portions into rectangular shapes. Roll the rectangles up to achieve some tautness and a shape resembling a baked potato. Place the rolls, seam side down, on 2 oiled baking sheets. Allow rolls to rise, covered loosely with a kitchen towel, in a warm (80° to 85°) location until puffy and almost double their original volume, about 1 hour.

Preheat the oven to 450° for 15 to 20 minutes. Brush the rolls with the beaten egg and bake for 15 to 20 minutes, until golden brown all over. Remove from the oven and cool on a wire rack.

EVENING FOOD

SOUPS

• S O U P S •

Asian-Flavored Grilled or Roasted Eggplant Soup / 56

Black and White Corn Soup / 58

Brandied Pumpkin Soup with Tomato, Onion, Proscuitto,
and Rye Croutons / 61

Tyrolean Garlic Soup / 63

Dried Shrimp Pozole / 64

Roasted Tomatillo and Tomato Soup / 66

Zanzibar Fish Soup / 68

This soup does not have its origins in the cuisine of any specific country. It came about one day at the restaurant when we had a run on the soup we were serving and needed another that could be thrown together quickly with what we had on hand. Because it was so well received and so easy to make, we have featured it on our menu several times since. Originally, we roasted the eggplant and puréed it; lately we have been grilling and coarsely chopping the eggplant for a country-style texture, which I prefer. The flavors represent an amalgam of some of the Asian ingredients that are more readily available in American markets: soy sauce, sesame oil, and coconut milk combine with the eggplant for a rich, smoky base; while the coriander and garam masala provide a perfumy counterpoint. The chili paste with soy oil and shao-hsing, recent additions to the recipe, are the only ingredients not commonly available in supermarkets. If they aren't already in your pantry and a trip to an Asian market isn't practical, substitute dry sherry for the shao-hsing, with a little extra
(continued on page 57)

Asian-Flavored Grilled or Roasted Eggplant Soup

Makes 6 servings

1 large or 2 small globe eggplant

2 tablespoons soy sauce

6 tablespoons sesame oil

2 tablespoons chili paste with soy oil

1 tablespoon shao-hsing or dry sherry

1 (14-ounce) can (1½ cups) coconut milk

4 cups chicken stock or water

2 teaspoons coriander seeds, toasted and ground in an electric spice mill (or with a mortar and pestle)

2 teaspoons garam masala (page 27) or ½ teaspoon freshly ground cardamom seeds

1 teaspoon fine sea salt, or to taste

1 tablespoon sesame seeds, toasted, for garnish

3 to 4 tablespoons coarsely chopped cilantro, for garnish

Start a charcoal fire in a barbecue or preheat the oven to 375°. Trim the cap(s) off the eggplant and trim off the skin on two opposing sides, discarding the trimmings. Slice the eggplant lengthwise ¼-inch thick, cutting parallel to the skinless sides so that each slice has skin around its edge but no slice has all skin on one side. In a small bowl, whisk the soy sauce, sesame oil, chili paste, and shao-hsing together, and then brush the eggplant slices liberally with this mixture. Either grill the eggplant on the hot barbecue for 1 to 2 minutes per side, or lay the slices on a baking sheet and roast them for about 30 minutes, until richly browned and soft.

Roughly julienne the cooked eggplant slices. Combine them (and any left-over marinade juices) with all but ⅓ cup of the coconut milk, the stock, coriander, garam masala, and salt in a saucepan over medium heat. Simmer for 15 to 30 minutes, until the eggplant is very tender and the flavors have blended. Taste for salt, add if needed, and keep warm.

Meanwhile, pour the reserved coconut milk into a small pan and gently reduce to thicken it slightly (you'll want about 3 to 4 tablespoons for garnish). Warm soup bowls in a 200° oven for 10 to 15 minutes. Refrigerate the thickened coconut milk to cool it down.

When you are ready to serve, ladle the soup into the warmed bowls and drizzle with the coconut milk. (At Cafe Beaujolais, we put the coconut milk into a squirt bottle and draw a yin-yang design on top of the soup.) Sprinkle with the toasted sesame seeds and chopped cilantro. Serve warm.

soy sauce and a generous grinding of fresh pepper for the chili paste.

If I were pressed to name my favorite soup, this might well be it. A few years back, we prepared a dinner for Roederer Estate, the branch of the prestigious French champagne house that had recently established vineyards and a winery in nearby Anderson Valley. I had been fine-tuning a smoked corn soup and playing around with *huitlacoche*, an ingredient then fairly new to me, when it occurred to me to turn the huitlacoche purée that we'd been using as a sauce into a soup and combine the two corn soups in one bowl. Coincidentally, at that time huitlacoche was Paris' new food discovery, so what better way to try out my new idea than on the occasion of welcoming our new French neighbors? The soup was a great success at that meal and every time we've served it since, not just because of the novelty of two soups in one bowl, but because of the complex flavor interaction created in that presentation.

The flavors of each soup are tantalizing. The earthy flavor of huitlacoche is difficult to describe—its aftertaste reminds me of ginger and lemongrass—
(continued on page 59)

Black and White Corn Soup

Makes 6 to 8 servings

White Corn Soup

3 ears fresh white corn, husked

2 teaspoons unsalted butter

¾ cup chopped yellow onion

1½ teaspoons fine sea salt

1 small dried chipotle chile (see Glossary)

2 Kaffir lime leaves, fresh or frozen, coarsely chopped (see Glossary)

1½ tablespoons coarsely chopped cilantro stems

1 (14-ounce) can (1½ cups) coconut milk

1½ cups water

Black Corn Soup

3 ears fresh white corn, husked

5 teaspoons unsalted butter, home-rendered lard, or vegetable oil

1 cup chopped white onion

1½ teaspoons fine sea salt

2 teaspoons minced garlic (about 2 large cloves)

2 cups (8 ounces) huitlacoche kernels, fresh or frozen and thawed (see Glossary)

2 tablespoons chopped fresh epazote leaves (reserve stems)

3 cups pork or chicken stock, or water

1 to 2 (6-inch) corn tortillas, or more if you want to make extra chips

Vegetable oil for deep-frying

Fine sea salt to taste

½ large red bell pepper, roasted (page 6), peeled, seeded, and cut into ½-inch-wide, 1½-inch-long strips (rajas)

1 fresh poblano chile, roasted (page 6), peeled, seeded, and cut into ½-inch-wide, 1½-inch-long strips (rajas)

2 tablespoons coarsely chopped cilantro, for garnish

1 lime, cut into 6 to 8 wedges, for garnish

To prepare the White Corn Soup: Smoke the shucked ears either overnight in a home smoker or over a low fire in a covered barbecue until lightly browned by the smoke. Cut the kernels off the cobs. You should have 2 cups of kernels.

Heat the butter in a heavy-bottomed pan and add the salt, chipotle chile, Kaffir lime leaves, and cilantro stems. Sauté over medium heat until the onions are soft and golden, about 8 to 10 minutes. Add 1½ cups of the smoked kernels and sauté for another 3 to 5 minutes over medium-high heat, stirring constantly. Add the coconut milk and water. Place the remaining ½ cup kernels in a sieve or pasta insert and lower it into the soup to cook the corn separately from the rest of the soup. Bring the soup to a boil and then lower the heat to a simmer. Cover and cook for 30 minutes.

Meanwhile, prepare the Black Corn Soup: Cut the kernels of white corn from the cobs and measure 2 cups. Heat the butter in a heavy-bottomed pan and sauté the chopped white onion with the salt for 8 to 10 minutes, until soft and golden. Add the garlic and cook for a minute or two, until fragrant but not browned. Add 1½ cups of the corn kernels, all of the huitlacoche kernels, and the epazote stems and cook for 3 to 5 minutes. Add the stock. Place the remaining ½ cup corn kernels in a sieve or pasta insert and lower it into the soup to cook the corn separately. Bring the soup to a boil and then lower the heat to a simmer. Cover and cook for 25 minutes.

Remove the pan with the white soup from the heat and allow it to cool slightly. Remove the sieve and set the corn aside. Blend the remaining mixture, in batches (never fill a blender more than half full with a warm liquid or it may blow the top off and burn you), and pass it through a fine-mesh sieve to remove any fibrous matter. Use a rubber spatula to press the soup through the sieve. Add the reserved corn to the soup, add salt to taste, and set aside.

Add the epazote leaves to the black soup and simmer for another 5 minutes, covered. Allow the soup to cool slightly, and then remove the sieve and set it aside. Purée the remaining mixture in the blender, proceed as directed for the white soup, and set aside.

Heat the vegetable oil in an electric deep-fryer or medium, heavy-bottomed saucepan until it reaches 375°. (If you don't have a deep-fry thermometer, the oil is ready when a wooden spoon dipped in the oil begins sizzling almost immediately.) Using a 1-inch round cookie cutter (or any small round form and a knife), cut out 6 to 8 rounds from the tortillas (one round per person) and deep-fry them in the oil until golden brown. Drain on paper towels and add salt. (If you'd like to serve extra chips on the side, cut the remaining tortillas into diamond shapes, fry, drain, and salt.) Cut one ½ x ¼-inch strip per serving from the red bell pepper rajas, and set aside.

To assemble and serve, warm a shallow soup bowl for each person in a 200° oven for 10 to 15 minutes. Reheat both soups separately. Add the remaining red pepper rajas to the white soup and the poblano rajas to the black soup (approximately 1 tablespoon of each per serving). Put a 3-inch cookie cutter in the center of a warmed soup bowl. Pour ½ cup of the black soup into the center of the ring, and then the same amount of the white soup into the bowl outside the ring. Carefully lift the ring straight up and out of the bowl. Repeat with the remaining bowls until all are filled. Sprinkle the white soup with the chopped cilantro. Place 1 of the small reserved red pepper strips on top of a round tortilla chip and carefully float the chip in the center of the black soup. Place a lime wedge on the rim of the bowl. Repeat with the remaining bowls and serve at once, serving extra tortilla chips on the side if desired.

but it is a flavor that quickly grows on you. The soups can be tasted separately in the bowl, but tasted together in the same spoonful, their flavor union is fascinating, both contrasting and harmonious. This is achieved by putting the cilantro only in the white soup and the epazote only in the black soup. The flavors also play off the spicy, smoky, sweet flavor of the white soup (with its background tropical, floral creaminess from the coconut and lime) and the musty, elusive, pleasantly bitter flavor of the black soup. And while this flavor dance is happening on your palate, the textural contrasts of creamy soup, chewy corn, and crunchy tortilla chips add yet another element to contemplate. But enough philosophical taste analysis. Isn't it alarming how obsessive we cooks can get about food?

Finding huitlacoche should be the biggest challenge here (see Glossary). The other less familiar ingredients are readily purchased at Mexican and Thai markets. The recipe also calls for two round pastry rings or 1-inch diameter and 3-inch diameter cookie cutters, although these are not absolutely essential.

The size of your soup bowls will determine the size of the ring needed to divide the bowl evenly. A set of nested pastry rings is especially handy for serving two soups in one bowl because you can select a larger or smaller ring to adapt to soup bowls of varied sizes or if you want the flavor of one soup to dominate. The soup bowls we use at the restaurant hold 1 cup and are $6\frac{1}{4}$ inches wide at the top inside rim. We use a ring about 3 inches in diameter to divide the bowl roughly in half. The inside diameter of a standard tuna can is also, conveniently, about 3 inches.

Brandied Pumpkin Soup
with Tomato, Onion, Prosciutto, and Rye Croutons

Makes 8 to 10 servings

Soup

6- to 7-pound attractive pumpkin for presentation bowl (optional)

1 pound peeled and seeded fresh pumpkin (or 2 cups canned pumpkin)

4 cups light-bodied poultry broth (chicken, turkey, or duck, homemade, but not too reduced)

Fine sea salt to taste

Freshly ground white pepper to taste

Freshly grated nutmeg to taste

2 tablespoons unsalted butter

1 pound yellow onions, peeled and cut into quarters lengthwise, then sliced ¼ inch thick

4 to 5 ripe tomatoes, peeled, seeded, and coarsely chopped (2 cups), or 1½ cups canned whole tomatoes, drained, seeded, and coarsely chopped

¼ cup plus a dash of brandy

1 cup dry white wine

Garnish

2 ounces (approximately 1 large or 2 small slices, ⅛-inch-thick) prosciutto or other top-quality uncooked ham, trimmed of excess fat, then cut into ⅛-inch dice (When you purchase the meat, ask them to use setting #15 on the slicer.)

½ cup butter

8 ounces day-old light rye bread, preferably with caraway seeds, trimmed of crust and cut into ½-inch dice

2 tablespoons minced fresh chives

¾ cup crème fraîche or sour cream

2 tablespoons chopped fresh flat-leaf parsley

1 cup grated Gruyère or other Swiss cheese

Preheat the oven to 350° for 10 to 15 minutes. Cut out an attractive 5- to 6-inch-diameter lid from the large pumpkin. Scoop out the seeds and strings and bake for about 1½ hours while preparing the soup. (Don't let the pumpkin overcook or it will get too soft and collapse!) As soon as it begins to get tender, remove the pumpkin from the oven and set it aside. This will be the container for the soup.

Here's an example of the type of recipe development that I love to do: Take ingredients that have traditionally been combined in a popular regional dish, or sometimes in several variations of that dish, and experiment with recombining their proportions to each other, or their cooking methods, to create new taste and texture variations on a proven flavor marriage. I consider the new dish a success if it equals or surpasses my enjoyment of the original source of inspiration. In the case of this soup, I started with a few simple French pumpkin soup recipes. In addition to the pumpkin, each recipe called for some combination of tomatoes, stock, white wine, onions, gruyere cheese, leftover bread, and crème fraîche among its ingredients, although no single recipe combined them all. After several years of tinkering with these elements, I arrived at the following rendition, which I haven't been able to improve upon in the past eight years. All the flavors would taste comfortingly familiar to someone used to traditional French pumpkin soups, but hopefully such a

(continued on page 62)

Cut the fresh pumpkin into chunks and put into a large soup pot with the broth, sea salt, pepper, and nutmeg. (If the broth is already salted, you may not need additional salt.) Bring to a boil, cover, and simmer over low heat for 15 to 20 minutes until the pumpkin is very tender when pierced with a fork. Remove from heat and allow to cool. If using canned pumpkin, combine it with the broth in a large soup pot, bring it to a simmer, add the salt, pepper, and nutmeg, and set aside.

In a medium-large skillet over medium heat, melt the butter. Add the onions, season with salt and pepper, and sauté, stirring occasionally, for 15 to 20 minutes, or until the onions are soft and sweet but not browned. Add the tomatoes to the pan, bring to a simmer, stirring, and then add the brandy. Return to a boil, then reduce heat and simmer for 1 minute. Add the white wine and simmer briskly over medium-high heat for 10 to 15 minutes, uncovered, until some of the liquid has evaporated but the tomatoes still have distinct texture.

Meanwhile, blend the slightly cooled pumpkin-broth mixture in a blender until smooth. Pour through a sieve into a pot large enough to hold all of the soup. Add the tomato-onion mixture, return the soup to a simmer, and adjust seasoning to taste, keeping it slightly undersalted to allow the sweetness of the brandy and onions to remain prominent. If the soup seems too thick, it may be thinned with additional broth or water. Pour the hot soup into the whole baked pumpkin and place in a low (175° to 200°) oven to keep warm.

To prepare the garnishes: Sauté the prosciutto in the butter over medium heat for a few minutes, until crisp but not browned. Pour the contents of the pan through a sieve into a bowl, reserving both meat and butter. Toss the drained prosciutto in a paper towel to absorb excess fat and set aside.

Meanwhile, put the diced rye bread on a baking sheet in a medium-low oven (250° to 300°) to dry out but not brown. Remove when hard, 5 to 20 minutes, depending on the heat of the oven and the initial staleness of the bread. Wipe the pan clean and return the reserved prosciutto and butter to the pan. Heat until hot but not smoking, and then add the bread all at once. Sauté over medium-high heat, tossing and stirring constantly to coat the bread evenly with the butter and to keep it from burning. Cook until the croutons are an even golden brown. Drain immediately in a sieve or colander (if there is much butter left in the pan) or drain on paper towels. Set aside.

To serve: In a bowl, stir the minced chives into the crème fraîche and set aside with the chopped parsley, prosciutto, and rye croutons. Sprinkle 1 to 2 tablespoons of grated Gruyère on the bottom of each soup bowl and put the bowls in the oven for a few minutes to melt the cheese slightly. An additional dash of brandy, added just before serving, is often nice. If presenting the pumpkin at the table, sprinkle the top of the soup with some of the croutons, some of the minced prosciutto, and some of the parsley, and place a large dollop of chived crème fraîche in the center. After presenting the pumpkin tureen, ladle the soup into the warmed soup bowls and serve small bowls of additional garnishes. If you're not using the pumpkin for presentation, simply ladle the soup into the warmed bowls and garnish each bowl as described for the pumpkin bowl.

Tyrolean Garlic Soup

Makes 8 servings

- 1¼ pounds unpeeled garlic cloves, or 1 pound peeled garlic cloves
- ½ cup unsalted butter or olive oil
- 1 teaspoon sugar
- 2¼ to 2½ teaspoons fine sea salt
- ½ teaspoon freshly ground white pepper
- 1¼ cups dry white wine
- 1 bay leaf
- ½ teaspoon freshly grated nutmeg
- 5 tablespoons all-purpose flour
- 6½ cups chicken stock
- ¾ cup homemade croutons (use good sourdough or rye bread), for garnish
- 2 to 3 tablespoons chopped fresh flat-leaf parsley and/or minced fresh chives, for garnish

Coarsely chop the garlic cloves in a food processor. In a nonstick pan over medium-high heat, sauté the garlic in 4 tablespoons of the butter just until it begins to brown. Add the sugar, salt, and pepper, toss, and stir until nicely browned but not burned. Add the wine, bay leaf, and nutmeg and bring to a boil. Reduce by two thirds.

Meanwhile, in a 3- or 4-quart saucepan, heat the remaining 4 tablespoons butter and the flour together for 2 minutes over medium heat, stirring constantly, until the mixture is blond in color. (The cooked butter and flour mixture is called a roux.) Set aside. Add the stock to the garlic-wine mixture, bring to a boil, lower heat, and simmer for 15 to 20 minutes, until the garlic is falling-apart tender.

Warm the soup bowls in a 200° oven for 10 to 15 minutes.

If using unpeeled garlic, put the garlic-stock mixture through a food mill to remove the garlic skins. Return the roux to the heat and whisk in the hot garlic-stock, beating until smooth. Bring to a boil, stirring constantly. Remove the pan from the heat, adjust the seasoning, and serve garnished with croutons and chopped parsley.

If you have a food mill, you can use unpeeled garlic cloves; the soup will have a smooth texture. If you don't have a food mill, you must start with whole peeled garlic. If you don't feel like peeling the garlic yourself, you can buy peeled cloves in jars in supermarket produce sections. (If you do have to peel all of the garlic by hand, crush the cloves first with the side of a heavy knife to speed the process.) The soup made without the use of a food mill will retain the texture of the coarsely chopped cloves for a more rustic version.

The original Austrian recipe calls for butter and milk for the soup base, as the Tyrol is full of dairy cows but short on olive trees. I prefer this lighter version with stock replacing the milk, but as for the butter/olive oil dilemma, my allegiance is divided—the soup tastes great either way. The butter provides a more Tyrolean flavor, the olive oil a more Mediterranean one.

While visiting my friend Diana Kennedy at her home in Michoacán, Mexico, I had lunch in the nearby town of Zitácuaro. Diana, a renowned authority on Mexican cuisine and a fabulous chef, had recommended their dried shrimp soup, a spicy tomato-based vegetable soup accented by small dried shrimp, a recipe for which she includes in her book, *The Art of Mexican Cooking*. The soup was tasty and it got me thinking of my other favorite Mexican soup, really more of a brothy stew, called pozole. *Pozole* is the Mexican word both for whole hominy (dried field corn) and for a hearty soup of pork and hominy garnished with raw vegetables, herbs, and a dried chile-based salsa. This variation on that dried shrimp soup joins the unique flavor of dried shrimp with the texture and flavor panoply of a pozole.

Dried shrimp can be something of an acquired taste. Though I personally am fond of it, I was hesitant about including it on the menu. But a very positive response both in number of orders and recipe requests proved me wrong. Don't be

(continued on page 65)

Dried Shrimp Pozole

Makes 6 to 8 servings

- 1½ cups prepared hominy, preferably homemade, or 2½ cups canned and drained (see Note)
- 7 cups shrimp stock, fish stock, or 3½ cups clam juice mixed with 3½ cups water
- 1 medium sprig fresh epazote, leaves and stem separated and leaves finely chopped (if not available fresh, omit)
- 2 ounces dried shrimp (see Glossary)
- 5 to 6 ripe tomatoes (1¾ pounds), cored
- 1 ounce (about 10 to 12) dried cascabel chiles (see Glossary)
- 1 ounce (about 4 to 5) dried guajillo chiles (see Glossary)
- 1 teaspoon achiote seeds or paste (see Glossary)
- 3 cloves garlic, peeled and crushed
- 8 ounces young summer squash (about 3 crookneck, 16 pattypan, or 2 to 3 zucchini), preferably mixed colors and shapes (other vegetables, such as carrots, new potatoes, or green beans, may be added or substituted if desired)
- Fine sea salt to taste
- ¼ head napa cabbage, shredded (2 to 3 cups)
- 1 tablespoon dried Mexican oregano, for garnish
- ½ medium white or red onion, minced, for garnish
- ½ ripe avocado, cut into ½-inch dice, for garnish
- 2 tablespoons coarsely chopped cilantro leaves, for garnish
- 6 tablespoons sour cream, for garnish
- 2 limes, cut into wedges, for garnish

If using home-prepared hominy, put it in a pot with 6 cups of the stock and the epazote stem and simmer strongly, covered, for 45 minutes. Add half of the dried shrimp and simmer for another 45 minutes, still covered, until the shrimp and hominy are tender and some of the kernels have opened up like a flower. If using canned hominy, cook the shrimp by itself in the stock until tender and then add the drained hominy and epazote stem and simmer for another 10 minutes. Remove and discard the epazote stem. If using Mexican dried shrimp, chop them in half at this point if you'd like smaller pieces.

Meanwhile, put the tomatoes in a roasting pan and place them under a hot broiler until the skins are lightly charred and they are soft and cooked through, about 15 minutes. In a heavy, dry skillet over medium heat, toast the two types of chiles on all sides until fragrant but not burned, about 3 to 5 minutes. Stem the chiles and set them aside with the tomatoes.

Grind the remaining half of the dried shrimp and all of the achiote seeds to a powder in an electric spice mill, or with a mortar and pestle. (If using achiote paste, dissolve it in a little bit of the stock and add to the pot.) Combine the broiled tomatoes, toasted chiles, garlic, ground shrimp, and remaining 1 cup of stock in a saucepan. Bring to a boil, cover, reduce heat, and simmer gently for 30 minutes. Remove the pan from the heat and allow the mixture to cool slightly.

While the hominy mixture is cooking, cut the squash into $1/2$-inch rounds (for zucchini or crookneck) or wedges (for pattypans), toss with $1/2$ teaspoon salt, and drain in a sieve or colander for 30 minutes to concentrate their flavor. (Other vegetables, except eggplant, do not benefit from this preliminary salting before cooking.)

Allow the hominy mixture to cool. Purée it in a blender until smooth and pour it through a sieve into the hominy stock. Bring to a simmer and add the squash. Simmer gently for 10 minutes, or until the vegetables are barely tender. Add salt if desired (it should be peppery enough from the chiles).

To serve: Warm soup bowls in a 200° oven for 10 to 15 minutes. Place a small handful of the shredded cabbage into each of the warm soup bowls and ladle the pozole into the bowls. Garnish each bowl with a sprinkle of oregano and minced epazote leaves, a spoonful each of minced onion and diced avocado, a large pinch of chopped cilantro, a dollop of sour cream in the center, and a lime wedge on the rim. Serve hot with any extra garnishes on the side.

Note: Dried hominy and powdered lime, known as mais para pozole *and* cal, *respectively, are available in bulk in most Mexican markets and some tortille- rias. To prepare dried hominy for cooking, place 1 cup of hominy in a small pot with 2 cups of cold water. Dissolve 2 teaspoons of powdered lime in a little water and add it to the pot. Bring to a simmer and simmer strongly until the skins have turned bright yellow and can be easily rubbed off the kernels, about 20 to 30 minutes. Allow the hominy to cool slightly, then drain it in a colander and transfer it to a bowl of cold water. Rub the kernels between your hands until the skins have been removed. Change the water several times during this process to wash away the skin residue. Rinse the hominy again and, with the tip of a paring knife or with a strong thumbnail, remove the pedicels (the small hard tip of the kernel where it was attached to the cob). One cup of dried hominy will yield $1^{1}/_{2}$ cups of prepared hominy, which will expand to about $2^{1}/_{2}$ cups when cooked.*

alarmed upon your first taste of the chile-toma-to-shrimp base. Though it may seem extremely spicy alone, when it is eaten as an ensemble with all of its garnishes, the spiciness will be just right. (If you still find it too spicy, it can always be diluted with more stock or water.)

Roasted Tomatillo and Tomato Soup

Makes 8 servings

8 ounces (about 5 to 6) ripe tomatillos, husked and washed

2 tablespoons vegetable oil

1 cup chopped white onion (1 medium onion)

1½ teaspoons minced garlic (2 small cloves)

2 teaspoons chopped fresh epazote (if fresh is unavailable, omit)

½ teaspoon dried Mexican oregano, lightly toasted in a dry skillet

2 packed tablespoons chopped cilantro stems

1 serrano chile, stemmed and chopped

2½ cups chicken stock

2 teaspoons fine sea salt

1½ teaspoons cornstarch

1 pound (about 3 medium) ripe tomatoes

2 tablespoons vegetable oil

1 cup chopped white onion (1 medium onion)

1½ teaspoons minced garlic (2 small cloves)

2 teaspoons achiote paste (see Glossary)

1½ cups chicken stock

Grated zest of 2 oranges (rinsed in hot water before zesting)

½ small canned chipotle chile, rinsed (see Glossary)

2 teaspoons fine sea salt

Garnish

6 (6-inch) corn tortillas

Oil for deep-frying

Fine sea salt to taste

6 to 8 tablespoons crème fraîche or sour cream

⅓ cup roughly chopped cilantro leaves

To prepare the tomatillo soup: Place the tomatillos in a shallow metal baking pan and broil for 15 to 20 minutes, until lightly charred and soft. Turn once or twice to cook evenly.

In a 2-quart saucepan, heat the oil and fry the onion for 5 minutes over medium heat to soften. Add the garlic and cook for another minute, until fragrant but not browned. Add the epazote, oregano, cilantro stems, and chile and cook for a few more minutes, until fragrant. Add the tomatillos, chicken stock, and salt. Bring to a boil and simmer for 10 to 15 minutes. Dissolve the cornstarch in a little cold water, and then add it to the soup. Boil the soup for another 2 minutes and remove from heat. Allow soup to cool and then purée in a blender or food processor. Strain the soup into a pot through a sieve, and add more salt if desired. Set aside while preparing tomato soup and garnish.

To prepare the roasted tomato soup: Broil the tomatoes as instructed for the tomatillos, until they are lightly charred and soft on several sides. In a 2-quart saucepan, heat the oil and fry the onion for about 5 minutes to soften. Add the garlic and cook for another minute, until fragrant but not browned. Dissolve the achiote paste in some of the chicken stock, whisking until smooth, and add to the saucepan, along with the orange zest and chipotle chile. Cook for a few minutes over medium heat, stirring constantly.

Add the roasted tomatoes, salt, and stock and bring to a boil. Simmer for 10 to 15 minutes and remove from heat. Allow the soup to cool. Purée in a blender or food processor and strain into a pot through a sieve. Add more salt if desired. Keep warm over low heat. Rewarm the tomatillo soup, and warm soup bowls in a 200° oven for 10 to 15 minutes, while preparing the garnish.

Cut the tortillas into $^1/_2$-inch-wide strips. Turn the strips 45 degrees and cut them into small diamonds. Heat the oil to 375° and deep-fry until golden brown, about 3 to 5 minutes. (If you don't have a deep-fry thermometer, the oil is ready when a wooden spoon dipped in the oil begins sizzling almost immediately.) Remove the chips from the pan with a slotted spoon and drain on paper towels. Add salt to taste.

To serve, place a 3-inch-diameter pastry ring, a cookie cutter without a handle, or an empty tuna can with the top and bottom removed in the center of a warmed shallow soup bowl. Pour the red (tomato) soup into the inside of the ring and the green (tomatillo) soup outside the ring. When the soups are filled to the same height, remove the ring by lifting carefully and directly up and out of the bowl. Repeat with the remaining warmed bowls. Put the crème fraîche into a plastic squirt bottle and draw a sun-shape design, zigzagging around the border of the red center. (In the absence of a squirt bottle, spoon a dollop of crème fraîche in the center of the red soup.) Sprinkle chopped cilantro on the green soup, and serve the tortilla chips on the side.

Zanzibar Fish Soup

Makes 6 to 8 servings

4 cups canned tomatoes, with their juice

2 ounces (⅔ cup) dried shrimp (see Glossary)

4 cups fish stock, shrimp stock, or bottled clam juice

1 (14-ounce) can (1½ cups) coconut milk

2 cups chopped yellow onion (1 large onion)

1½ tablespoons minced garlic (4 to 5 cloves)

2 to 3 tablespoons minced small green chiles (serrano or
jalapeño, about 3 or 4 chiles)

2 tablespoons fish sauce (see Glossary)

½ pound boneless rockfish (see Note)

8 to 10 Kaffir lime leaves (see Glossary)

1 tablespoon freshly squeezed lime juice

¼ teaspoon sea salt

2 tablespoons coarsely chopped cilantro, for garnish

Cut the tomatoes in half and remove the seeds, reserving the juice. Coarsely chop the tomatoes and set aside. Grind half of the dried shrimp to a powder in an electric spice mill or with a mortar and pestle. Combine the tomato juice, fish stock, coconut milk, shrimp (ground and whole), onions, garlic, chiles, and 1½ tablespoons of the fish sauce in a 3- to 4- quart saucepan. Bring to a boil, reduce heat, cover, and simmer gently for 15 to 20 minutes, until the onions are tender.

Meanwhile, slice the rockfish crosswise into very thin, bite-sized pieces (about ⅛ inch thick). Place the fish in a medium bowl and toss with the remaining ½ tablespoon fish sauce and salt. Cover and allow to marinate at room temperature while the soup is cooking.

Add the reserved chopped tomatoes, lime leaves, and lime juice to the soup and simmer for another 5 to 10 minutes to allow the flavors to blend. Taste a dried shrimp to make sure it is tender. Add more salt if desired. Just before serving, remove soup from the heat and stir in the rockfish. Continue to stir until fish is opaque. Ladle soup into warm bowls and garnish with the chopped cilantro.

Note: The amount of fish in this recipe is for appetizer soup portions. To turn this soup into a stew that could be served as a main dish, increase the amount of fish and marinade as desired, using 1 tablespoon of fish sauce and ½ teaspoon salt for every pound of fish added. If using more than the amount of fish called for, keep the soup on the heat while stirring in the fish in order to cook it through and to prevent the soup from cooling off too much.

SALADS

• SALADS •

Tropical Spice-Marinated
and Grilled Flank Steak Salad / 72

Thai-Style Spicy Poached Seafood Salad / 74

Smoked Salmon "Caesar" Salad / 76

Joël Robuchon's Truffled Herb Salad / 78

Toasted Goat Cheese Salad with Lardons / 80

Smoked Pheasant Salad with Poached Pears
and Toasted Hazelnuts / 82

Marinated and Grilled Chanterelles
and Prosciutto-Wrapped Figs
on Arugula with Balsamic Vinaigrette / 84

This is a colorful, lively flavored meat salad that will transport your taste buds to a beach somewhere near the equator. It makes a perfect meal for an outdoor summer lunch or dinner. Don't be intimidated by the length of this recipe. Everything except slicing the avocado may be prepared up to several days in advance. If you don't want to fuss with the presentation described here (the way it's served at the restaurant), simply toss everything together in a big bowl and let people serve themselves, perhaps leaving the chiles and cilantro on the side for people to add to suit their taste. Assembling the exotic ingredients called for here may at first seem daunting, but a trip to a Mexican market and one to a Southeast Asian market will allow you to gather everything you need for this recipe and many other recipes in the book. Besides, most of these ingredients are inexpensive and will keep well in your pantry for months.

The wonderful tropical spice flavor at the heart of this recipe comes from the *Recado de Toda Clase*, a ground spice mixture adapted from chef Diana Kennedy's *The Art*

(continued on page 73)

Tropical Spice-Marinated and Grilled Flank Steak Salad

Makes 10 to 12 appetizer servings; 5 to 6 entrée servings

Marinade

1 tablespoon achiote paste
¼ cup Recado de Toda Clase (recipe follows)
3 tablespoons minced garlic (9 medium cloves)
2 tablespoons minced cilantro stems
2 tablespoons fish sauce (see Glossary)
⅓ cup Seville Orange Juice (page 7)

1 flank steak, about 2 to 2¼ pounds

Coconut-Onion Relish

2 cups pearl onions, peeled and halved
½ cup canned coconut milk
2 heads pickled garlic, broken into cloves, or substitute 2 teaspoons fresh minced garlic, or to taste
1 tablespoon pickled garlic brine, or substitute rice vinegar
1½ teaspoons light brown sugar
1 tablespoon rice vinegar
½ teaspoon fine sea salt

Dressing

1 tablespoon achiote paste
2 tablespoons Recado de Toda Clase (recipe follows)
1 tablespoon minced garlic (3 medium cloves)
3 small pieces dried galangal, toasted in a dry skillet and ground in an electric spice mill to yield 1 tablespoon, or substitute 1½ teaspoons ground ginger (see Glossary)
1 teaspoon fish sauce (see Glossary)
1 cup Seville Orange Juice (page 7)
½ cup freshly squeezed lime juice
1 teaspoon fine sea salt, or to taste
½ cup canola or light olive oil

1 red cabbage, cored and shredded
3 ripe avocados, peeled and sliced lengthwise ⅛ inch thick
3 medium ripe tomatoes, diced
4 serrano chiles or 3 jalapeño peppers, stemmed and sliced thinly into rings
Fine sea salt to taste
⅓ cup coarsely chopped cilantro leaves, for garnish

The day before you plan on serving this, combine all of the ingredients for the marinade in a bowl and blend thoroughly. Put the flank steak in a deep container, pour the marinade over it, cover, and marinate overnight in the refrigerator, turning the steak once or twice.

The next day, grill the flank steak whole over a hot fire for 3 to 5 minutes per side, depending on the thickness, for rare to medium-rare. Allow the steak to cool to room temperature before slicing.

To prepare the Coconut-Onion Relish: Combine all of the ingredients for the relish in a saucepan and simmer, covered, for 5 minutes over medium heat, and then uncovered for 8 to 10 minutes, or until the onions are tender and the liquid is reduced to a thick coating. Stir occasionally to keep the relish from burning. Set aside until ready to assemble salads.

To prepare the dressing and assemble the salads: Combine all of the dressing ingredients in a bowl or jar and whisk or shake to blend. Toss the shredded cabbage in some of the dressing and place a small mound in the center of each plate. Cut the flank steak thinly across the grain, slightly on the bias. Toss these strips with more of the dressing to coat them lightly and place 5 to 7 strips in a spoke-like pattern on each plate. Place the avocado slices between the meat slices. Place a spoonful of the relish in the center of each plate. Sprinkle the diced tomato over the avocado slices, and place the chile pepper rings on the meat slices. Sprinkle the meat and avocado lightly with salt and drizzle both with more dressing. Distribute the chopped cilantro over everything except the relish. Serve immediately.

Recado de Toda Clase

¼ cup black peppercorns
½ rounded teaspoon whole cloves
1 rounded teaspoon allspice berries
1 tablespoon crushed cinnamon bark
¾ teaspoon cumin seeds
¼ cup dried Mexican oregano, lightly toasted
   in a dry skillet
Water

Grind all of the spices to a powder in an electric spice mill or with a mortar and pestle. Mix in just enough water to form a paste.

of Mexican Cooking. It is used both to marinate the meat and to perfume the dressing. Traditionally, the spices for this blend, as with those in garam masala (page 27), would be ground to a paste using a mortar and pestle, but if you own an electric spice mill, it is a very effective tool for making this paste.

Sometimes the differ-
ence between a good
version of a dish and a
great version can be
slight, yet significant.
That is definitely the
case with this seafood
salad, which is one of
my favorite Thai appe-
tizers. In the spring of
1991, we began offering
a simple fixed price Thai
menu. A Thai woman
named Viraporn Lobell,
who had recently
moved to Mendocino,
heard of this and
applied for a cooking
position with us. I had
made a version of this
classic Thai dish several
times before, always
poaching the seafood,
usually squid, ahead of
time and keeping it
refrigerated until it was
ordered; it was good,
but somehow a little
flat. After Viraporn's
arrival, we put it on our
menu one week. I was
curious to taste her ver-
sion, to see if she had
any little tricks that
would improve upon
our current recipe. Sure
enough, she did: She set
up a fragrant poaching
broth and waited until
an order came in to
poach the squid. She
cooked the seafood to
order each time, tossing
it with the tangy dress-
ing and freshly chopped
herbs while it was still
warm! It was a small
change—otherwise her
recipe was basically the
(continued on page 75)

Thai-Style Spicy Poached Seafood Salad

Makes 4 to 6 servings

Dressing

2 garlic cloves, peeled

2 to 3 serrano chiles or jalapeño peppers, stemmed, or
  substitute 2 teaspoons dried red chile flakes or chile
  powder

⅓ cup fish sauce (see Glossary)

⅓ cup freshly squeezed lime juice

1 tablespoon brown sugar

½ to ⅔ cup peanut or canola oil

Poaching Liquid

2 quarts water

2 stalks lemongrass, cut into 2-inch lengths and lightly
  crushed with the back of a heavy knife

3 to 4 slices fresh galangal, or substitute fresh ginger
  (see Glossary)

4 to 6 Kaffir lime leaves, fresh or frozen (see Glossary)

2 tablespoons salt

½ cup white wine vinegar

1 pound rock shrimp or cleaned squid, fresh or frozen

1 stalk celery, thinly sliced

1 small to medium head napa cabbage, shredded

½ cup coarsely chopped fresh mint leaves

½ cup coarsely chopped cilantro leaves

¼ cup thinly sliced shallots

¼ cup chopped green onions

½ cup diced red bell pepper, cut into ¼-inch dice
  (about ½ pepper), for garnish

To prepare the dressing: Purée the garlic and chiles in a food processor with half of the fish sauce. Add the remaining fish sauce, the lime juice, and sugar. Set aside half of the dressing for the rock shrimp. Whisk the ½ cup of oil into the other half of the dressing and taste on a piece of cabbage; it should be strong but not overpowering. Add more oil if desired. Set aside.

To poach the seafood: Combine the water, lemongrass, galangal, Kaffir lime leaves, salt, and vinegar in a medium pot and bring to a simmer. Meanwhile, wash and drain the rock shrimp; if using squid, cut the tubes into ½-inch-wide rounds. Poach the shrimp with the sliced celery in a sieve or pasta insert low-ered into the simmering poaching stock for 20 to 45 seconds, until seafood is barely opaque and cooked through (taste a piece to be sure). Don't overcook! Put the cabbage in a bowl and toss with about ½ cup of the dressing, or enough to lightly coat the leaves. Divide among 4 to 6 room-temperature plates, clearing a small area in the centers of the plates for the shrimp.

Drain the shrimp in a colander as soon as it is cooked and put it in a bowl. Add the mint, cilantro, shallots, green onions, and reserved dressing. Toss to thoroughly coat and distribute among the cleared centers of the plates. Garnish the cabbage with the diced red bell pepper and serve.

same as what we'd been doing—but it was transformative. Suddenly the flavors were vibrant, the temperature and textures sensual; in short, it was now delicious.

In retrospect, this technique shouldn't have eluded me—on a visit to Thailand the previous winter, the best food I tasted there was the street food, which is always cooked to order in front of you. I think the secret of the allure of good Thai food lies in two things: the intrinsic appeal of a few characteristic flavors such as lemongrass, Kaffir lime, and coconut, and the freshness and vibrancy that comes through the immediacy of this kind of cooking. This is "fast food" as it should be.

Margaret: I like really spicy food occasionally and this fits the bill. Fresh, crunchy, full of cilantro, mmm....

(continued on page 77)

Smoked Salmon "Caesar" Salad

Makes 8 servings

Dressing

1 large egg

4 ounces smoked salmon (hot-smoked salmon made at home is best)

6 tablespoons freshly squeezed lime or lemon juice

1½ teaspoons minced garlic (2 small cloves)

¼ cup fruity extra virgin olive oil

¾ cup light olive oil

8 large handfuls young romaine, cut into 2-inch-wide strips (2 to 3 heads, depending on size)

½ cup freshly grated Parmesan cheese

24 thin baguette slices, brushed with Garlic Oil (recipe follows) and toasted in an oven until golden brown

4 ounces cold-smoked salmon or gravlax, thinly sliced and trimmed to fit the baguette croutons

1 tablespoon minced fresh chives

Freshly ground pepper to taste

To prepare the dressing: Cover the egg with cold water in a small pot and bring to a boil. Reduce heat and simmer for 1 minute, and then remove and refresh the egg in cold water. Peel the egg and add it to a food processor along with the 4 ounces smoked salmon, lime juice, and garlic. Process until smooth. With the machine running, slowly add the two oils.

Toss the romaine in a bowl with the dressing and ⅓ cup of the Parmesan to coat well. This dressing must be used liberally for the salmon flavor to come through—at the restaurant, we use twice as much dressing for this salad as we would on a regular green salad. Divide the salad among chilled salad plates and sprinkle the remaining Parmesan over the top. Place thin cold-smoked salmon pieces on the croutons, dot the salmon with some of the minced chives, and put 3 croutons on top of each salad. Garnish with freshly ground pepper and serve.

Garlic Oil

2 cups light olive oil
½ cup unpeeled garlic cloves

Combine the oil and garlic in a heavy 1-quart saucepan over low heat. Cook very slowly until the garlic is golden and very soft. Do not let the garlic burn or become darker than golden brown. Strain the oil through a fine-mesh sieve. Do not push down on the garlic in the sieve. Allow the oil to cool and store in an airtight container in a cool, dark place until needed. The cooked garlic cloves can be peeled and used in another recipe. They have a wonderful, mellow flavor and can be substituted for roasted garlic, used on croutons or pizza, or puréed into stock or the juices of roasted poultry or meat to create a mellow garlic sauce. The oil is also good for marinating meat before roasting or grilling.

salmon into mousse. So with an abundance of delicious hot-smoked salmon and the goal of creating a personalized Caesar-like salad for Margaret, I came up with this recipe. Essentially, it replaces the anchovies in the traditional version with a much larger amount of smoked salmon, so that the fish's flavor really comes to the forefront. The other adaptation that is important is replacing the traditional large, garlicky cube-croutons with flat croutons made from baguette slices, atop which you can then lay pieces of silken-textured cold-smoked salmon.

In this recipe I was able to capture the strong flavor of good home-smoked salmon and the sublime texture and flavor of good cold-smoked salmon, both in a familiar romaine salad. Something new for me, something Caesar-like for her. (The epilogue to this story is that, even though she did and does still like this salad, Margaret ended up prevailing upon me to serve the classic version at the restaurant as well.)

Usually I'm hard-pressed to name my favorite dish in any category. The ever-changing variables from meal to meal make absolute comparisons too difficult. Here, however, I make an exception. When chef Joël Robuchon prepared this salad for me, I thought it was the finest I'd ever tasted, and my sentiment hasn't wavered since. However, be forewarned; it requires a good deal of patience to meticulously remove all but the most tender of stems from the herbs, but don't ignore this essential part of the recipe, as large stems are too tough and harsh-tasting. A potential problem in preparing this recipe is that fresh truffles are in season during the winter when it is too cold for many herbs, except in the mildest of climates. The solution is to either make this dish in the summer with garden-fresh herbs, frozen truffles, and truffle butter, or splurge on a fresh truffle in the winter and settle for hothouse herbs. Also, unless you are preparing this salad for vegetarian guests, do not omit the roasted meat juices or stock from the dressing. These round out the flavor of the dressing deliciously.

Joël Robuchon's Truffled Herb Salad

Makes 6 to 8 small servings

18 small, tender sage leaves (scant 2 tablespoons)

36 small, tender basil leaves (½ cup)

1⅓ cups chervil leaves

Scant ⅔ cup tarragon leaves

⅔ cup marjoram leaves

1 cup plus 3 tablespoons mint leaves

⅓ cup dill leaves

3⅔ cups watercress leaves

9⅓ cups hearts of young chicory frisée leaves (white, yellow, or very pale green inner leaves only)

3 cups young arugula leaves

1 ounce black truffle, fresh or flash-frozen (optional) (see Note)

3 tablespoons juices from accompanying roast chicken, duck, beef, or lamb (or substitute reduced poultry stock)

1 tablespoon red wine vinegar

1 tablespoon sherry wine vinegar

½ teaspoon fine sea salt

Pinch of freshly ground pepper

7 tablespoons light olive oil

2 tablespoons truffle butter, black truffle juice, sauce, or oil (see Note)

3 tablespoons diced white or light rye bread (⅛-inch cubes), for garnish

2 tablespoons unsalted butter

Carefully wash and dry all of the herbs and greens, leaving the leaves intact and being careful not to bruise them. Stem all of the herbs by hand or with a scissors, and gently mix them together. Store them, refrigerated, in an airtight container until ready to serve. This step is best done the day of serving, but it can be done one day ahead if necessary.

If using fresh truffles, thoroughly scrub them clean with a soft vegetable brush and water. Cut a paper-thin slice for each serving and set aside in an airtight container. Mince the remaining truffle very finely and put it into a small bowl with the meat juice or stock, the red wine and sherry vinegars, salt, and pepper. Whisk to mix, and then slowly whisk in the olive oil. If using truffle butter, melt it gently in a small saucepan, just enough to liquefy it, and then add it to the dressing. If using truffle juice, sauce, or oil, simply add it to the dressing. Set aside.

To prepare the garnishes: Sauté the diced bread in 1 tablespoon of the butter in a small nonstick skillet until golden. Transfer bread to paper towels to drain.

To serve, toss the herb salad with the vinaigrette, gently yet thoroughly, until the leaves are well coated (approximately 1½ to 2 tablespoons dressing per 2 cup-sized handfuls of greens). Divide the salad evenly among chilled salad plates. Sprinkle salads with the mini croutons and top with a reserved truffle slice in the center of each salad. Serve immediately.

Note: Using a fresh truffle or the truffle butter, juice, oil, or sauce is indispensable to this salad, transporting it from the very good to the sublime. Fresh truffles are usually only available from mid- to late-November through February, from specialty food sources (page 207). If fresh truffles aren't available, look for flash-frozen ones, which are available year-round. They are almost as expensive as fresh and they are also usually only available in 7-ounce packages, so you may want to organize some friends for a communal purchase. Canned truffles are the least expensive type and the biggest gamble. If they are very high quality, or home-canned, they can be decent, but they often prove to be virtually tasteless.

Truffle butter is available from the same specialty food sources as truffles are. The butter is the most economical, consistently flavorful, and conveniently used and stored truffle "product" that I know of; I recommend it highly. The juice is of varying quality, similar to the canned truffles. If the juice was made from the first cooking of fresh truffles it can be sensational; unfortunately, it often ranges from mediocre to worthless. The sauce and oil are usually more consistent in flavor and more expensive than either the butter or the juice. If you are using fresh truffles, however, don't bother purchasing any of these other products. Instead, wash the truffle and let it marinate for a few days, refrigerated, in the olive oil you will use for the dressing—you will get plenty of flavor.

Toasted Goat Cheese Salad
with Lardons

Makes 6 servings

Several sprigs of fresh thyme and rosemary

Several bay leaves

½ cup fruity olive oil

9 to 12 ounces fresh goat cheese logs, cut into 6 even disks (see Note)

6 ounces well-smoked slab bacon, rind removed and reserved

2½ tablespoons red wine vinegar

1 tablespoon freshly squeezed lemon juice

1 tablespoon Dijon-style mustard

1½ teaspoons minced garlic (1 large or 2 small cloves)

¾ teaspoon fine sea salt

Freshly ground pepper to taste

⅓ cup unseasoned bread crumbs

Large pinch of herbes de Provence or dried thyme

6 thin slices baguette, lightly toasted

6 large handfuls of young chicory frisée (curly endive) or mixed lettuces of choice

Overnight or up to a week before serving, find a plate or platter large enough to just hold all of the goat cheese disks in one layer. Cover the bottom of the dish with half of the herbs and pour half of the fruity olive oil over them. Place the goat cheese rounds on top and cover with the remaining herbs. Drizzle with the remaining oil. Cover and place in the refrigerator to marinate, until shortly before serving.

When ready to serve, preheat the oven to 375°. Remove the marinated goat cheese from the refrigerator and allow it to come to room temperature. Cut the slab bacon into ⅜-inch lardons. Place the lardons and the reserved rind on a baking sheet and bake in the oven for 15 to 20 minutes, stirring occasionally, until lightly browned. Pour off the rendered fat into a small bowl and allow the bacon to cool slightly. Measure 3 tablespoons of the drippings into a separate bowl or a jar and discard the rind and remaining fat (or reserve for another use). Add the vinegar, lemon juice, mustard, garlic, and a large pinch of the salt to the bowl. Pour off 6 tablespoons of the olive oil from the goat cheese and add it to the bowl. Whisk or shake to blend the dressing and add pepper and additional salt to taste. If the dressing is too acidic, add another 1 or 2 tablespoons of olive oil. Keep in a warm place, such as above the stove (or the bacon drippings will solidify), until ready to dress the salad.

Combine the bread crumbs with the dried herbs in a medium bowl. Drain the goat cheese disks of any remaining oil and roll them in the bread crumbs to coat on all sides. Place the cheese rounds on top of the baguette croutons and put the croutons on a baking sheet. If your oven is separate from your broiler, first bake the goat cheese in the oven for 4 to 5 minutes, or until the cheese is just soft to the touch. Add the bacon lardons to the baking sheet and transfer it to the broiler. Broil close to the heat until the top of the cheese is richly browned and the lardons are browned and sizzling (if they start to burn before the goat cheese is ready, remove them first). If your broiler is in the oven, turn it on broil to begin with, put the cheese croutons on the lowest shelf and broil until soft, then add the bacon lardons to the pan and move the pan to a rack close to the heat to brown.

Toss the salad greens with the slightly warm dressing, using approximately 2 tablespoons per person. Distribute the greens evenly among room-temperature or slightly warm salad plates. Transfer the warm goat cheese croutons to the center of the salads and scatter the bacon lardons on the lettuce around them. Serve while the cheese is still warm.

Note: The goat cheese logs we use weigh 8 ounces and we usually cut them into 4 or 5 pieces. If you are following the salad with a substantial meal, use one 8-ounce log cut into 6 rounds, or cut 1 round from a second log and have some leftover. If you are serving big eaters or the salad is the focus of a light meal, cut larger rounds, using 1¹/₂ logs or more.

Smoked Pheasant Salad with Poached Pears and Toasted Hazelnuts

Makes 6 to 8 servings

2 lemons, halved

2 cups dry white wine

2 cups chicken stock or water

1 small smoked pheasant, about 1 pound (or substitute half a 2-pound smoked chicken)

2 firm ripe Bartlett pears

6 tablespoons hazelnut liqueur, such as Frangelico

5 tablespoons pear eau-de-vie

¼ cup pear vinegar (see Glossary) or white wine vinegar

½ cup hazelnut oil

½ cup light olive, canola, or vegetable oil

Fine sea salt and freshly ground pepper to taste

1 cup toasted hazelnuts, coarsely chopped

6 to 8 large handfuls mixed lettuces, such as mesclun, or other attractive greens, washed, dried, and chilled

One day before serving, squeeze 2 of the lemon halves to obtain ¼ cup of juice and set aside. Place the white wine and stock in a saucepan. Bone the pheasant, put the bones and skin into the pan, and simmer over medium heat for 15 minutes. Coarsely julienne the meat and set aside. Peel, core, and halve the pears, and add the peel and cores to the simmering stock. Strain the stock, discarding bones and pear peelings, into another saucepan and add 4 tablespoons of the hazelnut liqueur and 3 tablespoons of the pear eau-de-vie to it. Return the stock to a simmer, add the pear halves, and poach until tender when pierced with a knife. Remove the pears from the liquid and set them aside to cool.

Reduce the stock to 6 tablespoons, at which point it will be dark and syrupy. Remove the pan from the heat. Add the pear vinegar, the ¼ cup reserved lemon juice, the two oils, and salt and pepper. The vinaigrette should be slightly sweet, very tangy, and taste of pear and hazelnut. The amount of salt needed, if any, will depend on whether you are cooking with pheasant or chicken, how much salt was used curing it, and whether you use homemade or canned (salted) stock. Taste a small amount of dressing on some lettuce. It should be slightly saltier and more tart than you want the finished salad to be because it will be diluted with more liqueur before serving. Add more lemon juice and salt, if needed, with this in mind. Place the pheasant meat with the vinaigrette in a bowl, cover, and marinate in the refrigerator overnight. Cover and refrigerate the poached pears overnight.

The next day, remove the marinating pheasant from the refrigerator and bring to room temperature. Remove the pheasant meat from the vinaigrette and drain in a colander or sieve over a bowl to catch the dressing. Remove the pears from the refrigerator and slice them on the diagonal $\frac{1}{8}$-inch thick. Set $\frac{1}{4}$ cup of the hazelnuts aside for garnish. Put the drained pheasant meat, pear slices, and the remaining hazelnuts in a large sauté pan, keeping the meat and pears separate. Whisk the vinaigrette to make sure it is well blended, and add 3 table-spoons dressing per serving to the pan. Heat, covered, for 1 to 2 minutes to warm everything, shaking the pan gently several times. When the mixture is well warmed and coated with vinaigrette, add the remaining liqueurs and remove from the heat.

Put the mixed greens in a large bowl. Holding the pheasant, pears, and nuts back with the pan lid, drain as much of the dressing as possible into the bowl. Toss greens to coat them well with the dressing, supplementing with any leftover dressing not added to the pan if necessary. Avoid overdressing the greens, since they will begin to wilt quickly from the heat of the dressing. Distribute the greens among room-temperature or slightly warm salad plates. Distribute the pheasant meat, nuts, and pear slices attractively on top of the beds of lettuce, in a random pattern. Finish with a sprinkle of the reserved nuts over the top.

This is a simple, straightforward dish in which nearly every ingredient is mentioned in the title. Add a little fruity olive oil, salt and pepper, perhaps a few edible petals for garnish, and the ingredient list is complete. I have found that sometimes such simplicity is the secret to a great dish. Each year I look forward to the late summer onset of the Black Mission fig season and the first coastal fog-induced chanterelles, so that I can return this salad to our menu. It's the grilling technique that makes this dish memorable—the prosciutto is warmed and slightly crisped, the figs plumped and softened, and the mushrooms slightly caramelized, each permeated with the enticing flavor of wood smoke, which harmonizes all the flavors.

Margaret: The cook responsible for this dish always comes into the kitchen wrapped in a seductive smokiness after they've been grilling the fig and chanterelle skewers. If only we could bottle that aroma!

Makes 4 servings

6 to 8 ounces (about 3 cups) fresh chanterelles, as dry as possible (see page 31)

⅓ cup balsamic vinegar

⅔ cup fruity olive oil

Fine sea salt to taste

10 ripe but not squishy black Mission figs

Freshly ground pepper to taste

4 ounces good-quality prosciutto, thinly sliced

8 cups loosely packed young arugula, washed and dried

¼ cup mixed edible flowers, such as nasturtiums, borage, and calendula petals, for garnish (optional)

Four 6- to 8-inch bamboo skewers

Clean the chanterelles using a pastry or vegetable brush, a kitchen towel, and a paring knife. First, remove any loose dirt from the gills and caps with the brush, then wipe off any dirt remaining on the caps with the towel. Next, use the knife to cut away any deeply embedded grit. Cut the mushrooms in halves, quarters, or large bite-sized pieces, depending on their size. Mushroom buttons less than 1 inch in size should be left whole.

In a medium bowl, whisk the vinegar, oil, and salt together (when adding salt, bear in mind that the figs will be wrapped in prosciutto, which is salty). Set aside 6 tablespoons of the dressing for the arugula. Cut the figs in half vertically (stem to tail). Toss the fig halves and chanterelle pieces in a bowl with the remaining dressing, season generously with pepper, and set aside to marinate for about 30 minutes, tossing from time to time.

Start a charcoal fire in the grill. Soak the bamboo skewers in water for 10 minutes. Cut 20 broad strips from the prosciutto, approximately 1 x 3 inches. Wrap the fig halves with the prosciutto strips. Cut any remaining prosciutto into smaller strips and set aside, covered. Using bamboo skewers, skewer the prosciutto-wrapped figs, piercing the ham on both sides of the fruit to help keep it in place, and alternate with the chanterelles until all of the figs and mushrooms have been used. Any leftover marinade can be combined with the 6 tablespoons of dressing set aside for the arugula.

Grill the brochettes over a hot fire for 1 to 2 minutes on each side, covering them, if your grill has a cover, to get them well smoked. The prosciutto and chanterelles should be lightly browned but not charred and the figs should be warmed and softened a bit.

Toss the arugula in a bowl with the reserved dressing to coat lightly, and distribute among 4 room-temperature salad plates. Remove the figs and mushrooms from the skewers and distribute them evenly among the salads (there should be 5 ham-wrapped fig halves and 6 or 7 mushroom pieces per serving). Scatter the reserved prosciutto trimmings over the figs and chanterelles. Sprinkle the plates with the edible flowers and serve.

VEGETABLES & SIDES

My affinity for barley dates back to an oxtail and barley vegetable soup that my grandmother JoJo used to make for me. I find the chewy texture of the grains addictive. In this recipe, both that chewiness and the barley flavor blend well with the assertive texture and nutty flavor of wild rice to create a hearty pilaf that stands up especially well to full-flavored red meats, such as beef, lamb, and duck. It was the saucier at the Parisian restaurant Jacques Cagna who taught me the virtue of the pilaf technique: by sautéing grains (usually rice, but in this case barley) and then adding hot liquid to them, you minimize the amount of starch they release into the cooking liquid; the result is a pilaf with discreet, completely cooked, yet al dente grains, with no mushiness or gluiness to them.

Barley and Wild Rice Pilaf

Makes 6 servings (about 5 cups)

2 tablespoons light olive or canola oil
1 tablespoon unsalted butter or oil
1 cup chopped yellow onion
1 cup pearl barley
3 tablespoons wild rice
½ cup chicken stock
½ cup white wine
2½ cups water
2 teaspoons minced garlic (2 cloves)
1 teaspoon sea salt

In a heavy 2-quart pot, heat the oil and butter and fry the onions for 3 minutes over medium heat to soften slightly without browning. Add the barley and continue to cook, stirring constantly, for another 3 to 5 minutes, until barley is golden. Add the wild rice to the barley and cook, still stirring, for 1 minute.

Meanwhile, in a separate pot, bring the stock, wine, water, garlic, and salt to a simmer, covered. Remove the pot with the barley from the heat and stir the simmering liquid into the grains. Return the pot to the heat. Cover, and simmer gently over very low heat for 50 to 55 minutes, or until all of the liquid is absorbed. Turn off the heat, wrap the lid with a kitchen towel, replace the lid, and allow pot to sit for 10 minutes. Uncover the pot and fluff the grains with a fork or a wooden spoon. Serve warm.

Root Vegetable Gratin

Makes 12 servings

- 1½ pounds (weight after peeling, slicing, and trimming—about 2 pounds before) of 2 or more of the following root vegetables, in equal proportions: celery root, turnips, parsnips, Jerusalem artichokes (3 packed cups, thinly sliced)
- 1 tablespoon freshly squeezed lemon juice
- 1½ pounds yellow potatoes, preferably yellow Finns (3 packed cups, thinly sliced)
- 4 cups milk
- 1½ cups crème fraîche or heavy whipping cream
- 1 tablespoon fine sea salt, or to taste
- 1 tablespoon minced garlic (3 cloves)
- ⅛ teaspoon ground cayenne pepper
- ½ teaspoon freshly ground black pepper
- ¾ teaspoon freshly grated nutmeg

Preheat the oven to 425°. Peel and slice the celery root and Jerusalem artichokes, if using, ¹⁄₁₆-inch thick with a mandolin or with a sharp knife and place in a bowl of acidulated water (add 1 tablespoon lemon juice to 1 quart of water) until ready to use. Peel and slice the parsnips and turnips, if using, the same thickness as the other vegetables, and set aside. Slice the potatoes to the same thickness crosswise and put them into a large, heavy-bottomed pot such as a rondeau. Add the milk, crème fraîche, and seasonings and bring to a simmer. Drain the celery root and Jerusalem artichoke slices, stir them into the pot with the potatoes, and continue to simmer gently for 10 minutes, or until they are almost tender. Stir occasionally to keep the vegetables from sticking and adjust seasoning as desired.

Stir the parsnips and turnips into the pot with the potatoes. The milk mixture should barely cover all of the vegetables. If it doesn't, add a little more crème fraîche or milk just to cover. Cook for another 5 to 8 minutes, or until the vegetables are barely tender, not still crunchy, and yet not so soft that they're falling apart.

Meanwhile, preheat the oven to 425° for 10 to 15 minutes. Butter a 17 x 10-inch baking sheet (or other gratin dish approximately the same size). Using a perforated skimmer or slotted spoon, transfer the vegetables to the pan, spreading the mixture out evenly. Pour or ladle the hot cream over the vegetables to fill the pan completely. Put the baking sheet on the top rack of the oven and bake for 30 to 45 minutes, or until golden brown all over. Serve immediately.

This gratin is a perfect late fall or winter accompaniment to a steak, chop, burger, lamb, or chicken roast. If you can't find yellow potatoes, substitute a red- or white-fleshed waxy potato (don't use a russet). The potatoes don't need to be peeled, but can be, if you prefer.

Each type of root vegetable gives a distinctive flavor to the gratin. Try to use at least two of the four called-for vegetables to achieve the flavor complexity that makes this gratin distinctive. You can substitute carrots for the parsnips since they contribute a similar, sweet component, but don't use only carrots and parsnips together or the dish will be too sweet. My favorite version combines all five root vegetables.

The gratin reheats well if you have leftovers, but if you prefer to make a smaller amount, just cut the recipe in half. Try to use a gratin dish approximately half the size of the baking sheet called for so the gratin will still be about ¾ inches thick. (For example, this recipe fits well in a 17 x 10-inch pan, which has a surface area of 170 square inches; a 9 x 9-inch coffee cake pan with 81 square inches is a pretty good choice for a half recipe.)

I'm a wild mushroom enthusiast and every fall I'm in pig heaven. The diversity of our fungal bounty in Mendocino is remarkable, and with each season I discover another edible species to play with in the kitchen. Unfortunately, most mushroom connoisseurs farther from the source must limit their indulgence to the big-reputation mushrooms—morels, cèpes, and chanterelles—not to malign these deservedly esteemed varieties. Fortunately, we are blessed not only with a great diversity of species but with a great abundance of two of the "big three"—cèpes (also known as porcini) and chanterelles. In European cuisines, the most common treatment of these varieties is a simple sauté in olive oil or butter with shallots, garlic, parsley, and maybe chives. Straightforward and satisfying. I think of this recipe as the Asian counterpart to the basic European recipe: It's a simple stir-fry, less familiar to Western palates perhaps, but no less delicious. If you have a wok, by all means use it for this dish.

Sautéed Chanterelles
with Sesame and Ginger

Makes 4 servings

8 ounces fresh chanterelle mushrooms, as dry as possible (page 31)

2 teaspoons canola, safflower, or peanut oil

Fine sea salt and freshly ground pepper to taste

1 teaspoon sesame oil

1 teaspoon minced garlic (1 clove)

2 teaspoons peeled, grated fresh ginger

2 tablespoons minced green onions (optional)

1 teaspoon soy sauce

1 tablespoon coarsely chopped cilantro

To prepare the mushrooms: Use a clean vegetable or pastry brush and a kitchen towel and brush and wipe the mushrooms clean. Be especially careful to brush away dirt in the gills. Any deeply embedded grit can be cut away with a paring knife. If the mushrooms are large, cut them into large bite-sized pieces (usually halving, quartering, or thickly slicing lengthwise leaves wild mushrooms most attractive and reminiscent of their original shape). If mushroom buttons are small, leave them whole.

Heat the canola oil in a 10- to 12-inch skillet, one large enough to hold all of the mushrooms. (They can be slightly crowded at first since they will shrink as they cook.) When the oil is hot, add the mushrooms all at once and cook quickly over high heat, stirring or tossing frequently, for about 2 minutes, until just beginning to soften. Season with salt and pepper, toss a few more times, then clear a space in the center of the pan and add the sesame oil, garlic, and ginger. Lower the heat to medium and continue to cook, stirring just the garlic and ginger for another minute until they are fragrant and just starting to color. Add the minced green onions, stir for another 15 seconds or so (do not let the garlic burn!), and stir or toss the seasonings together with the mushrooms. Add the soy sauce and chopped cilantro, toss a few more times, taste for seasoning, and serve.

Chive Mashed Potatoes

Makes 4 to 6 servings (about 5½ cups)

3 to 4 (1¾ pounds) large, yellow-fleshed, starchy
  potatoes, such as yellow Finn, Bintji, or Yukon gold
  (or substitute russets), peeled and quartered

1 tablespoon plus ½ teaspoon sea salt

1 quart cold water

2 cups half-and-half or milk

¼ cup (4 ounces) unsalted butter

1½ teaspoons minced garlic (1 large or 2 small cloves)

¼ teaspoon freshly grated nutmeg

⅛ teaspoon ground cayenne pepper

3 tablespoons minced fresh chives

Put the potatoes in a 3-quart pot. Add the 1 tablespoon salt and water and bring
to a boil. Reduce heat and simmer for 35 to 45 minutes, covered, until potatoes
are very tender and almost falling apart. Drain the potatoes and put them in a
heavy-bottomed pot over very low heat, or put them on a baking sheet in a
medium (300°) oven for 5 minutes, to dry out thoroughly.

Meanwhile, bring the half-and-half, butter, garlic, ½ teaspoon salt, nutmeg,
and cayenne to a simmer in a separate pan. While they are still hot, pass the
potatoes through a food mill or ricer, or mash them with a handheld potato
masher (do not blend in a food processor or the potatoes will become gummy).
Using a sturdy whisk or wooden spatula, slowly beat the hot liquid into the
potatoes. Test the consistency when two thirds of the half-and-half has been
added. The potatoes should be very light and fluffy yet still hold their shape in
soft peaks, like soft whipped cream. Add more of the half-and-half, little by little, as desired. Adjust seasoning and stir in the minced chives just before serving. (Reserve any additional half-and-half, because purée stiffens up as it sits,
and if it needs to be reheated, adding more warmed half-and-half will keep the
texture light and smooth.) Serve immediately.

*Notes: Here's a tip on the fastest and most successful way to reheat leftover
mashed potatoes. Line a steamer with damp cheesecloth or a damp kitchen
towel. Put the cold potatoes on top of the cloth, cover, and steam over high
heat for about 15 minutes, until hot. Remove the cloth and empty the potatoes
into a bowl. Whisk to fluff, and serve.*

*For a heart-healthy version, omit the butter and half-and-half and replace
them with 2½ cups 1 percent milk. Yellow-fleshed potatoes are essential to this
preparation.*

Here's a secret to preparing fabulous mashed
potatoes. In Paris, I
learned that to produce
the best-textured
mashed potatoes, start
by choosing the largest
potatoes you can find.
This ensures that they
will have developed the
most starch, providing
optimal fluffiness poten-
tial. But it was in
Mendocino that I found
out about potato vari-
eties—a factor that
wouldn't have even
occurred to me in
France, where delicious
potatoes seem to be a
given. It was only when
local organic farmers
Catherine and Charles
Martin began growing
old-fashioned European
varieties of yellow-
fleshed potatoes that I
learned what a flavor
difference starting with
such varieties makes.
Yellow Finn, Bintji, and
Yukon gold are three
varieties we have used at
the restaurant, the first
being my favorite.
Fortunately, this potato
news has spread quickly
and such good yellow-
fleshed potatoes are
now widely available
across America.

I love learning about foods—vegetables usually—that have fallen from popularity undeservedly. I think the most frequent reason for this is bad representation in supermarkets. Thanks to our local organic farmers, I've come to discover the health and flavor virtues of turnips, kohlrabi, kale, quince, and parsnips. This purée works well as a side dish with pork, duck, and venison, especially in conjunction with a fruity sauce such as Huckleberry Sauce (page 11). It may be prepared up to a week in advance. It also freezes well, so you can make it ahead and pull it out to defrost and reheat when you're ready to serve it.

Quince, Apple, and Parsnip Purée

Makes 8 servings (approximately 6 cups)

2 to 3 medium-large (1 pound) fresh quinces (or substitute pears)

2 to 3 medium (1 pound) tart apples

3 tablespoons freshly squeezed lemon juice

3 to 4 medium (1 pound) parsnips

1 teaspoon coarse sea salt

1½ cups sugar

2 cinnamon sticks

6½ cups water

2 tablespoons butter

2 tablespoons apple cider or pear vinegar (see Glossary)

Peel, core, and quarter the quinces and apples, covering them as they're done with enough water to barely cover. Add 1 tablespoon of the lemon juice to the water. Peel the parsnips, cut them into 1-inch-thick rounds, and put them in a 4- to 6-cup saucepan with water to cover. Add the salt and bring to a boil, and then reduce heat and simmer for 25 to 30 minutes, or until tender. When soft, drain the parsnips in a colander and set aside.

Meanwhile, bring the remaining 2 tablespoons lemon juice, the sugar, cinnamon sticks, and 6½ cups water to a boil in a pot large enough to also hold the fruit. Add the fruit, return the mixture to a simmer, and cook for 15 minutes, or until the fruit is tender. (Weight the fruit down with a small plate or pot lid to keep it submerged.) Drain the fruit in a colander, pressing lightly to extract syrup. The syrup may be reserved, refrigerated, and used in another dish. The cinnamon sticks may be discarded, saved in the syrup, or rinsed, dried, and used in another dish.

Return the pan to the stove. Add the butter, vinegar, drained fruit, and parsnips and cook over medium heat for 5 minutes, stirring with a wooden spatula to avoid browning. When the fruit is soft and breaks up easily, put it through a food mill or purée in a food processor. Taste for the desired sweet-sour balance and add more vinegar if it tastes too sweet or bland. Serve warm.

Rösti Potatoes

Makes 4 servings (one 12-inch diameter or two 8½-inch diameter röstis)

3 large or 4 medium russet potatoes, unpeeled
6 cups cold water
4½ teaspoons sea salt
1 teaspoon fine sea salt
⅛ teaspoon freshly ground pepper
⅛ teaspoon freshly grated nutmeg
Pinch of ground cayenne pepper
8 to 10 tablespoons duck fat or vegetable oil
1 to 2 tablespoons unsalted butter

Wash the potatoes, and put them in a medium pot with the water and salt. Cover and bring to a boil. As soon as the water boils, uncover, reduce heat, and simmer for 5 minutes. The potatoes are ready when a sharp knife pierces to the center fairly smoothly, without a crunching sound. Drain the potatoes immediately. If they still feel pretty raw inside, simmer for up to 5 minutes longer, until barely tender. (Test every minute or so, as the cooking time will vary depending on the age and size of your potatoes.) Set aside to cool for 5 to 10 minutes, and then peel the potatoes. Refrigerate the peeled potatoes to cool completely, at least 30 minutes, even overnight, before grating. Cut the potatoes into shreds with a grater or in a food processor fitted with the large grater blade. If the potatoes were cooked properly they will be very sticky and will not discolor.

In a small bowl, mix together the salt, pepper, nutmeg, and cayenne.

Heat one 12-inch or two 8½-inch-diameter nonstick or well-seasoned cast-iron skillets over high heat with 6 tablespoons of the duck fat (3 tablespoons in each pan if using two skillets) for 2 minutes. When the fat is hot but not smoking, add the grated potatoes and flatten them out with a metal spatula to cover the entire bottom of the pan in an even, ¼- to ⅜-inch-thick pancake. Make sure the edges are as thick as the center. (This evening and pressing process can take several minutes.)

Lower the heat to medium-high, season the pancake with half of the salt mixture, and cook for 6 to 8 minutes, until golden brown on the underside (check by lifting up an edge and peeking). Swirl the pan from time to time to make sure the pancake isn't sticking. If the underside is browning too quickly or unevenly, the heat is too high and there isn't enough fat in the pan; add another 1 or 2 tablespoons of fat and lower the heat to medium. If after 8 minutes the pancake is still very pale, increase the heat. The total cooking time can be 10 to 14 minutes, so be patient.

I've learned to neither underestimate nor underappreciate these potatoes. Known in France as pommes paillasson or pommes dauphin, and in this country as hash browns, these potatoes are a golden, crusty brown on the surface and are soft and creamy in the center. A perfectly made rösti is one of the great accompaniments to a beautiful, tender roast of lamb, beef, or chicken. It is also a wonderful vehicle to demonstrate the virtues of duck or goose fat, which has no equal as a cooking medium for potatoes. If you can't find duck fat, substitute light olive oil, but use extra butter for the best flavor. If you're concerned about the health effects of poultry fat, bear in mind that southwest France, where cooks commonly use poultry fat and where people consume the most foie gras—fattened duck liver—of any region in France, has the lowest incidence of heart disease in the country. (France has the lowest incidence of heart disease in the world, besides Japan.) The secret to making excellent röstis is to use enough salt, enough fat, and to not

(continued on page 96)

cook the potatoes too quickly; the best, most even crust develops with cooking the potatoes for 10 to 14 minutes over moderate heat on the first side.

For the next step, you will need a plate or a flat lid the diameter of the potato pancake. When the pancake is richly browned on the underside, place the plate on top of the potatoes and, holding the plate with an oven mitt, flip the pancake over onto the plate. Add another 1 or 2 tablespoons of fat to the pan and slide the pancake back into the pan, browned side up. Season with the remaining salt mixture and cook for another 4 to 6 minutes, until the bottom is lightly browned. Dot the top with the butter halfway through.

When the rösti is done, transfer it to several thicknesses of paper towels, pat off excess grease, and cut it into 12 wedges with a sharp knife or a pizza cutter (if you made 2 röstis, cut each into 6 wedges). Cover the röstis loosely with aluminum foil to keep them warm until ready to serve. If the röstis have cooled off too much by the time you're ready to serve, rewarm them in a hot oven for a few minutes on the plates they will be served on.

Quinoa Pilaf
with Carrots, Parmesan, and Chives

Makes 4 servings (2 cups)

2 tablespoons unsalted butter or light olive oil

½ cup diced carrots (¼-inch dice)

1 cup quinoa, rinsed and drained

¾ cup chicken stock

¼ cup white wine

1¼ cups water

1 teaspoon minced garlic (1 clove)

½ teaspoon fine sea salt

¼ teaspoon ground nutmeg or mace

¼ teaspoon freshly ground pepper

⅓ cup freshly grated imported Parmesan cheese

3 tablespoons minced fresh chives

In a heavy 2-quart saucepan, add the butter and fry the carrots for 2 minutes over medium heat until they begin to soften. Add the quinoa and cook for another 2 minutes, stirring occasionally.

Meanwhile, bring the stock, wine, water, garlic, salt, nutmeg, and pepper to a boil in a separate pan. Adjust seasoning if desired. Off-heat, stir the simmering liquid into the quinoa, then return the pan to the heat and simmer, covered, over very low heat for 18 to 20 minutes until all of the liquid is absorbed.

Wrap the lid with a kitchen towel, replace the lid, and allow pan to sit for 10 minutes. Uncover, fluff with a fork, and stir in the cheese and chives. Serve warm, by the spoonful; or, the pilaf may be packed into 3- to 4-ounce ramekins or other small molds and unmolded onto plates.

This is a dish with origins outside of Cafe Beaujolais. For a number of years my father penned a weekly syndicated food column entitled "The Practical Cook." With that ever-present deadline looming over him, it seemed like he was always either on the lookout for new column ideas or testing new recipes at home. One weekend while I was visiting, he was ensconced in the process of researching and recipe-testing the recently rediscovered grain of quinoa, the "wheat of the ancient Incas." In addition to filling my head with all sorts of history and facts about this nutritious grain, he impressed my palette. That evening, we played around with quinoa recipes for dinner, and came up with this pilaf. Later that year, Margaret and I traveled back to New York City to cook at the James Beard House. My dad joined us in the kitchen for one of our meals and the three of us prepared this quinoa to accompany an entrée of sweetbreads with lobster sauce. When we have since served it at the Beaujolais, we have paired it with less exotic fare, such as roast chicken and steamed fish. Either way, it's marvelously satisfying.

It's nice to have some foolproof recipes in your repertoire. Here is one of our favorites. At the restaurant, this straightforward pilaf, with its balanced blend of tomato, garlic, and oregano flavors, has been a staple on our menus and in our staff meals for years. We first served it as part of a multiple component, Mexican-inspired vegetarian entrée, which was extremely popular and only left the menu, after a lengthy run, because of the labor intensity of all those components. Before its departure, however, it inspired one of our Mexican line cooks at the time to concoct his own vegetarian creation (see Arturo's Vegetarian Special, in the Entrées chapter, in which this rice is also featured). If you have any leftover, it reheats well.

Mexican Rice

Makes 6 to 8 servings (about 6 cups)

2½ cups chicken or pork stock, or water (for vegetarians)

2 tablespoons tomato paste

2 teaspoons fine sea salt

1 teaspoon Mexican dried oregano

1 teaspoon minced garlic (1 clove)

6 tablespoons peanut or canola oil

1 cup chopped white onion

2 cups long-grain white rice

1 cup diced ripe tomatoes (or canned plum tomatoes, drained, diced, and then measured)

In a small pot, combine the stock, tomato paste, salt, oregano, and garlic and heat until simmering. In a 2-quart saucepan, heat the oil over medium heat and sauté the onions for about 2 minutes, until slightly softened. Add the rice and cook for another 1 to 2 minutes, stirring constantly.

Add the diced tomatoes to the rice and cook for 1 minute. Add the simmering stock mixture and bring to a boil. Reduce heat to a very low simmer, cover, and cook for 15 minutes over very low heat, or place in a medium oven for 30 to 45 minutes, until the liquid is completely absorbed and the rice is barely tender. Remove the pan from the heat, wrap the lid with a kitchen towel, replace lid, and let steam for 15 minutes. Uncover, fluff with a fork, and serve immediately.

Note: To reheat leftover rice, put it in an uncovered steamer or cover it tightly with aluminum foil and bake in a 300° oven until steaming hot, 10 to 20 minutes. The steaming goes faster on the stove top than in the oven.

Coconut Rice

Makes 6 servings (approximately 5 cups)

1⅓ cups water
1½ generous cups (14-ounce can) coconut milk
¾ teaspoon fine sea salt
1 tablespoon sugar
1½ cups jasmine, basmati, or other long-grain rice

Combine all of the ingredients in a 2-quart saucepan with a lid. Bring to a rolling boil and boil for 1 minute. Reduce heat, cover, and simmer for 18 to 20 minutes, until most of the liquid has been absorbed by the rice. Turn off the heat, wrap the lid with a kitchen towel, and let sit for 15 minutes.

Transfer the rice to a larger saucepan or bowl, stir gently and fluff with a fork, cover, and let sit in a warm place for another 15 minutes before serving. Test rice to make sure it is cooked through (but not mushy). If it is still chalky, put the pan, covered, in a 250° oven until done, testing every 5 to 10 minutes.

Pan-Wilted Winter Greens with Ginger

Makes 4 to 6 servings

½ cup water
2½ teaspoons peeled, grated fresh ginger
¾ teaspoon fine sea salt
20 cups loosely packed mixed greens such as chard,
  kale, or spinach, stemmed and cut into 1½-inch-wide
  ribbons, crosswise (if leaves are especially large,
  cut lengthwise first)

Combine the water, ginger, and salt in a large skillet over high heat. As soon as the water boils, add the greens, packing them down with a pan lid. Cook, covered, over high heat for about 5 minutes, until the greens are tender. Stir the greens and shake the pan to mix several times during cooking.

A funny thing about this rice is that I don't think I've ever seen or eaten it in a Thai restaurant. I first saw a recipe for coconut rice in a Thai cookbook and tried it out of curiosity. Coconut addict that I am, I loved it, although I should quickly add that its flavor is by no means overwhelmingly coconut-y. I fiddled with the proportions and procedure slightly to arrive at the following recipe that works well for us, and then proceeded to find innumerable applications for this delicious, slightly rich and subtly coconut-flavored rice. I really think of it as the Southeast Asian equivalent of mashed potatoes—completely satisfying comfort food that acts as a flavor foil for more assertive chiles and spices not only from Thailand, but from tropical cuisines around the globe. We serve coconut rice to accompany one entrée or another, usually along with Soupy (Black) Beans (page 100), practically year round. The apotheosis of this tropical flavor ensemble is the Yucatécan–Thai Crab Cakes (page 132), a wildly popular dish for us during the winter and early spring Dungeness crab season.

Here I must tip my toque once again to one of my food mentors, my dear friend Diana Kennedy. Before getting to know Diana and her food, I liked dried beans well enough, with a few favorite bean-based dishes like southwestern French cassoulet, but they were not a food I felt passionately about. Thanks to Diana and her impassioned caveats in *The Cuisines of Mexico* about how dried beans should be properly cooked and served, I am a born-again bean cooker and eater. This master recipe for cooking beans, adapted from her recipe and ancillary instructions, is virtually the only bean recipe we follow at the restaurant these days. The title emphasizes that their soupy texture is quite intentional, reflecting her contention, of which I am a staunch advocate, that beans should always be fully cooked and tender—never al dente—and served in their flavorful cooking liquid, which has been pleasantly thickened by the starch released by those fully cooked beans. As I often tell our cooks when teaching them this recipe, when it comes to beans, sludgy is OK— crunchy is not!

Soupy Black or White Beans

Makes 8 servings (approximately 6 cups)

1 pound (about 2½ cups) black turtle or navy beans

1 yellow or white onion, roughly chopped

2 tablespoons chopped garlic (6 cloves)

7 cups water

1 bay leaf

2 sprigs fresh thyme, leaves and stems separated, or 1 teaspoon dried and rubbed through a sieve

2 sprigs fresh oregano, leaves and stems separated, or 2 teaspoons dried and rubbed through a sieve

2 sprigs fresh epazote, leaves and stems separated, or 1 tablespoon dried and rubbed through a sieve

2¼ teaspoons fine sea salt

Pick over the beans carefully to remove any bits of dirt or small stones. Rinse and drain in a colander. Combine the beans, onion, garlic, water, bay leaf, and fresh herb stems, or the dried and sieved herbs, in the top of a double boiler or in a heavy-bottomed pot over very low heat. Cook slowly, covered, for 2½ to 3 hours, until the bean skins are tender and the beans are soft. The beans should remain soupy; add more water if they begin to get dry.

Meanwhile, chop the fresh herb leaves, if using fresh herbs. When the beans are fully cooked, their liquid should be cloudy and thickened. Add the fresh herbs and salt and cook for another 15 minutes. Remove and discard the herb stems before serving. If you will not be serving the beans the day you cook them, stir them to cool as quickly as possible, and refrigerate. (If the beans are allowed to sit at room temperature for long, they will sour.)

EVENING FOOD

Winter Squash or Yam Purée
with Citrus and Galangal

Makes 6 to 8 servings

1½ pounds orange-fleshed winter squash, such as butternut, buttercup, or Kabocha, or Garnet yams

Grated zest of 1 lemon or lime (wash skins in hot water before zesting)

1½ to 2 tablespoons peeled, grated fresh galangal (see Glossary) or fresh ginger

Fine sea salt and freshly ground pepper to taste

2 to 4 tablespoons unsalted butter

Sour cream or crème fraîche, for garnish (optional)

Preheat the oven to 375°. Cut the squash in half lengthwise and scoop out the seeds. Place the squash in a shallow baking pan with enough water to come ¼ inch up the sides. Place the pan in the oven and allow the squash to steam-bake uncovered for 1½ to 2 hours, adding more water to the pan if it all evaporates. Cook until the squash is very tender. If using yams, bake them whole in the pan with a little water (¹/₁₆-inch deep) until soft.

Remove the squash from the oven. When the squash is cool enough to handle, remove the squash flesh from the skin with a spoon and put the flesh in a medium saucepan. Beat the squash with a wooden spoon or a potato masher to purée. (This can be accomplished with a food mill or ricer also.) If the purée is too loose, cook over low heat, stirring constantly, to dry out slightly. Add the zest, galangal, salt, pepper, and butter. Serve warm, garnished with sour cream.

Variation: Galangal Glazed Yams

For the same flavor in another form, preheat the oven to 400°. Scrub the yams and slice them crosswise into ³/₄- to 1-inch-thick rounds. Place the yam slices on a baking sheet, mix the grated fresh galangal with a little canola oil, and brush the surfaces of the yams generously with the mixture. Pour about ¼ inch of water in the pan and bake on the top rack of the oven for 50 to 60 minutes, until the yams are tender and lightly browned on top. Serve warm.

If you eat yams or winter squash only at holiday feasts, you're missing out. They're highly nutritious, flavorful, and about as much work to prepare as a baked potato. Try this easy preparation with roast chicken, where the vegetables can be in the oven at the same time as the chicken (the squash might take slightly longer than the chicken, depending on size). Leave out the butter and crème fraîche for a low-cal, heart-healthy dish. For that matter, try baking and eating a yam, skin and all, as a baked-potato alternative sometime. For an informal meal at home, it's hard to beat.

ENTRÉES

• ENTRÉES •

Ham and Leek Cannelloni / 106

Oven-Steamed Salmon Fillet
with Fresh Herb Sabayon Sauce / 108

Roast Chicken with Fresh Ginger Sauce / 110

Osso Buco with Gremolata / 113

Rockfish, Crab, and Artichoke Ragout / 115

Crayfish and Seafood Ragout / 117

Swordfish Baked in Parchment
with Thai Herbs / 121

Striped Bass with Squash Scales
and Chive Blossom Sauce / 123

Thai-Style Panang Duck Curry
with Kohlrabi, Greens, and Basil / 125

Braised Pork Loin
with Prunes and Cream Sauce / 127

Roast Cornish Hen
with Apricot Marsala Sauce / 130

Yucatécan–Thai Crab Cakes / 132

Poulet au Verjus / 134

Simca's Lamb Stew with Mellow Garlic / 136

Seafood Couscous / 138

Pan-Roasted Halibut
with Prosciutto and Thyme / 142

Arturo's Vegetarian Special / 144

When Margaret was working on *Morning Food*, she asked me to contribute a few recipes that had originated on our dinner menu. Dishes like Strawberry-Rhubarb Pie, which we had begun offering during the day as well, were appropriate candidates. This cannelloni arrived on our dinner menu and in the present volume through a reverse migration. I created it as a special for our weekend brunch menu and was pleased enough with the results to also offer it in the evening. The flavors are a smooth combination I learned years ago in France—ham, leeks, Madeira, and tarragon—and the pasta is true European-style comfort food that harkens back to the beginning of my food education.

Ham and Leek Cannelloni

Makes 6 servings (12 cannelloni)

2 cups chopped leek whites and tender green parts

2 tablespoons unsalted butter or olive oil

2 tablespoons water

1¼ teaspoons salt, or to taste, plus ¼ cup

Freshly ground black pepper to taste

1 cup ¼-inch diced, cooked ham

2 tablespoons Madeira or marsala

1 (15-ounce) container ricotta cheese

¾ to 1 cup freshly grated Parmesan cheese

¼ teaspoon freshly grated nutmeg

1½ teaspoons chopped fresh tarragon

2 tablespoons chopped fresh flat-leaf parsley

½ pound dried imported cannelloni (about 14 cannelloni shells—only 12 are needed, but it's good to have a couple extra in case some break)

Olive oil for brushing

1½ cups Roasted Tomato Sauce (page 8), or canned tomato sauce

Combine the leeks, 1 tablespoon of the butter, the water, ¼ teaspoon of the salt, and pepper to taste in a covered skillet over medium-high heat. Braise the leeks until tender but not mushy, about 8 to 10 minutes. Uncover and raise heat to evaporate excess liquid. When the leeks are fairly dry, transfer them to a mixing bowl and allow them to cool while preparing the ham. There should be about 1 cup of braised leeks.

Return the skillet to the stove over medium-high heat. Add the remaining 1 tablespoon butter and the ham and sauté for 1 minute. Add the Madeira and simmer for another 1 to 2 minutes to reduce slightly. Transfer the ham and Madeira to the bowl with the leeks and allow to cool slightly. Add the ricotta, ½ cup of the Parmesan, the nutmeg, tarragon, 1 tablespoon of the parsley, 1 teaspoon salt, and pepper to taste. Stir to mix evenly and adjust seasoning.

Bring 4 quarts of water to a boil in a pasta pot and add the ¼ cup salt. When the water returns to a boil, add the cannelloni shells and cook until tender yet al dente. Drain the pasta in a colander and refresh it in ice water to stop the cooking process. Drain the pasta on a kitchen towel. If you are not ready to fill the cannelloni right away, rub their insides lightly with some of the olive oil to prevent them from sticking shut.

Preheat the oven to 425°. Using a pastry bag or a spoon, stuff each cannelloni with about 6 tablespoons of the filling. Place the cannelloni in a lightly oiled baking pan large enough to hold all the cannelloni in a single layer, or put two per serving in individual baking dishes. Cover with half of the tomato sauce and bake until heated through, about 7 to 8 minutes. Meanwhile, warm the remaining sauce in a pan. When the cannelloni are hot, remove the pan from the oven and top the cannelloni with the remaining sauce. Sprinkle with the remaining Parmesan and chopped parsley and serve.

Serving salmon free of
any bones is something
I attribute to my French
apprenticeship. The
French believe that in a
quality restaurant the
kitchen and waitstaff
should remove any pos-
sible inconvenience to
the diner, such as hid-
den bones. One might
say it's an "eater-
friendly" approach; you
would never be served
fish that has little
bones to watch out for.
It's very different from
the Asian approach,
where they hack up the
chicken, bones and all,
and you're expected to
pick them out of your
mouth as you go.

We use Japanese fish
tweezers to remove
what are called "pin
bones" in salmon. The
tweezers are not very
expensive and they
work wonderfully.
They're very strong, so
you can really grab
those little bones stick-
ing out of the flesh of
the fish. In Western
kitchens, some people
use needle-nosed pliers.
It's very elegant to
serve a salmon fillet
and sauce where
there's nothing on the
plate that you wouldn't
want to eat. This is part
of the French aesthetic,
and it's important to
us, too.

This recipe for oven-
steamed salmon
(continued on page 109)

Oven-Steamed Salmon Fillet
with Fresh Herb Sabayon Sauce

Makes 8 servings

Sabayon Sauce Base

¾ cup salmon (or whitefish) stock (if no stock or bones
  are available, you may substitute half clam juice and
  half water, but reduce the salt when seasoning)

¾ cup dry white wine

6 egg yolks

1 cup crème fraîche or heavy whipping cream

1½ teaspoons fine sea salt (start with 1 teaspoon if
  canned clam juice is used)

½ teaspoon freshly ground white pepper

2½ pounds fresh, boneless, skinless salmon fillet, cut
  diagonally into 8 equal portions

Fine sea salt and freshly ground white pepper to taste

Small handful of dried or clean, fresh seaweed (optional)

1 lemon, halved, or 1 stalk lemongrass, coarsely chopped
  (or a few tablespoons dried)

6 tablespoons unsalted butter, cut into pieces

1 to 2 tablespoons freshly squeezed lemon juice

2 to 3 tablespoons chopped fresh dill or a mixture of
  minced chives or garlic chives and chive blossom flowers (pluck the tiny individual purple flowers from their
  pompon cluster)

8 small sprigs dill, or additional chive blossoms,
  for garnish

To prepare the sabayon base: Combine the stock and wine in medium saucepan and reduce to ½ cup. Set aside to cool. In a medium bowl, whisk together the egg yolks, crème fraîche, salt, and pepper, then whisk in the reduced stock. Return the sauce to the saucepan and cook over medium heat, whisking or stirring with a wooden spatula constantly, until the mixture coats a wooden spatula or spoon lightly. To test the sabayon sauce for doneness, draw a line with your finger across the sauce coating the spatula or spoon; if it leaves a lasting trace, the sauce is sufficiently thickened. If you have an instant-read thermometer, the sauce should be between 176° and 178° at this point. Remove from heat immediately. (Do not allow the sauce to exceed this temperature or the yolks will begin to scramble. Should this occur, blend the sauce for a few seconds in a blender or with a handheld immersion blender and pass it through a fine-mesh sieve before continuing.) Put the saucepan into a bowl of ice water to stop the cooking process and allow the sauce to cool slightly. Whisk occasionally. The sauce base may be prepared ahead to this point, covered, and refrigerated for up to 1 week.

An hour before serving, remove the salmon pieces from the refrigerator, season lightly with salt and white pepper, and allow to come to room temperature for at least 30 minutes before cooking. Meanwhile, preheat the oven to 300°. Combine the seaweed and lemon in a saucepan with 6 to 8 cups of water and bring to a boil. Place a roasting or coffee cake pan on the center rack of the oven. When the water comes to a full boil, pour it into the roasting pan. Place the salmon fillets on a cake-cooling rack, allowing at least an inch between them, and transfer the rack to the top of the roasting pan, making sure that all of the salmon pieces are above the hot water. Close the oven and steam-bake the fillets for 8 to 9 minutes, until their surface is opaque and they are lightly springy to the touch. They will not turn as opaque as they would being steamed over high heat and they will stay very tender and juicy.

Meanwhile, finish the sauce by returning the saucepan to low heat and whisking in the butter, piece by piece, until it is just absorbed. Add the lemon juice and chopped herbs to taste. Do not let the sauce get too hot—it should be just warm enough to melt the butter. Remove the salmon from the oven. Pour the sauce onto slightly warm plates, top with the salmon fillets (1 piece per serving), and garnish with a small dill sprig or sprinkling of chive blossom flowers. Serve immediately.

showcases a cooking technique that I learned from Paula Wolfert's *World of Food*. It's an oven-steaming technique that produces the most incredibly textured salmon you've ever tasted. It's really very special. It is so moist and incredibly tender, you could cut it with a feather. It takes longer (about 8 minutes, instead of the 4 or so on the stove top), but it's truly worth the extra time.

Here's a recipe for roasting chicken with an elegant sauce that we sometimes serve at the restaurant, along with a recipe for a very basic roast chicken with natural juices that Margaret and I often have at home. This delicious sauce is one I learned as an apprentice at Restaurant Jacques Cagna in Paris. They served it with veal medallions, but I've found it equally complements other white-fleshed meats—sweetbreads, pork, and chicken. At the time, that restaurant was something of a bastion of nouvelle cuisine, and this style of sauce (a series of reductions of an infused alcohol, followed by stock, then cream, and finished with a touch of butter) was very popular. Nowadays, cream sauces are out of favor, being supplanted by salsas, broths, juices, vinaigrettes, and infused oils. Not to say that these new darlings of the sauce world can't be wonderful, healthy, and tasty, too; but, as anyone who has eaten in a Michelin three-star restaurant I believe will agree, a deftly made stock-based, cream-finished sauce is always a work of culinary magic. It reminds me of what "subtle" means when it
(continued on page 111)

Roast Chicken
with Fresh Ginger Sauce

Makes 4 to 6 servings

4- to 5-pound roasting chicken, rinsed and patted dry

Fine sea salt and freshly ground pepper to taste

1 (2-inch) length of fresh ginger (2 ounces), coarsely chopped

1 tablespoon unsalted butter

Fresh Ginger Sauce

¼ cup peeled and chopped (in a food processor) fresh ginger

6 tablespoons dry white wine

2 tablespoons dry vermouth (or substitute more wine)

1½ teaspoons good-quality cider, rice, or white wine vinegar

1 cup reduced veal stock, or 6 cups chicken stock reduced to 1 cup

1 cup heavy whipping cream

1 tablespoon unsalted butter

2 tablespoons peeled, finely julienned ginger

Fine sea salt and freshly ground white pepper to taste

Chopped fresh flat-leaf parsley, or freshly chopped chives, for garnish

Suggested Accompaniments

Chive Mashed Potatoes (page 93) or Barley and Wild Rice Pilaf (page 90)

Sautéed green vegetables, such as peas, green beans, broccoli, or spinach

Season the chicken inside and out generously with salt and pepper up to several days in advance, to allow the most flavor to develop. Refrigerate. (Seasoning a roast, especially poultry, well in advance of cooking is one of the simplest "marinades," and it will make a profound impact on the final flavor of the roast.)

When it is 2½ hours before you plan to serve, preheat the oven to 475°. Trim the chicken of its wing tips, neck, and feet (if included) and reserve for stock, along with the heart and gizzard. (The liver can be used for another purpose or lightly sautéed and eaten as a snack while the chicken cooks.) Remove excess fat from the inside cavity and put it in a small saucepan.

Rub the chicken skin all over with the freshly cut surface of the ginger, then put it in the inner cavity along with 1 tablespoon of butter.

To prepare the sauce, combine the chopped ginger, wine, vermouth, and vinegar in a small (1-quart) saucepan and reduce, over medium-high heat, to a glaze. Add the stock and lower the heat slightly. Reduce until very syrupy and black, to about $^1\!/_4$ cup. Whisk frequently to avoid scorching. Add the cream and return the sauce to a boil, watching to make sure it doesn't boil over.

Remove the sauce from the heat and strain it through a chinois or fine-mesh sieve, pressing down hard on the ginger with a wooden spatula to extract all the sauce. Discard the solids and set sauce aside. This sauce may also be kept refrigerated for up to a week or frozen for up to 2 months.

Truss the chicken with a 5-foot piece of cotton twine: Loop the legs together at the ankles with the center of the string, then bring both ends up the insides of the thighs and pin the wings to the sides of the breast; cross the string ends behind the back and finally bring them up the outsides of the thighs to tie off above the bound ankles, pinning them to the base of the back and closing the cavity (tuck the tail in under the ankles). Put the bird on a roasting rack, breast-side up, over a shallow roasting pan.

Add 1 tablespoon of butter to the saucepan with the chicken fat from the cavity and melt together over low heat. Brush the chicken skin all over with the melted butter and fat, and turn the chicken breast-side down. Roast the chicken at 475° for 20 minutes, then turn it onto its side, baste with the butter, lower the heat to 450°, and roast for 10 minutes. Turn the chicken onto its other side, baste with the butter, lower the heat to 400°, and cook for 10 minutes. There should be enough of the melted butter and fat mixture in the roasting pan to use for basting. Turn the chicken breast-side up, baste, lower the heat to 350°, and roast for another 30 to 45 minutes, basting once or twice, until the breast reaches 150°. (Use an instant-read thermometer. To test for doneness without a thermometer, poke the thick part of the thigh with the point of a knife or skewer. If the juices run yellowish-clear, the chicken is done; if they are red or pink, it needs more time. You can also learn to recognize the right doneness just by appearance—the skin on the drumsticks will have shrunk away from the ankles and be slightly wrinkled.)

Remove the bird from oven and let it rest, breast-side down, in a warm place, such as on top of the stove (if your oven is beneath it) or loosely covered with aluminum foil for at least 15 minutes, or up to 30 minutes before carving.

When ready to serve, transfer the chicken to a cutting or carving board. Pour off the juices from the roasting pan into a degreasing pitcher or a glass and pour or spoon off and discard excess fat. Deglaze the pan with a little water over medium heat, scraping the bottom of the pan with a wooden spatula to dissolve caramelized bits. Add the deglazed juices to the degreased pan juices and adjust seasoning. If not too salty, a tablespoon or two of the juices may be strained into the sauce. Reserve the rest for stock.

is used positively rather than pejoratively: it has a complexity of flavor in a silky texture that is unattainable in less labor-intensive sauces.

A word on temperatures and doneness: All white-breasted poultry (chicken, turkey, guinea fowl, and pheasant) taste best when the breast meat is cooked to 150° and the dark thigh meat to 165°. This can be tricky to achieve when the bird is roasted whole, which accounts for the common occurrence of dry breast meat or undercooked leg meat. At the restaurant, we allow the chicken to come to room temperature for several hours before cooking, and we turn the chicken breast-side down for the first 15 to 30 minutes of roasting time, which gives the legs a head start. We pull the chicken out when the breast meat reaches 150°. After allowing the bird to rest in a warm spot for 15 to 30 minutes, the legs have usually finished cooking as well. They will occasionally retain a pink blush, which can be easily remedied by another 5 minutes or less in a warm oven.

Rewarm the sauce in a small saucepan and taste. If the ginger flavor is not pronounced enough, add half of the julienned ginger. With a handheld mixer or in a blender, incorporate the butter into the sauce, until silky. Taste and correct seasoning if needed. Strain out the ginger if you prefer a smooth sauce. Serve warm. Garnish dish with remaining ginger.

Remove the trussing string from the chicken and cut the chicken into 8 serving pieces (dividing the drumstick and thigh and cutting the breast into 2 servings will give 4 people each some white and dark meat). Serve on warm plates, blanket with sauce, and sprinkle each dish with julienned ginger and parsley. After carving, save the carcass to make chicken stock, along with wings, neck, and feet trimmings. (The ginger may be left in the cavity or discarded, depending on whether you'd like a ginger-flavored stock or not.)

Note: The turning and basting are optional. They mimic the effects of a rotisserie, which, unless you have a convection oven, is the best way to produce more even browning and juicier breast meat. This is also the purpose of the descending oven temperatures. If this doesn't fit into your schedule or you need the oven at a certain temperature to cook another dish at the same time, the chicken can be roasted at 475° for 30 minutes, and then lowered to 350° until done, about 1½ to 1¾ hours for this size chicken.

Variation: Using this same roasting, basting, and deglazing technique, you can create a delicious and easy variation as we do at home without the cream sauce. Rub the surface of the chicken with 1 or 2 cut or crushed cloves of garlic and then fill the inner cavity with several crushed garlic cloves and a handful of either fresh tarragon or one or more pungent herbs, such as bay leaf, rosemary, sage, thyme, or oregano, saving about a teaspoon of herbs to chop for the sauce. Add the seasoning and butter and truss, roast, and baste as instructed above. Deglaze the pan as directed with either water or a mixture of water and wine, brandy, sherry, port, or Madeira: Reduce until well flavored but not too salty. Just before serving, stir in the freshly chopped herbs and an optional teaspoon of butter, pour over the chicken pieces, and serve.

Osso Buco with Gremolata

Makes 6 servings

Vegetable Base

1 tablespoon light olive oil

½ cup diced bacon (¼-inch dice)

2 yellow onions, cut into ¼-inch dice (3 cups)

2 large carrots, cut into ¼-inch dice (2 cups)

2 cups diced leeks (¼-inch dice), white part only

½ cup diced celery (¼-inch dice)

1 tablespoon minced garlic (3 cloves)

1 teaspoon fine sea salt

½ teaspoon freshly ground pepper

2 to 3 sprigs thyme, or ½ teaspoon dried thyme

1 bay leaf

½ cup dry white wine

2 cups good-quality canned tomatoes, drained and coarsely chopped

1 cup reduced veal stock, or 6 cups chicken stock reduced to 1 cup

6 large veal shanks, cut into 1-inch-thick slices

Fine sea salt and freshly ground pepper to taste

½ cup all-purpose flour

1½ tablespoons unsalted butter

1½ tablespoons light olive oil

1 to 2 cups chicken stock or water

Gremolata

3 tablespoons chopped fresh flat-leaf parsley

1 tablespoon finely minced lemon zest (wash lemon in hot water before zesting, then remove all white pith before mincing zest)

1 teaspoon finely minced garlic (1 clove)

Suggested Accompaniments

Polenta, risotto, or Chive Mashed Potatoes (page 93)

To prepare the Vegetable Base: In a heavy-bottomed 3- to 4-quart braising pan or saucepan, heat the olive oil and diced bacon over medium heat. Cook for a few minutes, until the bacon is just starting to color. Add the diced vegetables, garlic, salt, pepper, and thyme and cook for another 5 minutes, until vegetables are starting to soften. Add the wine, bring to a boil, and cook for several minutes to reduce slightly. Add the tomatoes and stock and return to a boil. Remove from heat and set aside. (The base may be prepared several days ahead and stored in the refrigerator.)

When we do a braise and we put in a pig's foot, or we make a stock with a whole bunch of chickens' feet, necks, and wing tips, we cook it way down so it's very thick and rich. People seem to think that means it's fatty, but what gives it that unctuous feel is actually the liquefied gelatin from the bones. Osso buco is another dish that people think is going to be very rich with fat when in reality, in a braised, long-simmered dish like that, virtually 90 percent of the fat is rendered into the cooking liquid, which is degreased (it is skimmed). Osso buco tastes very rich and meaty, but it's not fatty at all. It's definitely leaner than hamburger meat or steak.

This is probably one of the most-requested recipes we make. The gremolata is the traditional garnish. The vibrancy of the lemons, raw garlic, and parsley really wake up your taste buds and work as a wonderful counterpoint to the rich meaty flavor.

To cook the shanks: Preheat the oven to 275°. Pat the shanks dry, season them generously with salt and pepper, dredge them in the flour, and pat and shake off excess flour. Heat the butter and oil in a large skillet until the foam subsides. Add the shanks and brown over high heat, in two batches if necessary, until golden brown on both sides, about 3 to 5 minutes per side. Remove shanks from the pan as they brown and put them on top of the vegetables in the braising pan. (If you use a saucepan for the vegetable base, transfer it to a rondeau or enameled cast-iron pan or to a deep roasting pan large enough to hold the meat all in one layer.) Regulate the heat, raising and lowering it as needed, to prevent blackening.

When all of the shanks are browned, pour off the fat from the skillet and deglaze it with $1/2$ cup or more of water, scraping to dissolve browned bits. (If the pan has gotten too hot and burned on the bottom, do not deglaze.) Add deglazing water to the braising pan and enough of the chicken stock to barely cover the shanks. Bring to a simmer on top of the stove, then cover and transfer to the preheated oven (or cook on the stove top over very low heat) and braise for 2 to $2^1/_2$ hours, until the shanks are tender when pierced with a fork but not falling apart.

Meanwhile, prepare the gremolata. Mix all of the ingredients together in a medium bowl, place in an airtight container, and set aside.

Remove the shanks from the oven and, holding the shanks back with a lid, carefully pour off excess liquid from the pan through a fine-mesh sieve into a bowl or saucepan. Return any of the vegetables that slip into the sieve to the pan with the shanks, and cover with a lid or with aluminum foil.

Degrease the braising liquid in a degreasing pitcher or by skimming fat with a small ladle or a spoon. Put the degreased stock in a saucepan over high heat and reduce by one quarter to one third to thicken slightly. Adjust seasoning to taste. Stop reducing if the sauce starts to become too salty.

Put 1 shank on each plate on a bed of soft polenta, risotto, or potatoes and ladle the reduced sauce and diced vegetables over the meat. Sprinkle meat with the gremolata, surround with a green vegetable of your choice, and serve immediately.

Rockfish, Crab, and Artichoke Ragout

Makes 6 servings

- 4 cups water
- 3 lemons—1 halved and 2 juiced, yielding 6 tablespoons of juice
- 2 tablespoons olive oil
- 3 tablespoons milk
- 2½ teaspoons fine sea salt
- ½ teaspoon freshly ground pepper
- ½ teaspoon mixed dry herbs such as herbes de Provence, or dried thyme
- 1 bay leaf
- 6 large artichokes
- 12 ounces Jerusalem artichokes
- 1 (1½- to 1¾-pound) Dungeness crab, live or cooked
- 3 quarts fish stock (page 200) or water
- 1 cup thinly sliced shallots
- ½ cup Cynar (artichoke liqueur, see Note), or ¼ cup Pernod (or other anise-flavored liqueur) and ½ large fennel bulb, peeled, cored, and sliced or chopped
- ½ cup dry vermouth
- 1 cup dry white wine
- 2 pounds fresh rockfish fillets, trimmed and deboned
- 1 cup crème fraîche or heavy whipping cream
- Fine sea salt and freshly ground pepper to taste
- 1 tablespoon chopped fresh flat-leaf parsley, for garnish
- ½ cup fennel fronds, for garnish (optional)

Suggested Accompaniments

Cooked white or brown rice

1½ cups fresh peas, blanched for 2 to 3 minutes, refreshed briefly in ice water, drained, and added to ragout 1 to 2 minutes before serving to rewarm, or substitute frozen petits pois, thawed directly in ragout

Combine 2 cups of the water with 3 tablespoons of the lemon juice, the olive oil, milk, 1½ teaspoons of the salt, the pepper, herbs, and bay leaf in a medium saucepan and bring the mixture to a simmer over high heat. Remove from the heat and set aside: this is the "blanc" for cooking the artichoke hearts and Jerusalem artichokes.

This was the entrée I made for the restaurant's seventh anniversary meal—a meal that was basically a job interview. Margaret hired me after that meal. The recipe hadn't been written down, it was just a part of the whole meal, based on what I found fresh and available at the time.

Margaret: What struck me at the time was how much the sauce tasted like the sauce of the French chef I had worked with at the Great Chef's Program at Mondavi Winery in the Napa Valley. It had the same richness and intensity of flavor. No one else at the dinner knew anything about that similarity—they just kept saying, "Wow."

Put the remaining lemon juice and water into a container. Remove the hearts from the artichokes and drop them into the lemon water as you work. As soon as you have all the hearts, scrape out the furry chokes of the hearts with the edge of a spoon, rub the hearts with the lemon halves, and drop hearts into the blanc. Reserve the lemon water for the Jerusalem artichokes. Return the blanc with the artichoke hearts to a simmer, lower the heat, and cover the surface directly with plastic wrap or parchment paper (not aluminum foil). Simmer very gently for 10 to 15 minutes.

Meanwhile, peel and cut the Jerusalem artichokes into bite-sized pieces, dropping them into the reserved lemon water as you work.

When the hearts are barely tender when pierced with knife but still quite firm, remove them from the blanc with a slotted spoon and set them aside on a plate to cool. Poach the Jerusalem artichokes in the blanc, covered as with the hearts, for 10 minutes or until similarly tender but firm. Remove them with a slotted spoon to the plate with the artichoke hearts to cool. When the hearts are cool enough to handle, cut them into bite-sized wedges, 6 to 8 per heart, and set aside.

If using live crab, rinse it off and put it in a large pot with the fish stock to cover. Add 1 teaspoon sea salt and bring to a full simmer (200°). Cover, remove from heat, and let sit for 10 minutes. Remove the crab from the pot and refrigerate until cool enough to handle.

Open the crab with your hands, remove and discard the gills and sand sack in the head, then crack the shells with a nutcracker and pick out the meat with a skewer, reserving the meat. Return the shells to the pot of stock. (If beginning with precooked crab, start with this step, adding the shells to the fish stock along with the salt.) Bring the stock to a simmer, and cook for 15 minutes, skimming any scum that rises to the surface. Strain through a chinois or piece of damp cheesecloth, discard the shells, and set the liquid aside.

Meanwhile, combine the shallots, Cynar, vermouth, and wine in a medium nonaluminum saucepan and reduce to a loose glaze over the shallots. Add the strained stock and reduce to 3 cups over medium heat.

Cut the rockfish into bite-sized pieces and season it lightly with salt and pepper. Lower the reserved artichoke heart and Jerusalem artichoke pieces into the shallot reduction in a sieve or nonaluminum pasta insert. Simmer gently until both types of artichoke are just tender, about 5 minutes. Remove the artichokes to a small bowl. Add the crème fraîche to the pan, raise the heat to high, and reduce the liquid rapidly by one fourth to one third, or until thickened slightly. Adjust seasoning to taste, if desired. Transfer the sauce to a larger saucepan, with a lid, that will accommodate all of the seafood and vegetables.

Warm 6 shallow soup bowls. Add the rockfish to the saucepan and cook over medium heat, covered, until the fish is almost done, about 3 to 4 minutes. Add the crabmeat, artichoke pieces, and peas (if using). Stir well to mix, continuing to cook just until everything is hot again and the fish is barely cooked. Put a layer of rice in each bowl and ladle the ragout on top. Garnish with the chopped parsley and fennel fronds and serve.

Note: Cynar is an Italian artichoke liqueur available in stores that carry a broad range of imported spirits, as well as in Italian specialty markets.

Crayfish and Seafood Ragout

Makes 6 to 8 servings

Ragout

7½ pounds crayfish (about 24 crayfish)

7 quarts plus 1½ cups water

⅓ cup sea salt

1 cup plus 2 tablespoons white wine vinegar

2½ cups Franco-Thai Crayfish Bisque Sauce
(recipe follows)

1 pound fresh manila clams or other small clams
(18 to 24 clams)

1½ to 1¾ pounds mixed fresh whitefish, such as
rockfish, ling cod, sole, and/or halibut

¾ to 1 pound medium day-boat caught and dry-packed
sea scallops (12 to 16 scallops)

Fine sea salt and freshly ground white pepper to taste

Pepper Brunoise

¼ to ½ red bell pepper, seeded, deribbed, and cut into
⅛-inch dice (½ cup)

¼ to ½ yellow bell pepper, seeded, deribbed, and cut
into ⅛-inch dice (½ cup)

3-inch length fresh ginger, peeled and cut into 1/16-inch-
thick slices (½ cup)

1 poblano chile, seeded, deribbed, and cut into ⅛-inch
dice (½ cup)

1 pound fresh mussels (18 to 24 mussels)

2 cups white wine or water

Several dashes of fresh lime juice, or to taste

Reserved Pepper Brunoise, for garnish

Reserved julienned ginger, for garnish

1 to 2 tablespoons Kaffir lime leaves (see Glossary), cut
into very fine julienne, or coarsely chopped cilantro, for
garnish (optional)

Suggested Accompaniments

Cooked white rice, preferably basmati, or Coconut Rice
(page 99)

To prepare the crayfish: Soak the crayfish in several changes of water over a period of 2 to 3 hours to cleanse. Bring the 7 quarts of water to a rolling boil in a large pot over high heat. Add the salt and white wine vinegar. When the water returns to a full boil, add half of the cleaned crayfish all at once, cover, and poach for exactly 2 minutes, uncovering the pot only if the water returns to a

When people ask what kind of food we serve at the restaurant, what style, I want to say "transformational." This is a very personal thing. It's like having your home recipe box, where you've clipped out recipes from magazines or copied them from cookbooks and there are notes in the margins for things you've tried. A lot of our recipes have evolved like that. They start from a favorite cookbook or magazine recipe that sounded good, and they evolve over many, many times of appearing on the menu.

This dish came into being on the weekend *San Francisco Chronicle* restaurant critic Stan Sesser came up and gave us our three-star review. I had made this very traditional, elegant, butter-enriched, creamy crayfish soup, and he loved it. But as the years went by and I became interested in ingredients from Thailand, I started playing with combinations of ginger and lemongrass with seafood. Eventually, I realized I'd never come across a Thai recipe for crayfish. So I started experimenting. I began with the French recipe, but instead of using cream I used coconut milk, and then, in

(continued on page 118)

boil before 2 minutes are up. Remove the crayfish from the water and set them aside to cool. Allow the water to return to a rolling boil and repeat with the remaining crayfish. Alternatively, if you have a large steamer, the crayfish may be steamed in batches over a smaller quantity of the boiling vinegar water, but allow to cook for approximately 4 to 5 minutes per batch, or until the crayfish turn red. To test, remove one crayfish from the steamer, peel its tail, and check for doneness.

When the cooked crayfish are cool enough to handle, pick out 1 nice looking crayfish with two claws for each serving, and carefully peel the shell off the tail meat, leaving the tail attached to the body. If the claws are especially large they can be lightly cracked with a nutcracker so they can be opened by your guests; if they are small, don't bother. Separate the tails from the remaining crayfish bodies, then peel the shells off the tail meat and put these tail shells with the tailless bodies. Discard any black or off-smelling crayfish, since they were prob-ably dead before cooking and are therefore not good to eat. Any tails with promi-nent black digestive tracts should be deveined with a small knife. Cover the tail meat with plastic wrap and refrigerate it along with the whole crayfish garnish-es until ready to use.

Put the shells in a heavy-duty electric mixer fitted with the paddle attach-ment and collar, or in a food processor. Mix or process in batches to crush the shells thoroughly, and set aside for the bisque sauce.

Prepare the Franco-Thai Crayfish Bisque Sauce (recipe follows).

Put the clams in salted cold water (1 tablespoon salt for every quart of water) to soak and release sand for 1 to 2 hours. Trim the whitefish of all skin and bones and cut it into bite-sized pieces. Pull the small muscles off the sides of the scallops. Rinse and pat dry the fish and scallops. Season lightly with salt and pepper, cover, and refrigerate.

Mix the three-pepper brunoise (see sidebar) together in a bowl. Set aside 6 tablespoons of the mixed pepper brunoise and 2 tablespoons of the julienned ginger for garnish.

Wash, drain, and debeard the mussels. Drain the clams and put them into a heavy-bottomed pot over high heat. Add the wine, cover, and cook, shaking the pot, for 3 minutes, until the clams just begin to open. Remove the lid and trans-fer the clams to a bowl as they open—do not wait for them all to open or the first to open will overcook. Cover the pot if necessary, add a little water, and continue to cook until all of the clams have opened. If any seem particularly stubborn, check to make sure they aren't just shells full of mud.

Add the cleaned mussels to the pot and repeat the same process as for the clams, with one exception: Since mussels live on rocks or ropes and not sand, "stubborn ones" will never be full of mud, but they may be dead. After 5 minutes of cooking, any mussels that haven't opened more than they were when you start-ed cleaning them might have been dead for a long time and should be discarded.

Strain the cooking juices through a damp piece of cheesecloth or kitchen towel to remove any sand, and then swish the clams in the liquid to wash. Strain the liquid through the cloth again and add it to the crayfish base. Set the clams and mussels near the stove for easy access.

In a braising pan large enough to hold all of the fish, put the crayfish sauce, several dashes of lime juice, the 1½ cups water, the julienned ginger, and the pepper brunoise (except what you set aside for garnish). Heat to a simmer, and then add the fish and the scallops. Stir to coat evenly with the sauce, cover, and cook over medium heat for 3 to 4 minutes, stirring occasionally, until the fish is almost cooked through. Stir the crayfish tails into the ragout, add the clams and mussels, cover, and shake or toss the pan a few times while cooking for another 30 seconds. Add the whole crayfish, cover, remove from heat, and allow to sit for a minute to heat the whole crayfish in the steam of the pan.

Warm 6 to 8 large flat soup bowls. Put a layer of warm rice on the bottom of each bowl or a scoop of rice in the center of each. Uncover the ragout. Pick out the whole crayfish and as many of the clams and mussels as you can quickly find and set them aside. Distribute the ragout evenly among the bowls, putting 2 scallops and several types of fish in each bowl. Place the clams and mussels on top, 2 to 3 of each per bowl. Garnish each bowl with 1 reserved whole crayfish. Sprinkle the top with the reserved pepper brunoise and julienned ginger and a pinch of Kaffir lime leaves. Serve immediately, with side plates for the shells.

Note: Don't be alarmed if some or all of the mussels are slightly open before cooking. This is a reaction to temperature changes, such as being put into or removed from a refrigerator. It does not mean they're dead. Mussels should only be discarded if they do not open any more than this when cooked.

Franco-Thai Crayfish Bisque Sauce

Makes 2½ cups

1 cup coarsely chopped yellow onion
¾ cup coarsely chopped carrot
1 large stalk lemongrass, trimmed and coarsely chopped
1-inch length fresh galangal (see Glossary) or ginger (1 ounce), peeled and coarsely chopped
3 to 4 garlic cloves, crushed and peeled
¼ cup coarsely chopped cilantro stems
2 Kaffir lime leaves (see Glossary)
2 tablespoons unsalted butter or oil
1½ teaspoons sea salt
1 teaspoon white peppercorns
Crushed shells from cooked crayfish
¼ cup Armagnac or other brandy
¼ cup shao-hsing, sherry, or port wine (see Glossary)
3 tablespoons tomato paste
2 cups water
1½ cups canned coconut milk (one 14-ounce can)
2 tablespoons uncooked white rice
Fine sea salt and freshly ground white pepper to taste

Margaret: When staff members come and eat at the restaurant as customers, they always comment on the experience—how different it feels. Whether they work the front or the back of the house, they know all the people—they're probably with these people more than they are with anyone else—but when they get to dress up and be treated with the graciousness that we treat customers, everybody comments on what an incredible experience it is. One of our waiters said that when he came into the dining room as a customer and watched one of his co-workers work the floor, he said to himself, "I could never do that job. It's too complicated." Then he realized in the next second that it's the job he does every night of his working life!

Put the onions, carrots, lemongrass, galangal, garlic, cilantro stems, and lime leaves in the bowl of a food processor fitted with the metal blade. Pulse several times to chop everything fairly finely, but stop short of puréeing the vegetables.

In a large (4-quart) pot, melt the butter, then add the chopped vegetables, salt, and peppercorns. Cook, stirring, over medium heat for 5 to 8 minutes, until the vegetables are soft. Add the crushed crayfish shells, Armagnac, and shao-hsing, stir well, cover, and simmer for 5 minutes. Add the tomato paste, water, and coconut milk, cover, and simmer gently for 30 minutes more.

Remove the pan from the heat and allow to sit for 15 minutes. Strain through a colander or coarse-mesh sieve, pressing down hard with a ladle to extract as much liquid as possible. Discard the solids. Strain the liquid again, this time through a chinois or piece of damp cheesecloth, again squeezing out all liquid and discarding any solid residue or grit. This double straining process is tedious, but it is essential. Be patient—the result is worth it.

Return the sauce to the heat in a clean saucepan. Bring to a boil, add the rice, and simmer over low heat, covered, until the rice is completely cooked, about 20 minutes. Remove the sauce from the heat and allow it to cool slightly, then purée in a blender and strain through a fine-mesh sieve to make sure all of the rice is puréed and the sauce is very smooth. Add salt and pepper. Allow to cool and store refrigerated until needed, for up to 3 days. It may be frozen for up to a month.

Swordfish Baked in Parchment
with Thai Herbs

Makes 6 servings

Lemongrass Mixture

1 to 2 stalks fresh lemongrass, trimmed to inner core
and very finely sliced or chopped (½ cup) (see Note)

2 tablespoons peeled and grated fresh galangal (see
Glossary) or ginger

1 tablespoon minced garlic (3 cloves)

¼ cup freshly squeezed lime juice

6 large (18 x 12 inch) sheets of parchment paper

6 (5- to 6-ounce) skinless swordfish steaks (or fresh tuna)

Fine sea salt and freshly ground pepper to taste

12 to 18 Kaffir lime leaves (see Glossary)

1 tablespoon canola or peanut oil

6 tablespoons coarsely julienned fresh Thai basil leaves
(sweet basil may be substituted)

6 tablespoons very coarsely chopped cilantro leaves

¼ cup all-purpose flour

Water

Suggested Accompaniments

Cooked basmati or other white rice, Thai jasmine rice,
or Coconut Rice (page 99)

Blanched and sautéed broccoli, snow or snap peas, or
bok choy, tossed with a little sesame and/or chili oil
at the end

To prepare the Lemongrass Mixture: Mix the lemongrass together with the galangal, garlic, and lime juice in a medium bowl.

Fold the sheets of parchment paper in half so they measure 9 x 12 inches. Cut out half a heart shape from the sheets as if you were making a valentine (so that when the sheets are unfolded they form a full heart). Make the heart as large as you can within the sheet.

Season the swordfish steaks lightly with salt and pepper.

On a large work surface, open up all of the parchment hearts. Spoon 1½ to 2 tablespoons of the lemongrass mixture on the right side of the paper hearts, near the fold. Spread the mixture out to approximately the size of the pieces of fish. Lay 2 Kaffir lime leaves on top of each lemongrass bed, then lay the pieces of swordfish on the mixture, starting about ½ inch from the fold and keeping at least a 1-inch border of clean parchment around the fish. Brush the left half of the heart lightly with the oil, then sprinkle the tops of the pieces of fish with basil and cilantro.

I had never tasted Thai food before I came back to the West Coast in the early 1980s. I fell completely in love with some of the flavors—coconut, Kaffir lime leaves, lemongrass. I started reading Thai cookbooks and ate at Thai restaurants whenever I could, and I longed to go to Thailand and see what the flavors would be like at the source. In 1991, I did go, finally, and had a great time. If anything, the trip just reinforced my love of those flavors and gave me more ideas about possible ways to use them, like this dish.

One thing I really loved and could relate to in Thailand is that their culture is as food-obsessed as French culture is. In France, it seems as if every third shop is devoted to food in some form. It's either a bakery, charcuterie, or café. In Thailand, there are little street carts and kiosks selling food everywhere. People always seem to be snacking. There are huge outdoor markets with incredible arrays of produce. And they make it easy for people to cook well in their own homes. Some places sell little packages of a few slices of ginger, a stalk of lemongrass, and a couple of Kaffir lime leaves, like in France, where you can

(continued on page 122)

buy a little fresh bundle of bouquet garni for your soup. It was beautiful. In Thailand and in France, people who have no particular interest in being cooks still love to eat, and when they sit at a table to eat, they talk about the food, discussing whether it's fresh and how they like it.

Margaret: There's such tremendous delight in appreciation of food in some other cultures, and it's also about being in the here and now. I don't have experience with Thailand, but the French family talks about food. They make special meals into major social events, multigenerational ones, where they'll sit down and have three-hour meals. It's an extremely convivial thing. In the States, people seem more interested in how fast can I get my dinner, and did this cost 59 cents or 63 cents—many other things seem to be the issue besides the food.

Place the flour in a small bowl and add enough water to form a paste. Brush the rounded border of the right side of the hearts with the paste. Fold the left sides of the parchment over the fish and press to adhere the rounded top border to the lower border. Brush the outside of the top rounded border with more of the paste. Beginning at the top of the heart near the center fold, fold the border in small, overlapping folds, working your way around the fish and finishing where the tip of the heart is. The fish will be snugly secured in the parchment. These parchment packages (papillotes) may be made several hours in advance and stored in the refrigerator.

Thirty minutes before serving, preheat the oven to 350°. Bring the papillotes to room temperature for 15 to 20 minutes. Place them on 2 baking sheets and heat the sheets over a stovetop burner for a couple of minutes, just enough so that the pans are hot to the touch. Put the pans in the oven and bake for 10 to 12 minutes, or until the papillotes are puffed and slightly browned. Warm plates in the oven for the last 5 minutes of the cooking. Remove the papillotes from the oven and put them on the warmed plates along with the rice and broccoli. Serve immediately, inviting guests to cut the papillotes open themselves with sharp steak knives. (Half of the pleasure of eating a dish cooked in parchment is smelling the wonderful aroma as the package is cut open.)

Note: When preparing lemongrass to be eaten, cut off about ½ inch of the base and the top third of the stalk. Peel off several of the outer layers of reed, usually about four layers, and the top, greener part of the inner core. Only the paler, more tender inner core or heart should be finely sliced or minced. All of the trimmings, which are very fibrous, may be washed and used to infuse soup (unless they are very old and moldy or funky looking, in which case you should discard them).

Striped Bass with Squash Scales and Chive Blossom Sauce

Makes 6 servings

3 (1¾- to 2-pound) striped bass, filleted, skinned, and boned (reserve bones for fish stock), yielding 6 (4- to 6-ounce) boneless fillets

Fine sea salt and freshly ground white pepper to taste

3 to 4 (½-pound) small (approximately ¾-inch diameter) green zucchini

3 to 4 (½-pound) small (approximately ¾-inch diameter) yellow zucchini

1 teaspoon fine sea salt

¾ cup fish stock (page 200), preferably made from bass bones (if no stock or bones are available you may substitute half canned clam juice and half water, but watch for saltiness when seasoning)

¾ cup dry white wine

6 egg yolks

1 cup crème fraîche or heavy whipping cream

2 to 3 teaspoons freshly squeezed lemon juice

¼ teaspoon fine sea salt, or to taste

Freshly ground white pepper to taste

4 to 6 tablespoons unsalted butter

2 to 3 tablespoons chopped fresh chives, garlic chives, or chive blossom flowers

2 to 3 tablespoons minced chives, for garnish

Chive blossoms, for garnish

Suggested Accompaniment

Boiled new red potatoes, cut in halves or quarters and tossed with chopped fresh flat-leaf parsley

Season the bass fillets lightly on both sides with the salt and pepper and set aside at room temperature while preparing the squash scales.

Slice the squash into ⅛-inch-thick rounds or ovals (using a mandoline if available). Toss with the salt and set in a colander to drain for 1 hour.

This presentation is a showstopper. I first saw this technique used in the restaurant where I worked with Japanese fish chefs. Making it for six people doesn't take very long, and then you just pop it in the oven. The best way to cut the squash is with a mandoline (a traditional French slicing tool). It has a folding leg so you can put it in a couple of different positions and you can adjust the height or thickness of the cut. The European mandolines are stainless steel and very expensive, but there's a Japanese type available that's plastic with a metal blade that works very well.

Margaret: It's interesting that my friend, Barbara Tropp, was telling me that in an informal survey of women chefs she knows, when they were asked what their most important kitchen tool was, a number of them mentioned this device.

If you would like to try variations on this recipe, cucumbers, blanched carrots, or radishes can be substituted for the squash to make the scales. You can really play with it.

To prepare the sauce: Combine the stock and white wine in a small saucepan and reduce to ¹/₂ cup. Whisk together egg yolks, crème fraîche, lemon juice, sea salt, and white pepper in a small bowl, and whisk in the reduced stock. Fill a bowl, large enough to hold the saucepan, with ice. Return the mixture to the saucepan and cook over medium heat, whisking constantly, until the sauce reaches 176 to 178° on an instant-read thermometer, at which point it will thicken noticeably and coat a wooden spoon thickly. (Do not let the sauce get above this temperature or the yolks will begin to scramble! If the sauce does get a little too hot and begin to scramble, blend for a few seconds in a blender or with an immersion mixer and pass through a sieve before continuing.) Put the saucepan immediately into the bowl of ice to stop the cooking process and allow the mixture to cool to room temperature, whisking occasionally. When cool, adjust seasoning to taste and store the sauce in the refrigerator until ready to use, up to 2 days.

Place the bass fillets on a lightly buttered baking sheet. Place the squash rounds, alternating colors, in overlapping rows to resemble scales over the entire surface of each fillet. May be refrigerated, loosely covered with plastic wrap, as long as overnight, but no longer than that or the scales will begin to look tired.

If the fillets have been refrigerated, remove them from the refrigerator and bring them to room temperature 30 minutes before cooking. Thirty minutes before serving, preheat the oven to 300° and put a pot of water on to boil. Place an ovenproof pan with at least 1-inch-high sides on the lower shelf of the oven. When the oven is warm and the water is boiling, place the pan with the fillets on the top shelf of the oven. Pour boiling water into the pan on the lower shelf to fill the pan at least ¹/₂ inch deep. Steam-bake the fillets for 8 to 10 minutes, until they are just barely springy to the touch.

When ready to serve, gently rewarm the sauce, whisking in the butter by tablespoonfuls just until it is absorbed, and then whisking in the fresh chives, and salt and pepper to taste. Do not let the sauce get too hot or it will break. The rewarming and finishing of the sauce should be done while the fish is cooking and not before.

To serve, warm plates slightly (if they are too hot the sauce will break). Ladle 3 to 4 tablespoons of the sauce onto each plate and surround the perimeter with parsleyed potatoes. Using a metal pancake spatula, carefully transfer each fillet to the pool of sauce. Lightly sprinkle the sauce with minced chives and blossoms. Serve immediately.

Thai–Style Panang Duck Curry
with Kohlrabi, Greens, and Basil

Makes 4 servings

- 4 teaspoons panang (or red) curry paste
- 4 teaspoons light brown sugar
- 4 teaspoons freshly squeezed lime juice
- 4 to 6 teaspoons fish sauce (see Glossary)
- 12 Kaffir lime leaves, fresh or frozen and thawed, torn in half (see Glossary)
- 3 (14-ounce) cans (4½ cups) coconut milk
- 1 cup duck or chicken stock
- 2 to 3 cups fresh kale and/or Swiss chard, washed, stemmed, and cut crosswise into 1-inch-wide ribbons
- 2 kohlrabi or turnips, peeled and cut into 8 thin wedges each
- 1 (4- to 5-pound) roast duck, Chinese-style or home-roasted (see Note), boned and cut into 1-inch pieces
- 12 Thai basil leaves, torn in half if large, or sweet basil
- ¼ cup coarsely chopped cilantro, for garnish

Suggested Accompaniment

Steamed basmati, Thai jasmine, or Sticky Rice (recipe follows)

Bring the curry paste, sugar, lime juice, fish sauce, lime leaves, coconut milk, and stock to a boil over high heat in a wok or saucepan, whisking until smooth. Boil for a few minutes to reduce and thicken slightly. Taste for seasoning, adjust if needed, and set aside.

Bring 3 quarts of water to a boil in a large pot and add 3 tablespoons of sea salt. When the water returns to a boil, blanch the kale and/or chard until barely tender, about 2 to 4 minutes. Refresh in ice water, drain, and squeeze dry—you should have about ½ cup, packed.

Add the kohlrabi to the curry base and return to a simmer. Cook for 1 minute, then add the duck pieces, blanched greens, and basil leaves. Return to a simmer and cook gently for 2 minutes until the duck is heated through and the kohlrabi is barely tender. Taste and adjust seasoning again. Spoon the curry into warmed bowls with a scoop of rice in the center or on the side. Sprinkle with the chopped cilantro and serve.

This is a late fall or winter version of my favorite Thai curry, red duck curry with tomatoes, spinach, and basil. In the original version, which we prepare at the restaurant in summer and early fall, whole tomatoes are cut into wedges and cooked briefly along with the spinach in a red curry base. In this variation, we use panang curry paste, a blend I'm particularly fond of, and organic kohlrabi or young turnips in place of the tomatoes, a typically French pairing with duck. I also enjoy the robust flavor and texture of the kale or chard, which balances the richness of the duck and coconut milk. If you would like to try the tomato and spinach version, use young, tender spinach and skip the blanching step, cooking it directly in the curry for about 2 minutes. All of the Asian ingredients are described in the glossary and are commonly available in Thai markets.

Sticky Rice

2 cups glutinous short- or long-grain rice
Water

Soak the rice in cold water to cover for at least 1 hour and as long as overnight. Line a steamer with damp cheesecloth, add the soaked and drained rice, and steam over boiling water for 20 to 30 minutes, until the rice is translucent all the way through. Serve immediately.

Note: Thai restaurants traditionally prepare duck curries from Chinese-style roast ducks, which can be purchased in Chinese barbecue restaurants in the Chinatown district of most cities. However, if you live in the country as we do, far from any Chinese community, you can roast your own duck. Season the duck with salt, place it on a roasting rack in a roasting pan, and roast it to medium-rare, about 45 minutes in a 375° oven. Remove the duck from the oven and allow it to cool for 15 minutes or longer. When the duck is cool enough to handle, cut the breast and leg pieces off the carcass and brown them skin-side down in a hot, dry skillet (no additional fat will be needed) until crisp. Remove the duck pieces from the pan and allow to cool slightly, then bone the meat and cut it into 1-inch chunks.

Braised Pork Loin
with Prunes and Cream Sauce

Makes 6 servings

24 Brandied Prunes (recipe follows) or regular pitted
    prunes

2 cups dry white wine

2¼ to 2½ pounds boneless pork loin or shoulder roast,
    trimmed of excess fat and tied at 1- to 1½-inch intervals

Fine sea salt and freshly ground pepper to taste

2 tablespoons light olive oil, canola oil, or light peanut oil

1 to 2 tablespoons unsalted butter

¼ cup diced yellow onion (¼-inch dice)

¼ cup diced carrot (¼-inch dice)

¼ cup diced celery (¼-inch dice)

1 cup crème fraîche (or heavy whipping cream and
    1 teaspoon lemon juice)

2 teaspoons red currant jelly

Freshly squeezed lemon juice to taste

1 to 1½ tablespoons finely minced chives or chopped
    fresh flat-leaf parsley, for garnish

Suggested Accompaniments

Quince, Apple, and Parsnip Purée (page 94)

Chive Mashed Potatoes (page 93) or soft polenta

Pan-Wilted Winter Greens with Ginger (page 99),
    or fresh peas blanched and sautéed in butter
    with tarragon

If using brandied prunes, drain them from the brandy. Soak the prunes in the wine for several hours or overnight. Transfer the prunes and wine to a saucepan, bring to a simmer over medium heat, and cook gently for 10 minutes. Remove from the heat and set aside.

Preheat the oven to 325°. Season the pork generously with salt and pepper on all sides. Heat the oil in a heavy-bottomed casserole pan large enough to hold the roast. When the oil is hot, add the pork and sear the surface to a rich golden brown on all sides. Adjust the heat to avoid blackening the bottom of the pot. Set the loin aside on a plate and pour off and discard all but about 1 tablespoon of the fat.

Add 1 tablespoon of the butter and the chopped vegetables to the casserole pan and cook, stirring occasionally, for 8 to 10 minutes over medium-high heat, until the vegetables are golden. Do not allow the vegetables to burn—add another tablespoon of butter if they seem too dry.

Pork prepared with prunes and cream is a classic French combination from the Loire Valley. It can be prepared either with a whole loin, as described here, or with chops. Each preparation has its advantages: Chops cook faster and have a greater surface area, which offers more caramelized meat in each serving; a braised loin or shoulder requires less attention at the stove, especially close to serving time, and because it cooks more slowly, it is less likely to be overcooked, tough, and dry. Try this recipe in the fall, when fresh quinces appear, and accompany it as we do at the restaurant with Quince, Apple, and Parsnip Purée and Pan-Wilted Winter Greens with Ginger. If you can, try this recipe with Brandied Prunes, which require at least 2 weeks to develop full flavor, but are worth the wait.

Drain the prunes from the wine and reserve both. Add the wine to the casserole pan and deglaze over low heat, scraping the bottom with a wooden spatula to loosen any browned bits. Return the browned loin and any juices on the plate to the pan, resting the meat on top of the vegetables. Cover the casserole and bake in the oven for 45 to 60 minutes, until the internal temperature reaches 140° to 145°. (If you have more room on the stove top than in the oven, the pork may be braised over very low heat instead of roasted in the oven. Turn the loin over once or twice during cooking.)

Remove the pork loin from the oven and transfer to a platter or cutting board. Remove and discard strings and cover the pork loosely with aluminum foil. Prepare or warm the side dishes you will serve and warm plates in the turned-off oven.

Pour the liquid from the casserole through a fine-mesh sieve into a degreasing pitcher or small bowl, pressing down hard on any vegetables in the sieve to extract the maximum liquid. Reserve the vegetables in a small bowl. Degrease the strained liquid using a degreasing pitcher or by skimming fat off the surface with a spoon. Return the liquid to the casserole and reduce rapidly over medium-high heat, stirring and scraping any browned bits attached to the bottom, until the liquid is nut brown. Add the crème fraîche and reserved vegetables and return to a boil. Boil rapidly for 2 minutes, then remove from heat and allow to cool for 1 minute.

Using a handheld immersion mixer or a blender, purée the mixture until smooth, then strain it through a fine-mesh sieve into a medium saucepan, discarding any vegetable matter that doesn't pass through. If the sauce isn't thick enough to coat a spoon lightly, return to a boil and reduce rapidly for another minute or two. When the sauce is the desired consistency, remove it from the heat and stir in the currant jelly and lemon juice. Taste and adjust seasoning with salt, pepper, and lemon juice if desired. Add the soaked prunes to the saucepan and heat gently, stirring, until prunes are just heated through.

To serve, place a generous dollop (⅔ cup) of the Quince, Apple, and Parsnip Purée, Chive Mashed Potatoes, or polenta in the center of each warmed plate and surround with the suggested greens. Slice the pork thinly and place 4 slices on the bed of purée, potatoes, or polenta on each plate. Spoon sauce and prunes over the pork slices, sprinkle with chives or parsley, and serve.

Note: Trichinella bacteria, which cause trichinosis, are killed by freezing pork for three weeks prior to cooking, or by cooking the meat to an internal temperature of at least 137°. Fresh pork is safe to eat when it is cooked to an internal temperature of 140°, at which point it will still be slightly pink, juicy, and delicious. If you want it less pink, cook it to an internal temperature of 145° to 150°, but no longer, or it will become tragically tough and dry.

Brandied Prunes

1½ cups freshly brewed hot black tea, such as Earl Grey
1 pound large pitted prunes
½ cups sugar (optional)
1 to 1½ cups Armagnac or other brandy

Pour the hot tea over the prunes and soak overnight. The next day, drain the prunes and discard the tea. Place the prunes in a clean jar, add the sugar to the jar, and stir or shake to mix. Pour the Armagnac over the prunes to cover and shake gently to dissolve the sugar. Cover the jar and store in a cool, dark place, or in the refrigerator, for at least two weeks before using. Check from time to time to make sure prunes stay covered by the brandy. Brandied prunes keep almost indefinitely, improving with age.

Roast Cornish Hen
with Apricot Marsala Sauce

Makes 4 servings

4 small Cornish hens (1 to 1¼ pounds each), rinsed and patted dry

Fine sea salt and freshly ground pepper to taste

6 tablespoons unsalted butter

5 large bay leaves

1 small bunch fresh thyme, about 1½ inches in diameter

½ teaspoon allspice berries

1 teaspoon black peppercorns

½ cup dried apricots

¾ cup marsala

1½ cups white wine

6 cups chicken stock

½ cup thinly sliced shallots

Garnish

1 tablespoon almonds

1 tablespoon chopped fresh flat-leaf parsley

1 teaspoon finely minced orange zest (wash orange in hot water, then peel the orange and carefully trim any white pith from the peelings before mincing)

2 tablespoons water

Suggested Accompaniments

Chive Mashed Potatoes (page 93) or soft polenta

Pan-Wilted Winter Greens with Ginger (page 99) or sautéed green beans

At least several hours before roasting, or up to three days in advance, season the hens liberally with salt and pepper all over, including the cavities. Add ½ teaspoon of butter, a bay leaf, and a two sprigs of fresh thyme to the cavity of each bird. Store the hens, covered, in the refrigerator.

One hour before roasting, bring the hens out of the refrigerator and allow them to come to room temperature. Preheat the oven to 475°. Pat the birds' skin dry again, and melt 2 tablespoons of butter in a small saucepan. Brush the skin of each bird all over with the melted butter and set them breast-side down on a rack placed over a baking sheet or shallow roasting pan. Leave as much space as possible around each hen for optimal browning.

Roast the hens on the top rack of the oven for 15 to 20 minutes, until the skin begins to turn golden. Remove the pan from the oven, turn the birds over, and baste the breasts with any fat that has dripped into the pan. Lower the temperature to 425°, return the pan to the oven, and roast for another 25 to 30 minutes. Baste the breasts with pan drippings after 15 minutes. If the pan drippings begin to burn or smoke, add a cup of water to the pan.

Meanwhile, prepare the sauce. Strip the leaves off the stems of the remaining thyme sprigs and set the leaves aside for the garnish. Place the stems and the remaining bay leaf, allspice, and peppercorns in a small piece of cheesecloth or paper coffee filter and tie securely with kitchen twine. Place the herb bundle in a 1-quart saucepan along with the dried apricots, marsala, and white wine. Bring to a boil and then reduce heat and simmer, uncovered, for 15 minutes, until the apricots are tender. Remove from the heat.

In a 2-quart saucepan, bring the stock to a boil and reduce to $^{3}/_{4}$ cup. It will become very dark and strong. Strain the apricots from the marsala mixture and reserve. Return the liquid and herb bundle to the smaller saucepan. Return the saucepan to the stove and reduce the liquid to $^{1}/_{2}$ cup. Add the shallots and cook for another 10 minutes, until the shallots are wilted and tender. Remove the pan from the heat. Add the reduced stock and reserved apricots. Remove the herb bundle, squeezing all juices into the saucepan, and discard. Set aside until the hens are ready.

Toast the almonds in a moderate (300°) oven on a baking sheet, until golden brown (about 10 minutes). Allow them to cool, and then coarsely chop. Finely chop the reserved thyme leaves and measure out 1 teaspoon. Combine this teaspoon of thyme in a small bowl with the parsley, almonds, and orange zest.

When the hens are done (the inside of the thigh should read 165° to 170° on an instant-read thermometer) remove the pan from the oven. Cool the birds breast-side down on the roasting rack for 5 to 10 minutes before serving. Pour off any juices from the roasting pan (deglaze with a little water if caramelized) and degrease with a degreasing pitcher or with a spoon. Return the sauce to the stove over low heat and add the degreased juices to the sauce. Swirl in 2 tablespoons of water, and adjust seasoning.

Place the hens on a bed of mashed potatoes or polenta surrounded by greens. Ladle warm sauce over the birds and sprinkle generously with the herb-almond mixture. Serve immediately.

These crab cakes are wildly popular at the restaurant. We've had nights where more than a third of our diners order this entrée. We usually offer them from January through April or May, depending on the Dungeness crab season. This recipe is an example of my affinity for mixing Southeast Asian and Mexican flavors. It is also clearly a dish whose total effect is greater than the sum of its parts. It's very beautiful to look at, too, with the bold contrasting colors of the white coconut rice and the black beans, the bright red achiote tomato sauce, the green Avocado Salsa, and the golden brown cakes.

Yucatécan–Thai Crab Cakes

Makes 6 servings (12 cakes)

Crab Cakes

1½ cups coconut milk (1 14-ounce can)

1 pound crabmeat, squeezed dry and picked over for bits of shell and cartilage

¼ cup crab "butter" and fat (the pale green liver and fat inside the body shell if picking your own crabmeat) (optional)

3 large egg whites

1 tablespoon fish sauce (see Glossary)

1½ tablespoons freshly squeezed lime juice

2 tablespoons chopped shallots

1 tablespoon minced garlic (3 cloves)

1½ tablespoons peeled and grated fresh galangal (see Glossary) or ginger

1 tablespoon shao-hsing (see Glossary) or dry sherry

1 tablespoon grated orange zest

¼ cup minced cilantro stems

6 to 8 tablespoons unseasoned bread crumbs

Avocado Salsa

2 ripe Haas avocados, cut into ½-inch dice

½ cup Seville Orange Juice (page 7)

½ cup finely chopped red onion

1 habanero chile or 4 serrano chiles, stemmed and minced (including seeds)

1 tablespoon finely chopped epazote leaves (see Glossary) or cilantro

½ teaspoon fine sea salt

1½ cups Achiote Sauce (page 7)

Unseasoned bread crumbs, for coating crab cakes (approximately 2 cups)

4 to 6 tablespoons unsalted butter

2 to 3 tablespoons canola oil

4 to 6 tablespoons coarsely chopped cilantro, for garnish

Suggested Accompaniments

Soupy Black Beans (page 100)

Coconut Rice (page 99)

To prepare the crab cake batter: In a small, heavy-bottomed saucepan over medium heat, cook the coconut milk, whisking occasionally, until it is reduced to $^3/_4$ cup, at which point it will be very thick and beginning to sputter. Remove the pan from the heat. If the milk has separated, emulsify it with a handheld immersion blender. Transfer the milk to a mixing bowl to cool to room temperature. Add the crabmeat (and crab butter, if desired), egg whites, fish sauce, lime juice, shallots, garlic, galangal, shao-hsing, orange zest, cilantro stems, and 6 tablespoons of bread crumbs. Taste and adjust seasoning. Chill the mixture in the refrigerator for 10 to 15 minutes to firm up (the bread crumbs will absorb moisture). Remove batter from the refrigerator and test the consistency. Try squeezing a small handful of the mixture into a $^1/_4$-cup patty; it should be light and moist. If it seems too wet and fragile, stir in another tablespoon or two of bread crumbs. Return the batter to the refrigerator.

To prepare the salsa: Combine the diced avocado, orange juice, onion, chile, epazote, and salt in a bowl and stir well to blend. If making in advance, cover the surface with plastic wrap to prevent browning.

Prepare the Achiote Sauce.

Remove the batter from the refrigerator and prepare the crab cakes. Shape the batter into $^1/_4$-cup cakes. Dredge each cake in the bread crumbs and flatten using the bottom of a measuring cup to approximately $^1/_2$-inch-thick disks about $2^1/_2$ inches in diameter. Heat the butter and oil over medium-high heat in 2 large nonstick skillets. Add the cakes to the pans. Because these cakes are light on filler, they are delicate and can be tricky to flip over if there are too many in the pan, so don't crowd them during cooking. If your pans are not big enough to fit all the cakes comfortably, cook them in batches and keep the first batch warm in a low (200°) oven while finishing the rest. You may need to use more butter and oil if cooking in batches. Sauté the cakes until they are evenly browned and crisp on the bottom, about 2 to 3 minutes. Using a pancake spatula, carefully flip cakes over to brown the other side, another 2 to 3 minutes. Remove the cakes from the pans and drain on paper towels.

To serve the cakes: Ladle 2 to 3 tablespoons of warm Achiote Sauce in a band across each warmed plate. Place 2 cakes, overlapping, on the sauce and top them with 2 to 3 tablespoons of avocado salsa. Place some black beans on one side of the cakes and Coconut Rice on the other side. Sprinkle cilantro over the top and serve.

For the past few years,
our friends at Navarro
Vineyards in the
Anderson Valley have
been making verjus for
us to use in a wonderful
sea bass dish from chef
Joël Robuchon. Verjus,
the juice of underripe
wine grapes, has been
used extensively in
sauces and marinades
since as long ago as the
Middle Ages. Except for
its continued use in
Dijon mustard, it has
waned in popularity to
the position of near
obscurity. It's a shame
because its flavor is an
intriguing combination
of the acidity of mild
vinegar and the fruiti-
ness of grape juice—
definitely worthy of culinary consideration.

   When I was a teen-
ager, I catered my first
meal, a dinner party for
my stepfather and three
friends. For the entrée, I
prepared poulet au
vinaigre, or chicken with
vinegar, an old bistro
dish recommended by
my dad as being very
"in" at the time. Well,
this type of homey fare
always tastes "in" to
me. When Ted Bennett
and Deborah Cahn, the
owners of Navarro
Vineyards, asked me to
come up with some
recipes using their verjus
to help spread the word
about its value, poulet
au vinaigre leapt
instantly to mind. This
(continued on page 135)

Poulet au Verjus

Makes 4 servings

1 medium roasting chicken (about 3 to 4 pounds), cut
   into 8 pieces, at room temperature
Fine sea salt and freshly ground black pepper to taste
2 tablespoons canola or light olive oil
2 tablespoons unsalted butter
⅓ cup unbleached all-purpose flour
1 cup verjus (or ¾ cup good-quality wine vinegar)
4 medium shallots, thinly sliced
1 cup peeled, seeded, and coarsely chopped tomatoes
1 tablespoon tomato paste
1 cup chicken stock
2 tablespoons mixed chopped fresh parsley, chervil,
   and tarragon

Suggested Accompaniments

Chive Mashed Potatoes (page 93)
Barley and Wild Rice Pilaf (page 90)
Blanched and sautéed green beans

Season the chicken pieces on both sides generously with salt and pepper. Heat
the oil and 1 tablespoon of the butter in a heavy-bottomed, nonreactive 10- to
12-inch skillet or casserole with a lid until the foam subsides. Meanwhile, pat
the chicken pieces dry with a kitchen towel and dip them in the flour, turning
to coat them on all sides, and pat off the excess. When the pan is hot, add the
chicken pieces, skin-side down, and cook over high heat until richly browned,
about 5 to 7 minutes. Turn the pieces to brown on all sides, adjusting the heat
as necessary to keep the chicken and the pan from blackening. When the pieces
are well browned on all sides (about 15 minutes total), remove the chicken to a
plate. Pour off the fat from the pan, and use a paper towel to blot up fat that
doesn't pour off. Still off-heat, add the verjus to the pan. Place the pan over high
heat and deglaze by scraping up any browned bits with a wooden spatula. Add
the shallots, tomatoes, and tomato paste to the pan, lower heat to medium, and
bring to a simmer. Add the chicken pieces and any juices that have collected on
the plate. Turn heat up to high again and simmer for 5 minutes to reduce the
liquid by half, turning the chicken pieces over once to coat them with the sauce
and cook evenly. Add the stock, return to a simmer, and then lower the heat to
a gentle simmer. Cover and cook for another 5 to 8 minutes, turning the pieces
over after 3 to 4 minutes. Remove the pan from the heat. The dish may be prepared in advance to this point. If prepared ahead, to reheat, warm the chicken in
the sauce until heated through.

   Remove the chicken pieces to a warm serving platter and put the platter in
a low (200°) oven to keep warm while you are finishing the sauce. Return the

EVENING FOOD

sauce to the pan and, with a small ladle or soup spoon, skim any fat from the surface. Reduce over high heat for a few minutes to concentrate flavors and thicken the sauce slightly. Taste and adjust seasoning if desired. Off-heat, swirl in the remaining 1 tablespoon butter and the chopped fresh herbs. Remove the serving platter with the chicken from the oven and pour the sauce over the chicken pieces. Serve with mashed potatoes or rice pilaf, and green beans.

Note: Unlined cast iron and aluminum can react with acids such as those in verjus to form off flavors, so an enameled cast-iron, stainless steel, or lined copper pan is preferred here.

adaptation goes especially well with pinot noir wines. (For sources of verjus, see Glossary.)

So often when you make a stew, it can be tricky to get all of the vegetables cooked through but not mushy at the same time that the meat is ready. I've seen recipes that suggest that you cook everything together for an hour or so and then strain it through a colander and pick out the blah-blah-blah and you end up spending 45 minutes picking out something that's completely mixed in with the other components. For this stew, we developed a technique that solves both problems. Our method involves cooking the vegetables in the perforated insert that's used to cook pasta. You can use it to lower the vegetables into the cooking liquid. This way you get all the benefits of cooking the vegetables with the meat: the flavors of the vegetables get into the stew base, and the vegetables benefit by absorbing the flavors from the meat as they cook. And the minute they're done, you just pull the vegetables out, set them aside, and cook the next vegetable. You can cook one vegetable after another and then, at the end, put everything together and all the components are perfectly cooked.

Simca's Lamb Stew
with Mellow Garlic

Makes 4 to 6 servings

- 2 tablespoons light olive or canola oil
- 2 pounds boneless lamb shoulder, cut into 1½-inch chunks
- 2 cups chopped yellow onion
- 1 cup dry white wine
- 2 cups lamb or chicken stock
- 1½ teaspoons fine sea salt
- Freshly ground pepper to taste
- Bouquet garni: 1 bay leaf, 1 teaspoon peppercorns, 2 tablespoons fresh thyme sprigs, and ¼ cup parsley stems combined in a piece of cheesecloth or a paper coffee filter and bound into a packet with kitchen twine
- ½ (generous) cup crushed garlic cloves (20 to 25 cloves)
- 1 large celery root, peeled and cut into 1-inch cubes (1⅔ cups)
- 3 to 4 medium carrots, cut in 1-inch chunks (1⅔ cups)
- 5 tablespoons all-purpose flour
- 5 tablespoons unsalted butter, softened
- 3 cups blanched broccoli (optional)
- 2 tablespoons chopped fresh flat-leaf parsley, for garnish

Suggested Accompaniment

Barley and Wild Rice Pilaf (page 90), brown rice, or Chive Mashed Potatoes (page 93)

Heat the oil in a rondeau or similar heavy, wide-bottomed pan over high heat until almost smoking. Dry the lamb chunks on a paper towel and add them to the pan. Brown the lamb chunks on all sides. (Don't crowd the lamb pieces or they will steam and take too long to brown; if you don't have a pan wide enough to fit them comfortably in one layer, brown them in two batches.) Transfer the lamb pieces to a deep 6- to 8-quart pot as they are browned. Regulate the heat (medium-high) so that the bottom of the pan browns without blackening. Once all of the lamb has been browned and transferred to the pot, add the onions to the lamb fat and oil left in the pan and cook over medium heat, stirring, to brown. Add the wine to the pan with the onions and bring to a boil, scraping the bottom with a wooden spatula to deglaze.

Transfer the wine and onions to the pot with the lamb. Add the stock, salt, pepper, and bouquet garni. Bring to a simmer over medium-high heat. Using a metal pasta insert or other metal sieve, lower the garlic cloves into the stew, making sure the insert is nestled deep enough in the stew to keep the cloves submerged. If needed, add water to bring the liquid level high enough to cover both the lamb and garlic. Adjust the heat to maintain a very low simmer. Cover and cook until the garlic is tender enough to be easily crushed between your thumb and forefinger, about 20 minutes. Remove the garlic from the stew and set it aside in a small bowl to cool slightly. Purée the cooled garlic until smooth in the bowl of a food processor fitted with the metal blade. Pass the garlic through a sieve and set aside.

Put the celery root in the pasta insert, lower it into the stew, and cook for about 20 minutes, until the celery root is tender when pierced with a knife. Remove the celery root to a plate and refrigerate to stop the cooking process. Repeat this procedure with the carrots, refrigerating them with the celery root.

Continue to allow the stew to barely simmer, until the lamb is tender when pierced with a fork but not falling apart (about another 20 to 30 minutes; total cooking time should be about 1½ hours). Remove the pan from the heat and allow the lamb to cool in the stock, for 15 to 30 minutes. Strain the lamb and onions through a colander, reserving the stock. Squeeze out any liquid from the bouquet garni, adding the liquid to the stock, and discard the packet. Cover the lamb with a damp kitchen towel to avoid its drying out while you degrease and thicken the stock. (If you will not be serving the stew immediately, refrigerate the lamb to stop the cooking process.) Degrease the stock with a degreasing pitcher or a small ladle.

Knead the flour and softened butter with your fingertips into a smooth paste to make a *beurre manié*. Put the degreased stock in a 4- to 6-quart saucepan and bring to a boil. Whisk in the reserved garlic purée and the beurre manié. Continue to simmer for about 1 minute, whisking to dissolve all of the beurre manié and keep the stock from sticking to the bottom of the pot as it thickens. Taste for seasoning and adjust with more salt and pepper if desired.

If serving immediately, add the reserved lamb, onions, carrots, and celery root to the stock and cook until everything is heated through. Stir in the blanched broccoli, if using. Serve the stew in wide bowls over rice pilaf, brown rice, or mashed potatoes, and garnish with the chopped parsley. If preparing stew ahead of time, put the reserved lamb and vegetables in a bowl, pour the thickened stock over them, stir to mix evenly, cover, and refrigerate for up to 1 week or in the freezer for as long as 2 months.

This is a kind of Mediterranean/North African-style seafood stew that has a number of parts, some of which, like the Harissa and the garbanzo beans, may be made ahead to save time. The fresh herbs sprinkled on at the end are a nice addition. A defining feature of our cuisine at the restaurant is the use of fresh herbs. One of our cooks spends an hour or two each day washing, drying, and chopping fresh herbs. It makes such a difference. If you take an herb that was used in the cooking of a dish and sprinkle a little of it, finely chopped and maybe mixed with a little fresh parsley, over the dish, it really brings out the dish's flavor.

Seafood Couscous

Makes 6 servings

Charmoula Marinade

½ cup cilantro leaves and stems, loosely packed

¼ cup freshly squeezed lemon juice

¼ cup fruity olive oil

5 crushed garlic cloves

1 teaspoon ground toasted cumin seeds

1 tablespoon paprika

1 teaspoon fine sea salt

¼ teaspoon freshly ground black pepper

¼ teaspoon ground cayenne pepper

1¼ pounds trimmed fresh swordfish, tuna, sea bass, or other meaty white-fleshed fish, cut into 6 (1-inch thick) portions

18 large day-boat caught and dry-packed sea scallops, trimmed of small tough side muscle

18 medium to large shrimp, shelled (reserve shells for stock)

Spiced Garbanzo Beans

5 tablespoons dry garbanzo beans, soaked overnight in 1 cup cold water, or ¾ cup canned cooked garbanzo beans, drained

2 tablespoons pitted and coarsely sliced oil-cured black olives

2 tablespoons peeled, finely julienned fresh ginger

Zest from 1 lemon (wash lemon in hot water, zest with a zester or vegetable peeler, then julienne the zest)

Harissa

1 small fresh habanero chile, stemmed and charred on all sides in a dry skillet, or 3 to 4 small canned chipotle chiles, drained (see Glossary)

1 cup Roasted Tomato Sauce (page 8) reduced to ½ cup, or ½ cup canned tomato purée

½ teaspoon fine sea salt

Couscous

2½ cups couscous, regular or precooked ("quick-cooking")

1 teaspoon fine sea salt

2½ tablespoons fruity olive oil

1½ teaspoons orange flower water

Broth

¼ teaspoon saffron threads

1 cup dry white wine or vermouth

Reserved shrimp shells

2 tablespoons anchovy oil from can of anchovies or fruity olive oil

2½ cups chopped yellow onion

2 tablespoons chopped anchovies

2 tablespoons coarsely chopped garlic (6 cloves)

Spice bouquet: 1 tablespoon Ras el Hanout (see Glossary) or curry powder and 1½ tablespoons garam masala (page 27) combined in a small piece of cheesecloth or in a paper coffee filter and tied in a small bundle with kitchen twine

1 (28-ounce) can peeled plum tomatoes, coarsely chopped, and their juice

3 cups fish stock (page 200) or 2 (12-ounce) bottles clam juice

2 medium to large carrots or 1 large Garnet yam, peeled and cut into chunks approximately the size of the zucchini (18 to 24 pieces)

2 small to medium zucchini, halved lengthwise, then cut into 1½-inch-long pieces (18 to 24 pieces)

2 tablespoons chopped fresh flat-leaf parsley, for garnish

2 tablespoons chopped cilantro, for garnish

To prepare the Charmoula Marinade: Combine all of the marinade ingredients in the bowl of a food processor fitted with the metal blade and blend until smooth.

Place all of the seafood in a shallow nonaluminum dish and pour the charmoula over it. Rub the marinade into the seafood, cover loosely with plastic wrap, and marinate for several hours at room temperature or overnight, refrigerated.

To prepare the garbanzo beans: Put the soaked beans in a medium saucepan, cover with 2 cups of cold water, and bring to a boil. Reduce heat and simmer until tender, about 45 minutes. Drain in a colander and transfer the beans to a medium bowl. If using canned garbanzo beans, begin their preparation at this point. Mix the beans with the olives, ginger, and lemon zest and set aside.

To prepare the Harissa: Purée the chile with the tomato sauce in a blender until smooth. Strain through a sieve into a small saucepan to remove any seeds and large skin pieces. Reduce the sauce over medium heat, stirring, for about 3 to 5 minutes, until thickened. Season with the salt, transfer to a small serving bowl, and set aside.

To prepare the Couscous: If using regular couscous, wash with enough water to cover, drain in a sieve, and empty it into a shallow pan. Allow it to sit for 10 minutes to swell. Break up any lumps with your fingertips, and then transfer couscous to a steamer lined with a damp kitchen towel or cheesecloth. Steam, uncovered, over boiling water for 20 minutes. Return the steamed couscous to the shallow pan. Dissolve the salt in 1 cup of cold water and add the olive oil and orange flower water. Sprinkle the couscous with this mixture and toss with your fingertips to mix evenly. Cover with a damp kitchen towel and set aside. If using precooked couscous, put it into a shallow pan. Bring 2½ cups of water to a boil with the salt in a small saucepan and pour over the couscous. Cover and allow couscous to swell for 5 to 7 minutes. Uncover and stir with a fork or with your fingers to break up any lumps. Drizzle with the olive oil and orange flower water. Stir to mix evenly and break up any lumps with your fingertips. Cover and set aside in a warm place.

To prepare the Broth: Steep the saffron threads in the wine in a small bowl for 30 minutes. Put the shrimp shells in a medium saucepan with 2¾ cups water and a pinch of salt and bring to a boil. Lower heat and simmer for 20 minutes. Strain out and discard shells, reserving strained shrimp stock. Meanwhile, in a heavy-bottomed 3- to 4-quart pot, heat the anchovy oil. Add the onions and cook over medium heat for 5 minutes until slightly softened. Add the anchovies, garlic, and spice bouquet and cook for another few minutes, stirring, until fragrant. Add the saffron-wine, tomatoes and their juice, reserved shrimp stock, and clam juice and bring to a boil. Place the spiced garbanzo beans in a pasta insert or sieve and lower the mixture into the broth. Cover and simmer gently for 15 minutes. Remove the insert with the garbanzo beans from the broth and set aside. Strain the broth through a fine-mesh sieve, reserving the tomatoes, onions, and broth. Discard the spice bouquet.

Put the carrots and the strained broth in the bottom of a steamer and simmer gently over medium heat for 10 minutes. Put the couscous into the top of a steamer lined with a damp kitchen towel or cheesecloth (or into a colander that fits above the pot with the simmering carrots and broth). Add the zucchini to the broth and return to a simmer over medium heat. Cook for 20 minutes, until the vegetables are tender. Transfer the couscous to a bowl, cover, and set aside until ready to serve. Drain the vegetables, reserving the broth, and set aside in a separate bowl, also covered. Return the broth to the saucepan. The dish may be prepared to this point up to several hours ahead. When ready to finish and serve, warm the broth in the saucepan and warm the couscous either in an ovenproof bowl, covered, in a low (200°) oven, or in a steamer, while you cook the seafood.

To prepare the seafood: If the seafood has been refrigerated, allow it to come to room temperature for 1 to 2 hours before cooking. Transfer the reserved tomatoes and onions to a rondeau or similar wide, heavy-bottomed pan large enough to hold the seafood in a single layer. Lay the fish pieces on top of the tomato mixture and add enough of the reserved broth to come halfway up the sides of the fish. Bring the liquid to a very low simmer over high heat, cover the pan, and then lower the heat and simmer gently for 1 minute. Uncover, turn the fish pieces over, and add the scallops and shrimp, along with their marinating juices, poking as much of the shellfish as will fit in between the swordfish pieces. Scatter the reserved carrot and zucchini pieces and the garbanzo bean mixture over the surface. Return to a simmer, cover, and cook at a very low simmer until the seafood has turned opaque almost all the way through, about another 5 to 6 minutes. Be careful not to overcook. (Don't worry that the vegetables aren't covered by the broth—if the pan is covered they will rewarm in the steam.)

If serving family style, transfer the seafood and vegetables, using a slotted spatula or spoon, to a large platter and moisten with some of the broth. Sprinkle the chopped parsley and cilantro over the top. Serve the Couscous in a separate bowl and serve the Harissa and the remaining broth on the side. If serving individual plates, ladle the Couscous onto warmed plates and form a basin in the center of it with the back of a ladle. Carefully place a piece of swordfish into the center of each basin and surround it with some of the shellfish and vegetables. Moisten the seafood with a little of the warm broth from the pan and sprinkle the top with the chopped herbs. Serve the remaining warm broth and the Harissa in serving bowls for everyone to share.

This is a simple recipe that I like to make when we can get fresh tomatoes, although canned tomatoes will work too. People seem to think the mixture of fish and meat is unusual, but smoked pork products often work very well with certain white-fleshed fish like halibut, swordfish, rockfish, and ling cod.

Margaret: We've included this dish in our classes many times. People are always struck by the intensity of the aromas because first you cook it with the lid on and then the lid is taken off and the smell just fills the classroom. It's a recipe with a simple but very elegant presentation that's quite satisfying.

Pan-Roasted Halibut
with Prosciutto and Thyme

Makes 4 servings

1¼ to 1½ pounds fresh halibut fillet, cut into 4 (1-inch-thick) portions

Fine sea salt and freshly ground pepper to taste

3 tablespoons chopped fresh flat-leaf parsley leaves, stems reserved

1 bunch fresh thyme, leaves stripped and minced (to yield 1 tablespoon), ~~stems reserved~~

3 ounces prosciutto, cut into ¼-inch dice

4 tablespoons unsalted butter

¼ cup chopped shallots

1½ tablespoons minced garlic (4 to 5 cloves)

1 cup white wine

1 cup fish stock (page 200) or clam juice *or chicken*

1 cup chicken stock

2 teaspoons Pernod or other anise-flavored liqueur *(Sambuca)*

2 medium ripe tomatoes, peeled, seeded, coarsely chopped into ½-inch dice, and drained, to yield 1 cup (substitute 1 cup canned tomatoes if fresh tomatoes are unavailable)

Suggested Accompaniments

Pan-Wilted Winter Greens with Ginger (page 99)

Soupy White Beans (page 100) or French lentils

Season the halibut fillets with the salt and pepper. Mix the chopped parsley with half of the chopped thyme. Set aside 4 pinches of the mixture for garnish, then sprinkle the fish all over with the remaining herb mixture.

In a 2-quart saucepan over medium heat, sauté the prosciutto in 1 tablespoon of the butter for 3 to 5 minutes to render any fat from the ham and color it lightly. Add the shallots and cook for 2 to 3 minutes to soften. Add the garlic and the remaining chopped thyme and cook for another minute, until fragrant. Add the wine and herb stems and reduce to a loose glaze over the shallots and prosciutto, about 5 minutes. Add the fish and chicken stocks and reduce to 1 cup, another 7 to 10 minutes. Remove and discard herb stems. Remove the pan from the heat and season with freshly ground pepper. (The mixture should be sufficiently salted from the prosciutto.)

In a skillet with a tight-fitting lid that is large enough to hold the fish comfortably, combine the reduced cooking stock, Pernod, diced tomato, and remaining 3 tablespoons butter. Bring to a boil over high heat. Add the fish fillets to the pan, cover, and cook over high heat for 2 to 3 minutes, until the fish is cooked almost through (it should be slightly soft to the touch and barely translucent at the center, not dry and flaky).

Place the fillets on top of a bed of greens and surround with white beans or lentils. Taste the pan sauce for seasoning, adjust if needed, and gently pour over halibut, keeping some of the tomatoes on top of the fish. Sprinkle the reserved parsley and thyme mixture over the top and serve.

Margaret: The type of food we prepare tends to have some complexity to it, and we try to bring that same level of complexity to our vegetarian dishes. Frequently, vegetarian dishes take even more work than meat or poultry dishes, and that is why vegetarian dishes are often high-priced even though they don't contain what is thought of as a high-priced main ingredient.

Chris: People expect to pay more for a steak than for a plate full of vegetables, but the cost reflects the labor involved much more than the price of the ingredients. Making a dish from scratch, using ingredients that have just been harvested from the garden, entails far more labor than preparing any meat product does.

Margaret: We don't want to run the kind of restaurant that is always serving pasta primavera. Of course, there's nothing wrong with pasta primavera— but we don't want it to be the only thing a vegetarian can look forward to at our restaurant.

Chris: We want people to feel they're getting something worth going out for. Arturo's Vegetarian Special is one of those worthy

(continued on page 145)

Arturo's Vegetarian Special

Makes 4 servings

Country Salsa

6 to 7 (2 pounds) ripe tomatoes, or 1 (28-ounce) can whole peeled tomatoes
2 tablespoons light olive or canola oil
½ cup chopped white onion
2 teaspoons chopped garlic (2 cloves)
3 small green chiles, such as serranos or jalapeños, stemmed and chopped (to yield 1 tablespoon)
½ cup chopped green bell pepper
1½ teaspoons dried oregano
1 large bay leaf
½ teaspoon fine sea salt, or to taste
1 tablespoon freshly squeezed lime or lemon juice

Tortilla Cakes

¼ cup light olive or canola oil
½ cup chopped white onion
2¼ cups coarsely chopped button mushrooms
Kernels from 1 large ear of corn (¾ to 1 cup)
2 teaspoons chopped garlic (2 cloves)
1½ teaspoons achiote paste (see Glossary) (optional)
2 bay leaves
1 teaspoon fine sea salt
½ teaspoon ground cayenne pepper
1 cup chopped tomatoes (reserved from salsa)
¾ cup tomato juice (reserved from salsa)
2 packed cups young spinach, stemmed and coarsely chopped
8 (7-inch) corn tortillas

2 ounces Muenster or Monterey jack cheese, cut into 4 slices (or ½ cup grated)
1 medium stalk broccoli, stem peeled of outer fibrous layer and stem and florets cut into bite-sized pieces
12 baby carrots, peeled, or 2 medium carrots, peeled and cut into 2 x ¼-inch sticks
12 green onions, greens trimmed 5 inches from root end
3 cups button mushrooms, halved or quartered as needed for bite-sized pieces
½ recipe (2 cups) Soupy Black Beans (page 100)
1 recipe (4 cups) Mexican Rice (page 98)
4 tablespoons chopped cilantro, for garnish

To prepare the Country Salsa: If using fresh tomatoes, bring a medium pot of water to a boil. Cut a crisscross pattern on the tomatoes opposite the stem. Dip the tomatoes into the boiling water for 5 to 15 seconds, depending on their ripeness, just to loosen the skins. Remove the tomatoes, refresh briefly in ice water, and then drain them. Remove and discard skins. If using canned, peeled tomatoes, begin the recipe at this point. Cut the tomatoes in half horizontally and squeeze them over a sieve placed over a bowl to remove the seeds, reserving the juice. Coarsely chop the tomatoes and drain in a sieve to collect any additional juice. You will need approximately $1\frac{1}{2}$ cups of chopped tomatoes and $1\frac{3}{4}$ cups of juice in total. Set aside 1 cup of tomatoes and $\frac{3}{4}$ cup juice for the tortilla cake filling, then continue preparing the salsa.

In a medium saucepan, heat the 2 tablespoons oil. Add the onions, garlic, chiles, bell pepper, oregano, bay leaf, and salt and sauté for 5 minutes over medium heat, stirring occasionally. Add the lime juice, $\frac{1}{2}$ cup of chopped tomatoes, and 1 cup of the juice. Simmer for 10 to 15 minutes over medium-high heat, stirring occasionally, until the salsa is thick but not dry. Remove the pan from the heat, remove and discard bay leaf, taste for salt, adjust if desired, and set aside.

To prepare the tortilla cake filling: Heat the oil in another saucepan or skillet. Add the onions, mushrooms, corn, garlic, achiote paste, bay leaves, and salt and cook, stirring occasionally, for 5 to 7 minutes over medium heat to soften everything. Add the cayenne and the 1 cup reserved tomatoes and $\frac{3}{4}$ cup tomato juice. Return to a simmer and cook for another 5 minutes, stirring occasionally. Add the spinach to the pan, cover, and simmer for 2 minutes, without stirring, to wilt the spinach. Stir the spinach into the other vegetables in the pan, remove pan from the heat, cover, and let sit for 5 minutes. Taste and adjust seasoning if desired. Transfer the vegetable mixture to a colander set over a bowl to drain; reserve the juice for cooking the vegetables. Allow the filling mixture to cool slightly.

To assemble the Tortilla Cakes: Using a $2\frac{3}{4}$-inch round cookie cutter, cut out 24 rounds from the tortillas, 3 per tortilla. Set 4 rounds aside and lay the rest on the work surface. Spread 1 heaping tablespoon of filling on each round, and then assemble 4 stacks of 5 rounds each. Top each stack with one of the reserved plain rounds and, using a metal spatula, carefully transfer the tortilla cakes to an oiled baking sheet. (The recipe may be prepared up to two days in advance to this point and kept covered in the refrigerator.)

Preheat the oven to 350°. Warm 4 large plates. Place 1 slice of cheese or a heaping tablespoon of grated cheese on top of each tortilla cake. Put the cakes in the oven to warm through and melt the cheese, about 12 minutes. If the cakes have been refrigerated, remove them from the refrigerator 30 minutes before you plan to serve them, preheat the oven to 350°, and warm the plates. Bake the tortilla cakes for 5 minutes before adding the cheese, and then bake for an additional 15 to 18 minutes.

Meanwhile, combine the prepared broccoli, carrots, green onions, and mushrooms with the reserved filling juice in a large skillet and cook over high heat until the vegetables are tender but not mushy, about 10 to 12 minutes. Rewarm the salsa, Soupy Black Beans, and Mexican Rice.

dishes. Arturo's creation is a variation on another meatless entrée, which I had concocted previously—Vegetarian Special for Diana—developed by Arturo, a Mexican cook who worked with us for a year and a half before returning to Michoacán, Mexico, where he runs a little restaurant on his dad's ranch.

Margaret: This is Arturo's take on Chris' take on chef Diana Kennedy's take on Mexican cuisine. It's a multilayered approach to a multilayered dish!

To assemble the plates: Place ½ cup of Soupy Black Beans in the center of each plate and surround them with rice. Place a tortilla cake on top of the beans and spoon some of the salsa generously over the cake. Using a slotted spoon, place the vegetables on top of the rice and arrange them decoratively around the tortilla cake. Sprinkle the chopped cilantro over the top and serve.

DESSERTS

• DESSERTS •

As long as we've lived in a house with a fruit orchard, we've brought crate after crate of pears and apples into the restaurant. Sometimes, the simplest desserts, the ones I just throw together, end up becoming staples in our repertoire, like this favorite. We make three or four of these crisps every day during apple season. We make the crumble topping in a giant Hobart mixing bowl. The crumble is also a wonderful pie topping. This recipe makes enough for two pies. The cooking time varies so much because apples cook at very different rates.

Pear and Apple Crisp

Makes 10 to 12 servings

Topping

¾ cup all-purpose flour

1 cup nuts, lightly toasted and coarsely chopped (walnuts, hazelnuts, pecans, almonds, or a mixture of your choice)

¾ cup packed light brown sugar

½ cup unsweetened dried coconut

1¼ cups unseasoned bread crumbs

⅔ cup unsalted butter, cut into ½-inch dice

Filling

4 pounds tart apples such as Gravensteins, peeled, cored, and sliced ¼-inch thick

2 pounds ripe pears, such as Bartletts, peeled, cored, and sliced ¼-inch thick (or use all apples)

¼ cup freshly squeezed lemon juice

½ cup vanilla sugar (see Glossary)

1 tablespoon Calvados or other apple brandy

1 teaspoon orange flower water (optional)

Suggested Accompaniment

Cinnamon Bark Ice Cream (page 171) or Vanilla Bean Ice Cream (page 195)

To prepare the Topping: Combine the flour, nuts, sugar, coconut, and bread crumbs in a large bowl or in the bowl of a heavy-duty electric mixer fitted with the paddle attachment. Stir to blend. Add the butter cubes and blend with your fingertips or with the paddle attachment, if using an electric mixer, just until the mixture holds together when squeezed in the palm of your hand, but still crumbles easily. If it seems too moist, add more bread crumbs; if it seems too dry, knead in a little more butter. Store refrigerated in an airtight container until needed, up to 2 weeks, or freeze for up to 2 months.

Preheat the oven to 375°. Put the apples and pears in a bowl and toss with the lemon juice, vanilla sugar, Calvados, and orange flower water.

Grease a 13 x 9-inch baking pan with unsalted butter. Spread the fruit evenly in the pan and cover the fruit generously with the crumble topping. (The fruit should not be visible.) Bake on the lower rack of the oven for 45 to 75 minutes, until the pears and apples are soft and juices are starting to bubble through the topping. Move the pan to the top rack and continue baking for another 5 to 15 minutes, just long enough to turn the topping a rich golden brown, watching it closely; it browns quickly. Remove the pan from the oven and allow the crisp to cool slightly before serving. Serve warm on individual plates with a scoop of ice cream.

Wedding Cake

Makes one 9- to 10-inch cake, 12 servings

Cake

1¾ cups ground hazelnuts or 1½ cups whole hazelnuts (see Note)

¾ cup granulated sugar

Salt and distilled vinegar, for cleaning copper bowl

8 large egg whites

1 tablespoon freshly squeezed lemon juice

1 teaspoon Frangelico or other hazelnut liqueur (optional)

¼ cup vanilla sugar (see Glossary) or granulated sugar

Confectioners' sugar, for dusting

Buttercream

6 tablespoons water

6 tablespoons unsweetened, dried, shredded coconut

1 teaspoon crushed cinnamon bark or 1 (¾-inch) stick

2½ tablespoons chopped or grated, peeled fresh ginger

½ teaspoon cardamom seeds

1 cup vanilla sugar (see Glossary) or granulated sugar

Few drops of lemon juice

8 large egg yolks

1½ cups unsalted Plugras (see Glossary) or other unsalted butter, at room temperature

Chocolate Glaze

4 ounces bittersweet chocolate, shaved or chopped

2 tablespoons water

1 tablespoon Frangelico or other hazelnut liqueur

1 tablespoon Armagnac or other brandy

1½ teaspoons instant espresso or coffee

¼ cup whole hazelnuts, lightly toasted and skins removed

To prepare the Cake: Preheat the oven to 300°. Cut parchment paper to fit the bottom and sides of two 15 x 10-inch baking sheets. (If parchment paper isn't available, butter, flour, and chill the baking sheets—do not substitute waxed paper!) Also have ready either an 8-inch pastry ring, 8-inch springform pan with the bottom removed, or a pastry bag fitted with a large (½- to ¾-inch) plain round tip.

Margaret: This is not just any wedding cake. This was *our* wedding cake.

Chris: We had 250 people at the wedding but I'd made enough cake for 800, so we saved a whole cake in the freezer for the traditional one year. Of course, it tasted much better fresh.

Toast the ground nuts on a baking sheet in the 300° oven until they are lightly browned and nutty smelling, about 12 to 15 minutes. Remove the pan from the oven and allow the nuts to cool completely, then mix them with the sugar in a small bowl and set aside.

Clean the inside of a large copper bowl with salt and distilled vinegar then rinse with hot water and dry with a towel. Combine the egg whites, the 1 tablespoon lemon juice, and the Frangelico in the copper bowl and whisk slowly directly over very low heat to warm whites to the temperature of a hot bath (test the temperature on the inside of your wrist). Whisk constantly or shake the pan during this gentle warming. Do not leave the pan unattended even for an instant or the egg whites will cook where they touch the copper bowl. Remove the bowl from the heat and increase whisking speed to medium-fast for another minute or two, until the whites are frothy. Transfer the whites to the bowl of a heavy-duty electric mixer (preferably) or leave them in the copper bowl and beat with a handheld electric mixer. Beat at high speed for 3 to 4 minutes, until the whites reach the soft peak stage. Add the vanilla sugar to the bowl in a steady stream and continue to beat at high speed until the whites form stiff peaks when the beater is lifted from the bowl, about 2 to 3 minutes more. Make sure the meringue is nice and stiff, but don't beat too long or the whites will begin to break down and become grainy. Sprinkle the nut-sugar mixture over the meringue and fold together quickly and thoroughly (no longer than 1 minute). The batter should still be quite stiff and not runny.

If working with a pastry ring or a springform pan, set it down on one of the parchment-lined pans (dab a little meringue in each corner to adhere the parchment to the pan), leaving room to fit the second ring beside it. Fill the ring with one third of the batter, spreading it out with a rubber or plastic spatula to fill the ring with an even 1/2- to 3/4-inch layer. Carefully lift the ring straight up off the pan, leaving the meringue round intact on the pan. Repeat this process twice to use up all of the meringue. You should have two rounds on one sheet and one round on the other sheet. Space the rounds at least 1 inch apart to allow for expansion as the meringue bakes. If using a pastry bag, draw three 8-inch circles on the parchment with a pencil, using the bottom of a cake pan or a plate as your guide. Flip the parchment over so the penciled circle is on the underside. Fill the pastry bag with the meringue and pipe a spiral to completely fill the inside of each circle, trying to make as even a layer as you can.

Raise the oven temperature to 375°. Dust the rounds generously with the confectioners' sugar either with a dredger or through a fine-mesh sieve. Carefully place the pans in the oven and bake for 25 to 30 minutes, turning and rotating pans halfway through the baking time so they brown evenly. The meringues are ready when they are golden brown and feel lightly firm to the touch in the centers. Remove the pans from the oven and transfer the meringues to cooling racks. Allow to cool to room temperature. (Don't be alarmed when they deflate—this is normal.) When cool, carefully peel the parchment paper off the backs of the layers. The cake rounds are ready to use that day or they may be covered with plastic wrap and refrigerated for several days or frozen for up to a month.

To prepare the Buttercream: In a small saucepan, combine the water, coconut, cinnamon, ginger, and cardamom. (If using sugar and $1/2$ vanilla bean separately, add the bean now and the sugar when vanilla sugar is called for.) Bring to a simmer and cook for 2 minutes. Cover, remove from heat, and allow the mixture to infuse for 15 to 30 minutes. Strain the liquid through a chinois or piece of damp cheesecloth into a small bowl, pressing firmly on the coconut and spices to extract as much liquid as possible. Discard the coconut and spices. Rinse out the saucepan and return the infused liquid to it. Add the vanilla sugar and a few drops of lemon juice and place the pan over low heat. Stir to dissolve the sugar. Meanwhile, begin beating the egg yolks at medium speed in the bowl of a heavy-duty electric mixer. Let the mixer run while you finish the sugar syrup. When the sugar has dissolved, cover the pan and bring to a simmer over medium heat. Simmer for 1 minute, then uncover the pan and simmer for another 2 to 3 minutes, until the syrup reaches the soft ball stage (238° on a candy thermometer). Simmering covered for 1 minute should have caused enough condensation to wash the sides of the pan of any undissolved sugar crystals, but if you see any remaining sugar when you uncover the pan, wash it down with a pastry brush and a little water. (To test for the soft ball stage without a thermometer, dip the end of a wooden implement into the simmering syrup, and quickly move it over a small dish of cold water. Allow a drop of syrup adhering to the wood to fall into the water—it should form a distinct but malleable ball.) When the syrup reaches this stage, the beaten yolks should be pale and doubled in volume.

Remove the sugar syrup from the heat and increase the mixer speed to high. Carefully pour the hot syrup into the mixer bowl in a steady stream, keeping the stream of syrup between the whip and the side of the bowl so it doesn't splatter. Continue beating at high speed for 2 more minutes, then reduce the speed to medium and beat for 3 to 5 minutes, until the mixture is cool, pale, and thick enough to form a ribbon. Set aside until the yolk mixture is cooled to room temperature and then transfer it to another bowl.

Place the softened butter in the mixer bowl and beat on high speed until it is light and fluffy. Beat in the yolk mixture on high speed a little at a time. When all of the yolk has been incorporated and the Buttercream is completely blended, shiny, and smooth, you are ready to assemble the cake.

To assemble the cake: Place one of the cake rounds on a cardboard disk or a plate covered with strips of parchment or waxed paper. Cut 4 strips of parchment or waxed paper, 2 inches wide and 9 to 10 inches long, and tuck them under the bottom layer to protect the serving plate or cardboard disk while you spread the buttercream around the sides of the cake. Using a flexible metal spatula dipped in warm water, spread a $1/4$- to $3/8$-inch layer of buttercream on the cake as evenly as possible (use about $1\frac{1}{2}$ cups). Top with a second layer of cake and spread with the same thickness of buttercream. Top with the third cake layer, flat (bottom) side up, and spread enough of the remaining buttercream around the sides to cover them so that no cake shows through. There should be about $1/2$ cup of buttercream left. Put the remaining buttercream in a pastry bag fitted with a star tip and set it aside for decorating the top after the cake has been glazed. Refrigerate the cake while you make the glaze.

To prepare the glaze: Combine the bittersweet chocolate, the water, Frangelico, Armagnac, and espresso in a bowl placed over simmering water, in the top of a double boiler, or in a small pan over very low heat. Cook, stirring constantly, until the mixture is completely smooth.

Remove the cake from the refrigerator. Pour the chocolate glaze in a large puddle on the top of the cake. Lift the cake and tilt it carefully to cover the entire top with a smooth layer of glaze. Refrigerate to set the glaze. When set, remove the cake from the refrigerator. If any glaze has spilled onto the buttercream sides, trim it off with a spatula or small knife. Remove the paper strips protecting the serving plate. Decorate the top border of the cake with buttercream stars at twelve equidistant points to mark slices. Top each star with a toasted hazelnut. Refrigerate uncovered for 10 minutes to set the buttercream stars, then cover the cake loosely with plastic wrap and continue to refrigerate until 30 minutes before serving. The cake may be frozen, wrapped, for up to a month.

Note: Try specialty food stores for ground hazelnuts; if they are unavailable, you can grind your own in a food processor using raw hazelnuts. Grind the nuts with 1 tablespoon of cornstarch or cake flour and 6 tablespoons of the ³/₄ cup sugar using the pulsing method to keep the nuts from getting too oily. Do not grind the mixture for too long; stop the instant it starts to become oily. If you want to create a true nut powder, stop the machine a little way into the grinding and shake and rub the partially ground nuts through a sieve—the powder will go through the sieve, the coarser pieces will stay behind. Save the powder and return the coarser nut pieces to the processor to grind a little more. Repeat this process until you get enough powder and before the remaining ground nuts become too oily to pass through the sieve.

Simca's Bittersweet Chocolate Raspberry Bavarian

Makes one 9-inch tart, 8 to 10 servings

Bavarian Base

1 cup plus 1 tablespoon sugar

½ cup water

4½ ounces unsweetened chocolate

4 ounces bittersweet chocolate

2 cups (2 half-pint baskets or 12 ounces) fresh or frozen (unsweetened) raspberries, puréed in a food processor and passed through a sieve to remove all seeds and yield 1 cup plus 1 tablespoon seedless purée

4 to 6 teaspoons unflavored gelatin (see Note)

¼ cup raspberry liqueur, preferably St. George Spirits's or other imported brand (see Note)

1 cup heavy whipping cream

1½ teaspoons pure vanilla extract

Raspberry Sauce

2 cups (2 half-pint baskets or 12 ounces) fresh or frozen (unsweetened) raspberries

7 to 10 tablespoons sugar

1 tablespoon freshly squeezed lemon juice

1 tablespoon raspberry eau-de-vie (brandy), preferably St. George Spirits's or other imported brand (optional) (see Note)

1½ cups fresh raspberries, for garnish

Confectioners' sugar, for dusting

In a medium saucepan, bring the sugar and water to a simmer. Cover and simmer for 1 minute, then uncover and simmer for another 2 to 3 minutes, until syrup reaches the soft ball stage (see page 153).

Meanwhile, melt the unsweetened and bittersweet chocolates in the top of a double boiler, or in a bowl set over a pan of hot water.

When the syrup is ready, add the raspberry purée, whisking to combine. Return the mixture to a boil for 2 minutes, whisking constantly. Dissolve the gelatin in the raspberry liqueur in a small bowl. Whisk the melted chocolate into the heated raspberry syrup, and then whisk in the gelatin mixture. Pour the mixture into a bowl and let it cool to room temperature, whisking occasionally.

I love this dessert. I could eat it every day. It isn't one of those tall, traditional Bavarians. It looks like a crustless tart. With its incredibly intense chocolate-raspberry flavor and with fresh raspberries on top, it's absolutely to die for.

The way I discovered this recipe is actually a sweet little story. I was about to teach my first cooking class, a course on French desserts at the local community college, when I visited Simca (Simone Beck, a close family friend and coauthor of *Mastering the Art of French Cooking*, among other cookbooks). I asked her if she had any new dessert recipes that she would let me teach. She readily produced several recipes in their original typed form. Our time together was often like this: We'd get absorbed in talking about a recipe and before we knew it we were preparing it together. That's what ended up happening with the Bavarian.

Make this elegant Bavarian in the summer, when fresh raspberries are sweet and especially abundant. You will need to start with six half-pint baskets: two for the Bavarian Base, two for the sauce, and two for decorating the top and for eating.

When the chocolate-raspberry mixture is cool but not yet set, whip the cream with the vanilla in a chilled bowl or over a bowl of ice until soft peaks form. Fold the whipped cream into the chocolate, quickly and carefully, until no trace of cream remains.

Line a 9-inch tart pan with a removable bottom with plastic wrap. Spread the chocolate mixture in the pan, leveling it with a metal spatula dipped in warm water. Refrigerate to set for several hours or overnight.

Meanwhile, prepare the sauce. Purée the fruit in a food processor for 1 to 2 minutes, until completely smooth. Pass the raspberries through a chinois or fine-mesh sieve to remove the seeds, pressing and scraping the seeds vigorously with a rubber spatula, small ladle, or plastic pastry scraper, to obtain as much fruit as possible. Discard the seeds. (If using a larger-mesh sieve, you may want to strain a second time, pressing more lightly this time to make sure you remove seeds that were pressed through the first time.)

Whisk in the smaller amount of sugar, the lemon juice, and eau-de-vie, and taste for a sweet-tart balance. Don't worry if you taste undissolved sugar; it will dissolve shortly. Add the remaining sugar, to taste. (The amount of sugar will vary depending on the ripeness of the fruit, but remember to always taste sauce just before serving, since freshly puréed fruit tastes sweeter than puréed fruit that has been sitting for a while. Puréed fruit becomes more acidic while in storage. If only presweetened frozen fruit is available, just purée and strain it, then taste for sweetness—it may not need any additional sugar.) Refrigerate the sauce until needed, for up to five days, or freeze for longer. Frozen sauce may need to be whisked well or mixed in a blender or food processor after thawing to restore its smooth texture.

When the Bavarian is set, lift the removable bottom of the pan from the outer ring of the tart shell. If presenting the Bavarian whole, trim off excess plastic wrap from the edges and put the Bavarian on a serving plate. Score the top to mark 8 to 10 pieces and then cover the surface in between the lines with the fresh raspberries. Dust the top with the confectioners' sugar.

To serve, cut the Bavarian where you scored its surface using a thin knife dipped in warm water. With the knife and a metal spatula or chef's knife, scoop up each slice, being careful not to take the plastic underneath it, and transfer it to a dessert plate. Surround each slice with some of the raspberry sauce and serve the remaining sauce on the side. If you are not presenting at the table whole, it is easier to slice the Bavarian first and then top it with the raspberries.

Note: Because of its higher alcohol content, eau-de-vie requires more gelatin to set than liqueur does. If using only raspberry liqueur, use 4 teaspoons gelatin; if using half liqueur and half eau-de-vie, use 5 teaspoons gelatin; if using all eau-de-vie, use 6 teaspoons gelatin.

Raspberry eau-de-vie is clear raspberry brandy. It should not be confused with raspberry liqueur. The liqueur contains much less alcohol, is sweetened, and has a rich, red color. Try to use either a top-quality American brand, such as St. George Spirits's Framboise, or an imported brand.

Raspberry Gâteau (Summer Pudding)

Makes 8 servings

- 4 cups (1½ pounds) fresh raspberries or unsweetened frozen raspberries
- 1¾ cups granulated sugar
- ¾ cup raspberry eau-de-vie (brandy), preferably St. George Spirits's or other imported brand
- ¼ cup dry white wine
- 1 tablespoon unsalted butter, melted
- 30 ladyfingers (recipe follows), or substitute store-bought ladyfingers or 8 to 10 slices good-quality fine-textured bread, crust removed
- 1 to 1½ cups heavy whipping cream
- 2 tablespoons confectioners' sugar, or to taste
- 1 teaspoon pure vanilla extract

If making homemade ladyfingers, do so before proceeding with the gâteau.

Put the raspberries in a bowl, pour the sugar evenly over them, and then pour the eau-de-vie and wine evenly over the sugar. Let the raspberries steep for 10 to 15 minutes, gently tossing occasionally. Strain the raspberries over a bowl. Pour the reserved raspberry syrup into a saucepan and set over medium heat to completely dissolve the sugar, about 2 to 3 minutes. Pour the syrup over the berries. Put the berries into a colander or sieve placed over a bowl and drain for 5 to 10 minutes. Reserve both berries and syrup.

Paint a 2-quart charlotte mold or bowl with the melted butter. Dip each ladyfinger in the syrup, soaking for 5 to 10 seconds, and line the sides of the mold with 12 to 14 whole ladyfingers. Line the bottom of the mold with enough ladyfingers to cover (use broken pieces as needed to fill gaps). Put one third of the raspberries in the mold and cover with another layer of dipped ladyfingers, another one third of the raspberries, another layer of ladyfingers, and continue the layering, finishing with a layer of ladyfingers. Cover with plastic wrap and top with a plate that fits the top of the mold. Put a 1-pound weight (use a can or two) on the plate. Place in the refrigerator overnight. Strain any remaining syrup through a fine-mesh sieve to remove crumbs, and reserve in the refrigerator.

The next day, dip the mold in a bowl of hot water for 30 to 60 seconds, then unmold the gâteau onto a serving plate. Whip the cream in a chilled bowl until soft peaks form, adding sugar and vanilla to taste (keep the cream only lightly sweetened to balance the sweetness and richness of the pudding). Cut the gâteau into wedges and serve with the reserved syrup drizzled over the cut pieces and a large dollop of whipped cream on top.

This variation on an English dessert comes from a bistro that was just around the corner from where I apprenticed in Paris. I used to make it with all raspberry brandy (eau-de-vie), which was good, but quite alcoholic and pretty intense. The white wine mellows out the alcohol a bit and makes the dish a little more affordable.

Margaret: You can use a very good-quality, fine-grained white bread with the crust removed instead of the ladyfingers (and I do *not* mean presliced white bread). We've also made this gâteau with trimmed challah, an egg bread. Let it sit in the fridge for 24 hours, and sure enough, you've got this wonderful dessert.

Ladyfingers

Makes 30 ladyfingers

5 large eggs, separated

1 cup sugar

Pinch of fine sea salt

1½ teaspoons pure vanilla extract

6 tablespoons cake flour

6 tablespoons cornstarch

Salt and distilled vinegar, for cleaning copper bowl

2 teaspoons freshly squeezed lemon juice

Confectioners' sugar, for dusting

Preheat the oven to 325°. Assemble the following: one 15 x 10-inch baking sheet, parchment paper, and a large pastry bag fitted with a large (⅝ x ¾-inch) round tip. Cut the parchment paper to fit the pan. If you don't have parchment, butter and flour the pan.

In a heavy-duty electric mixer, beat the yolks with ½ cup of the sugar, the salt, and vanilla until very pale and tripled in volume, about 3 to 5 minutes. Sift the flour and cornstarch together into a small bowl. Fold the flour mixture into the yolk mixture with a rubber spatula until well blended. It will be very stiff. Transfer the mixture to a small bowl.

Rinse a copper bowl with salt and vinegar and pat dry with a paper towel. Put the egg whites and lemon juice into the bowl, hold the bowl directly over low heat, and whip slowly until the whites are body temperature or slightly warmer, about 60 to 75 seconds. Off-heat, whisk a little faster until frothy, then transfer to the cleaned mixer bowl and beat until soft peaks form. Add ¼ cup of the sugar and continue whisking until stiff but not dry.

Fold one third of the egg whites into the yolk mixture to lighten it, and then fold the mixture into the remaining whites, working as quickly as you can. Fold just until no streaks of white remain. Do not overfold. Put the mixture into the pastry bag.

Put the parchment paper on the baking sheet, using dots of batter at the corners to help it adhere to the pan. Pipe out ladyfingers on the parchment in approximate 1- by 3- to 4-inch lengths, spacing them at least ½ inch apart. Dust the ladyfingers generously with confectioners' sugar using a dredger or sieve. Bake for 15 minutes on the top rack of the oven and then rotate the pan and bake for another 10 to 15 minutes, until barely dry to the touch so that the ladyfingers will be light and crisp when cool. Remove the pan from the oven and transfer to a cooling rack. When cool, peel off the parchment. The ladyfingers can be stored in airtight containers in a cool, dark place for several weeks.

JoJo's Christmas Pudding

Makes 8 to 12 servings

- 1 cup diced chopped beef suet or unsalted butter
- 1 cup packed dark brown sugar
- 1 cup peeled and grated carrot
- 1 cup peeled and grated waxy potato (yellow, white, or red)
- 1 cup raisins or currants, or coarsely chopped, toasted nuts, or ½ cup of each
- 1 large egg, separated (optional)
- 1 tablespoon freshly squeezed lemon juice
- 1 cup cake flour (or substitute all-purpose flour)
- 1 teaspoon baking soda
- ½ teaspoon salt
- 1 teaspoon ground cinnamon
- ½ teaspoon allspice
- 1 tablespoon sugar (if using egg)
- Brandy-Flavored Whipped Cream (recipe follows) or White Chocolate–Rum Sauce (page 189)

Fill a pot large enough to hold a 6- to 8-cup pudding mold, tube pan, or deep ovenproof bowl, with enough water to come halfway up the mold. Cover the pot and bring the water to a boil. Grease the mold with unsalted butter and refrigerate. Cream the suet and brown sugar together in a mixing bowl. Stir in the carrot, potato, raisins, egg yolk, and 2 teaspoons of the lemon juice. Sift together the flour, baking soda, salt, cinnamon, and allspice and stir them into the carrot mixture. Blend everything together with a spoon or with your hands until well mixed.

If using the egg, whip the white, preferably in a copper bowl, with the remaining teaspoon of lemon juice, until soft peaks form. Add 1 tablespoon of sugar and continue beating until stiff peaks form, then fold into the batter. Fill the mold with the batter and cover tightly with a lid or with a piece of aluminum foil. Put the pan in the pot of boiling water, adjust the heat to a strong simmer, cover the pot, and steam for 2 hours. Check the water level occasionally and replenish if necessary. (If you don't have a large pot, you can bake the pudding in a 375° oven in a water bath for approximately the same amount of time.) While the pudding is cooking, prepare the Brandy-Flavored Whipped Cream or White Chocolate-Rum Sauce. The pudding is done when it is fragrant, dark, and set. Remove the pan from the water bath and allow it to cool slightly, then unmold and serve warm with the whipped cream or sauce.

My family does not have a prodigious culinary heritage. In fact, after thinking about family meals from childhood, this is the one recipe from either side that really stands out as a family heirloom, so I would be terribly remiss not to include it. It has been passed down from my father's mother, Josephine Kump, known endearingly as JoJo in our family. It has a couple of earmarks of a "family" recipe from years gone by: The quantities are arranged for easy memorization (to prevent the recipe being lost on a piece of paper somewhere), and the fat called for is suet, which, though delicious, has fallen out of popularity in the last generation. Substitute butter if you don't have suet on hand, and if you'd like to lighten it a bit, include the egg, my one "improvement." I pass this recipe along here as I received it, a good, old-fashioned, stick-to-your-ribs holiday steamed pudding.

Brandy-Flavored Whipped Cream

2 cups heavy whipping cream, chilled
½ cup confectioners' sugar, or ¼ cup granulated sugar
2 to 4 tablespoons brandy
1 teaspoon vanilla extract

Chill a 6-cup metal bowl and the beaters of a handheld electric mixer, or the bowl and whip attachment of a heavy-duty electric mixer in the refrigerator for 10 to 15 minutes.

Pour the chilled cream into the chilled bowl and beat the cream at high speed for 2 to 3 minutes, until it begins to thicken. Add the sugar, brandy, and vanilla and continue to whip for another minute, or until soft peaks form when the beaters or whip is lifted from the bowl. Transfer the whipped cream to a serving bowl and refrigerate, covered, until ready to serve.

Chocolate Marmalade Cake à la Simca

Makes one 9¹/₂-inch cake; 10 to 12 servings

Cake

1 thin-skinned seedless orange
1½ cups sugar
¾ cup water
¼ cup freshly squeezed orange juice
1 tablespoon Grand Marnier or other orange-flavored
   liqueur
7½ ounces bittersweet chocolate, shaved or chopped
1 ounce unsweetened chocolate, shaved or chopped
½ cup unsalted butter, cut in pieces
½ cup canned coconut milk
1½ teaspoons Stroh or Myers's rum or other dark rum
½ teaspoon pure vanilla extract
⅛ teaspoon almond extract
¾ cup ground toasted almonds
2½ tablespoons cornstarch
4 large eggs, lightly beaten

Glaze and Garnish

4 ounces bittersweet chocolate
¼ cup reserved orange poaching syrup (from cake
   preparation)
¼ cup (½ stick) unsalted butter, cut in pieces
1 tablespoon Grand Marnier or other orange-flavored
   liqueur
1 tablespoon Stroh, Myers's, or other dark rum
4 reserved candied orange slices (from cake preparation)
¼ to ⅓ cup unsweetened, dried, shredded coconut
¼ cup toasted sliced almonds
Whipped cream

To prepare the Cake: Bring a pot of water to a boil and dip the orange into it for 3 to 5 seconds. Refresh the orange in cold water, drain, and slice into very thin cross-sections. Combine ¾ cup of the sugar, the water, orange juice, and Grand Marnier in a medium saucepan and bring to a boil, stirring to dissolve the sugar. Add the orange slices and return the liquid to a simmer. Cover and simmer gently until the white part of the orange slices is translucent, about 20 to 30 minutes. Remove the pan from the heat and carefully lift the orange slices out of the syrup, transferring them to a cooling rack set over a pan to drain. Reserve the poaching liquid. Separate the slices, selecting the 4 most attractive slices to set aside for the garnish. Coarsely chop the remaining slices and measure them; add poaching syrup as needed to make ¾ cup. Reserve this mixture and an additional ¼ cup of the syrup for the glaze.

I developed this recipe in honor of my dear friend Simca and the influence she had on my cooking. In 1961 together with Julia Child and Louisette Bertholle, she published a recipe for this style of cake, called *La Reine de Saba*, in *Mastering the Art of French Cooking*. This style of cake is a dense single layer, very moist, rich, and chocolatey, made with ground nuts and often very little or no flour, iced with a thin, dark chocolate glaze. At the time, such a cake was essentially unknown in the United States, for it was a French housewives' cake, not a restaurant or pastry-shop cake. In her later cookbooks, Simca went on to create many variations on this theme, all of them scrumptious. In the United States today, similar cakes have become common in restaurants and pastry shops alike, a tribute to Simca's lasting influence here. This version uses several of her favorite flavors (orange, coconut, almond) in a way that was very much her style; it is especially popular at the restaurant.

I've never had any

(continued on page 162)

formal training in dessert decoration. I can create great flavor combinations, but my cake-decorating skills aren't up to great presentation so what I do is usually fairly simple. But I do believe that the garnish for a sweet or a savory dish should be edible and should reflect the flavors of the dish. The natural garnishes I like to use for this cake are toasted almonds, coconut, and orange in some form.

Preheat the oven to 325°. Cut a piece of parchment paper to fit the bottom of a $9\frac{1}{2}$-inch springform or other cake pan. Melt the bittersweet and unsweetened chocolates together with the butter and coconut milk in a bowl over simmering water, stirring continuously. When the chocolates are almost melted, remove the bowl from the heat and continue to stir until smooth. Add the reserved chopped candied orange, the rum, vanilla and almond extracts, almonds, and cornstarch. Stir well to blend.

Whisk the eggs and remaining $\frac{3}{4}$ cup sugar by hand in the bowl of a heavy-duty electric mixer over simmering water for 1 to 2 minutes. Off-heat, fit the mixer with the whip attachment and beat the egg mixture at high speed for 3 to 5 minutes, until the foam is pale, quadrupled in volume, and thick enough to form a ribbon. Fold one quarter of the egg foam into the chocolate mixture to lighten it, then fold this mixture back into the egg foam, folding until well blended. Pour the batter into the parchment-lined pan and bake on the top rack of the oven for 30 to 45 minutes, until the center is set but still moist and the cake is starting to pull away from the sides of the pan. A toothpick inserted in the center of the cake should come out oily but not wet with batter. Remove the cake to a cooling rack and allow it to cool for 15 to 20 minutes. Remove the cake from the pan and remove and discard the parchment.

To glaze the cake: Combine the bittersweet chocolate with the $\frac{1}{4}$ cup orange poaching syrup, the butter, Grand Marnier, and rum in a small bowl over simmering water, stirring constantly. When chocolate is almost melted, remove the bowl from the heat and continue to stir until smooth. Allow the mixture to cool to the consistency of heavy cream (90° to 92°). Meanwhile, set the cake on a cardboard round or serving round and protect the plate with parchment paper strips. Slowly pour the glaze over the top of the cake, turning and tilting the cake to cover the top in a smooth, even layer, then spread the glaze around the sides with a metal spatula. Refrigerate for 5 minutes to set the glaze.

Cut the reserved orange slices into quarters. Press 10 or 12 of the nicest quarters, point-side down and evenly spaced, onto the sides of the cake, to mark where the slices will be cut. Using your hands, gently press the coconut to the sides of the cake and around the orange quarters. Arrange three toasted almond slices in a fan around each orange quarter. Refrigerate the cake, covered, until ready to serve, for up to 2 to 3 days, or freeze, well-wrapped, for up to 2 months. Serve slightly chilled with whipped cream on the side.

Bittersweet Chocolate Raspberry Millefeuilles

Makes 6 servings

Chocolate Raspberry Cream

5 tablespoons sugar

2 tablespoons water

1 ounce bittersweet chocolate, shaved or chopped

1 ounce unsweetened chocolate, shaved or chopped

¼ cup seedless raspberry purée (from approximately ¾ cup, or 3½ ounces, fresh or frozen (unsweetened) berries, puréed in a food processor and passed through a fine-mesh sieve to remove seeds)

1 teaspoon unflavored gelatin

1½ teaspoons raspberry eau-de-vie (see Glossary), preferably St. George Spirits's or other imported raspberry liqueur (or substitute 1½ teaspoons additional raspberry purée)

5 tablespoons heavy whipping cream, chilled

½ teaspoon pure vanilla extract

¼ recipe Chocolate Puff Pastry

Chocolate Puff Pastry

1 cup plus 3½ tablespoons unbleached all-purpose flour (5 ounces)

1 cup plus 2½ tablespoons pastry or cake flour (4½ ounces)

½ teaspoon fine sea salt

5 tablespoons unsalted butter, chilled and diced

9 tablespoons ice water mixed with ¼ teaspoon freshly squeezed lemon juice

¾ cup unsweetened cocoa

Pinch of baking soda

1⅛ cups unsalted Plugras (see Glossary) or other unsalted butter, cut in large dice and at room temperature (if Plugras is not available, you will need an additional ¼ cup plus 1 teaspoon pastry or cake flour)

Confectioners' sugar, for dusting

2 cups fresh ripe raspberries

1 to 1¼ cups Coconut Sauce (recipe follows)

1 to 1¼ cups Raspberry Sauce (page 155)

To prepare the Chocolate Raspberry Cream: In a small saucepan, bring the sugar and water to a simmer over medium heat. Cover and simmer for 1 minute, then uncover and simmer for another 2 to 3 minutes, until the syrup reaches the soft ball stage (see page 153 for description of soft ball stage). Meanwhile, melt the bittersweet and unsweetened chocolates in the top of a double boiler, or in a small bowl set over a pan of hot water. When the syrup is ready, add the raspberry purée,

This is an exquisite dessert with a beautiful presentation. The millefeuilles are demanding to make, and you wouldn't want to make dozens of these plates all on your own, but for a very special dinner, it is worth it. The recipe involves caramelizing powdered sugar on the top of squares of chocolate puff pastry. They have a wonderful crunch and, with the cream filling and fresh raspberries, they are sweet and absolutely ethereal.

Good puff pastry takes time, patience, and finesse—there's no getting around it. But then, there's nothing quite like the results, either. If you have little or no experience working with pastry, don't start here! Break yourself in with flaky pie dough, then, when you feel comfortable with rolling out pastry in general, return to this recipe for ultimate gratification. When you are ready to tackle this recipe, read the "General Guidelines When Working with Puff Pastry" (page 167) twice before you get started, and refer back to them during down time between rolling out the dough. The most important variable to pay close attention to is temperature, which affects

(continued on page 164)

texture: keeping the pastry not too warm (and soft) and not too cold (and hard) is critical to its success. Be patient. Allow the dough time to chill and relax or warm and soften as needed between steps. The material of the work surface where you roll out your pastry is also important: it should be cool and nonporous. Polished marble is the optimal surface because it stays several degrees cooler than room temperature and is perfectly smooth, which is why portable marble pastry slabs are sold at many kitchen supply stores. More common counter surfaces, such as granite, stainless steel, and plastic laminate (Formica), are also acceptable. Wood is a poor choice because it doesn't stay any cooler than room temperature, it offers more friction resistance to rolling out the dough, and because of its porousness, it has a tendency to collect foreign particles that then become incorporated into your dough.

whisking by hand to combine. Bring the mixture to a boil, then lower the heat and simmer for 2 minutes, whisking constantly. Dissolve the gelatin in the raspberry liqueur in a small bowl. Whisk the melted chocolate into the raspberry syrup, and then whisk in the gelatin mixture. Pour the mixture into a bowl and let cool to room temperature, whisking occasionally.

When the chocolate raspberry mixture is cool (80° on an instant-read thermometer) but not yet set, whip the cream with the vanilla in a chilled bowl over a bowl of ice, until soft peaks form. Fold the whipped cream into the chocolate, quickly and carefully, until no trace of cream remains. Cover the bowl of Chocolate Raspberry Cream and store in the refrigerator for several hours or overnight before using it to assemble the millefeuilles.

While the cream is chilling, prepare the Raspberry and Coconut Sauces.

The Chocolate Raspberry Cream and Raspberry and Coconut Sauces may be prepared in advance to this point and refrigerated for up to 1 week or frozen for up to 2 months. (If frozen, thaw the ingredients overnight in the refrigerator before using.)

To prepare the puff pastry: Combine the all-purpose flour, pastry flour, and salt in the bowl of a food processor fitted with the plastic S-blade. Pulse to blend. Add the 5 tablespoons of diced butter and process just until sandy in texture. With the machine running, slowly add the ice water and lemon juice in a steady stream. Continue processing until the dough begins to ball up. Remove the dough to a lightly floured, cool work surface and knead as necessary to obtain a smooth, homogeneous, and slightly elastic dough. With a rolling pin, flatten into a 5½-inch square approximately ½- to ¾- inch thick. Slash the top of the square in a grid pattern with the tip of a knife. Cover the dough in plastic wrap and refrigerate for 45 to 60 minutes.

Meanwhile, sift the cocoa and baking soda together (with the additional ¼ cup plus 1 teaspoon flour if not using Plugras) into a bowl and set aside. Put the butter into the bowl of a heavy-duty electric mixer fitted with the paddle attachment and beat until soft. Beat in the cocoa mixture gradually and continue mixing until well blended, about 3 to 5 minutes. Transfer the mixture to a piece of plastic wrap, spread it into an evenly thick slab 5½ inches square (approximately the same size as the dough), and refrigerate for 30 minutes.

Remove the dough and butter block from the refrigerator. (They should be about the same firmness.) Roll the dough out with a rolling pin (on a work surface dusted with pastry flour) to a square large enough to fit the butter block inside it at a 45-degree angle, so that it looks like a diamond inside a square. Fold the corners of the dough up and seal them on top of the block to enclose it. Carefully flatten out the dough-covered block and roll it into a rectangle ⅜-inch thick. Give the dough a turn (fold it in thirds like a letter and rotate a quarter-turn clockwise), give it another turn, or fold and rotate, roll it out a little more, brush off excess flour, cover, and refrigerate for 30 to 45 minutes.

Remove the dough from the refrigerator and place it on a lightly floured work surface. Give it another 2 turns, refrigerate for 30 to 45 minutes, remove from the refrigerator and give it another 2 turns, and then refrigerate overnight. The next day, roll the dough out to ⅜-inch thick and cut it into pieces to freeze until needed. The dough may be frozen, well-sealed with plastic wrap, for up to 2 months.

At least 1 hour, but no more than 3 hours before you serve the millefeuilles, preheat the oven to 375°. Butter a 17 x 10-inch baking sheet and refrigerate it until ready to use. On a cool, smooth work surface lightly dusted with cake flour, roll the puff pastry out to a rectangular band about 5 by 14 inches and approximately $\frac{1}{8}$ inch thick. Lift the dough frequently off the work surface to be sure it isn't sticking or stretching as you roll (or it will shrink excessively in the oven). Refrigerate the dough for 30 minutes. Remove the baking sheet and dough from the refrigerator and lay the band of dough on the sheet. Place the baking sheet and dough in the freezer for 15 minutes. Then remove from the freezer, sprinkle with cold water, and bake on the top rack of the oven for 12 to 15 minutes, until slightly puffed and dry. Remove the pan from the oven and cool on a wire rack. If the pastry deflates and appears dark and soft or moist in the center while cooling, put it back in the oven and bake for 3 to 5 minutes longer.

When the pastry band has cooled to room temperature, carefully transfer it to a clean cutting board. Use a ruler to guide you in cutting twenty-four $1\frac{1}{2}$-inch squares (3 horizontally across the band and 8 down the length). Cut straight down with a large, sharp knife. (Do not use a sawing motion or you will tear the pastry.) Preheat the broiler for 5 minutes. Turn the squares over so that their bottom, flatter side, is facing up and dust the tops generously with confectioners' sugar using a dredger or a sieve. Carefully transfer the dusted squares back to the baking sheet and place the pan under the broiler, watching constantly, for 15 to 30 seconds, until the sugar just melts and starts to caramelize. This usually happens unevenly. Rather than waiting for the sugar on all of the squares to melt evenly, by which time some will have burned, immediately remove the squares as they are done, returning the rest to the broiler for as long as needed until all the squares are shiny but not blackened.

When you are ready to assemble and serve, remove the Coconut and Raspberry Sauces from the refrigerator and put them into small pitchers or plastic squirt bottles. Remove the Chocolate Raspberry Cream from the refrigerator. Select the 12 nicest looking pastry squares and set them aside for tops. Using a small metal spatula, spread a $\frac{3}{8}$-inch-thick layer (about $1\frac{1}{2}$ tablespoons) of chocolate cream on each of the remaining 12 squares. On top of each bed of cream, crowd 4 to 9 fresh raspberries (enough to cover the square in a single layer) standing upright. Dab the tops of the raspberries with a pinch more cream and place the reserved pastry squares on top of the berries, shiny sides facing up. Pour about 2 tablespoons of each sauce side by side on each plate so they meet in a straight border down the center. Draw 2 thin concentric lines of Raspberry Sauce about $\frac{1}{2}$ inch apart around the outer inch of the rounded part of the Coconut Sauce (squirt bottles work best for this, but if you have a steady hand it can be done with a small, narrow-spouted pitcher). Repeat with the Coconut Sauce around the outer inch of the Raspberry Sauce so that the two halves of the plates look like negative mirror images of each other, with the lines meeting at the center border. With a toothpick or skewer, trace lines through the concentric sauce lines at 1-inch intervals, alternating your strokes toward and away from the center of the plate, to create a spider web pattern. Carefully transfer 2 millefeuille squares with a metal spatula to the center of each plate, placing one on each sauce, turned so that their corners rather than their flat edges meet at the center of the plate. Serve at once.

Coconut Sauce

¾ cup milk

6 tablespoons canned coconut milk

¾ cup unsweetened, dried, shredded coconut

3 large egg yolks

5 tablespoons vanilla sugar (see Glossary)

2 tablespoons cold heavy whipping cream

In a small saucepan, bring the milk, coconut milk, and coconut to a boil. Turn off the heat, cover, and let sit for 15 minutes to infuse. In a bowl, beat the yolks with the sugar until they are very pale yellow in color and form a ribbon when the beater is lifted above the bowl. Add the milk mixture and stir to combine. Scrape the sides of the bowl to make sure all of the yolk-sugar mixture is dissolved in the liquid. Pour through a fine-mesh sieve back into the pan, pressing on the coconut with a spatula or wooden spoon to squeeze it dry. If you want to stir some of the coconut back into the sauce for texture, set it aside while you thicken the sauce; otherwise, discard it. Put the heavy cream in a large bowl and set it over a larger bowl of ice. Return the sauce to the saucepan and cook over medium heat, whisking constantly with a wooden spatula, until the mixture coats the spatula thickly. While stirring, be sure to scrape the bottom of the pan thoroughly. To test for doneness, draw a line with your finger across the sauce coating the spatula; if it leaves a lasting trace, it is sufficiently thickened (it should register 185° to 187° on an instant-read thermometer at this point). Remove the pan from the heat immediately. (Do not allow the sauce to exceed this temperature or the yolks will begin to scramble. Should this occur, blend the sauce for a few seconds in a blender or with a handheld immersion blender and pass it through a sieve before continuing.) Continue to stir briskly off-heat for 2 minutes more, then pour the sauce through the sieve into the bowl with the cream. Allow the mixture to cool completely, stirring occasionally. Store, refrigerated, until needed for up to 1 week, or freeze for up to 2 months. If frozen, after thawing, whisk well or blend in a blender or with a handheld immersion mixer to restore the sauce's smooth texture.

General Guidelines When Working with Puff Pastry

1. Always keep the dough from sticking to the work surface and rolling pin by using sufficient pastry flour, but diligently brush off excess flour before every turn.

2. Puncture any air bubbles and flour any butter spots, brushing off excess flour.

3. Constantly maintain the dough's shape with a plastic or metal dough scraper and a rolling pin.

4. Always chill the dough before cutting it and cut with a sharp knife dipped in cold water (cut cleanly—don't saw or drag).

5. If the dough becomes elastic, allow it to relax in the refrigerator for 30 to 45 minutes before continuing.

6. Use a ruler to help you roll the dough out to proper thickness at each stage. The dough should be $^3/_8$-inch thick between turns; $^1/_8$-inch for tops or bottoms of tarts or millefeuille layers.

7. Always take the dough directly from the freezer and bake it on a buttered, chilled baking sheet sprinkled with water, until it is golden brown on the sides as well as on top (usually 10 to 15 or 20 minutes, depending on thickness).

Rice pudding can't help but be evocative of childhood meals, yet I never had one this good until a few years ago in a Parisian bistro. The distinctive French touch is caramelizing the mold as you would for a crème caramel. The one I was served came flavored simply with vanilla and sat in a pool of vanilla crème anglaise. I loved the custard sauce idea, since the pudding itself is eggless. But I thought it would be even more interesting perfumed with orange, considering that flavor's affinity for caramel. I also added a splash of orange flower water, which gives it a Moroccan accent.

There are two types of rice puddings: those set with eggs and those thickened only by the rice's starch. The eggless version is about as simple as desserts get—rice, milk, and sugar are cooked together to a thick porridge. In old European cookbooks, eggless rice pudding is often simply called "rice with milk." Start with leftover rice. Nothing could be easier to whip up when you're short on time.

Caramelized Rice Pudding

Makes 8 servings

Caramel

1 cup sugar

¼ cup water

A few dashes freshly squeezed lemon juice, or 1 pinch cream of tartar

Rice Pudding

3½ cups milk

Grated zest from 2 oranges (rinse oranges in very hot water before zesting), or 2 teaspoons pure orange extract

1 cup uncooked Thai jasmine, basmati, or other long-grain rice, or 3 cups leftover cooked white rice

1½ cups water

⅔ cup vanilla sugar (see Glossary) or granulated sugar

2 teaspoons orange flower water

2 teaspoons pure vanilla extract (if not using vanilla sugar)

¼ teaspoon fine sea salt

To prepare the Caramel: Combine the sugar, water, and lemon juice in a small, unlined copper saucepan, if available, and bring to a boil, stirring to dissolve the sugar. Cover and simmer for 1 minute to wash down the sides of the pan with condensed steam, then uncover and boil over medium-high heat for 4 to 5 minutes more, until the syrup turns an attractive amber caramel color. Lower the heat as the syrup starts to turn blond since it will keep cooking for a little while off-heat and if it becomes too dark, it will taste bitter. Using oven mitts or gloves to protect your hands, pour the caramel into eight 4-ounce ramekins, lifting and swirling each ramekin to coat the bottom and about halfway up the sides (excess can be poured into the next ramekin). Work quickly and be sure to save enough caramel to coat all of the ramekins. Divide any extra caramel among any filled ramekins that seem too light. Alternatively, you can pour the caramel into a single 4-cup mold, tilting the mold to coat its sides with the caramel. Set aside the ramekins or mold and immediately put a little water into the pan used for heating the caramel and return it to the stove over low heat to soften what's left in the pan for easier cleaning.

To prepare the pudding: Bring the milk and orange zest to a boil in a heavy-bottomed 2-quart pan. Cover and set aside to infuse while cooking the rice. If using leftover rice, skip the next step. Rinse the excess starch from the rice in several changes of water. Put the rice in a 1-quart saucepan with the 1½ cups water and bring to a strong boil. Boil for 1 minute and then reduce the heat to very low. Cover and simmer for 15 to 17 minutes. After 15 minutes, uncover and check the rice. When the water has all been absorbed and the top grains are just barely cooked through (a little al dente is good), turn off the heat, wrap the lid with a kitchen towel, and let the rice sit for 10 to 15 minutes. Uncover and test the rice again; it should be perfectly done. Empty the rice into a bowl and fluff it with a fork to separate grains.

Stir the rice into the milk mixture, and then stir in the vanilla sugar, orange flower water, vanilla extract (if using), and salt. Return the milk mixture to a boil over high heat, then reduce the heat to medium and simmer, stirring occasionally, for 25 to 35 minutes, until the mixture resembles a thick porridge, spitting as it simmers. Pour the rice mixture into the reserved, caramel-lined ramekins and refrigerate for at least half an hour, or up to two days before serving.

To serve, unmold the pudding onto dessert plates and serve a pitcher of Crème Anglaise (recipe follows) on the side, or simply present the pudding as is, surrounded by its own caramel sauce.

Crème Anglaise

2 cups whole milk

½ vanilla bean, split lengthwise and scraped clean
  (reserve seeds)

5 large egg yolks

⅔ cup sugar

Put the milk and vanilla bean and seeds into a saucepan and bring to a boil. Cover, remove from heat, and let sit for 15 minutes to infuse. In a bowl, beat the egg yolks with the sugar until they are a very pale yellow and form a ribbon when the beater is lifted above the bowl. Strain the hot milk through a fine-mesh sieve into the mixture, whisking to blend and scraping the sides well to completely dissolve all of the egg-sugar mixture.

Return the sauce to the saucepan. Fill a bowl larger than the one used for beating yolks and sugar halfway with ice cubes. Take the bowl that the egg-sugar mixture had been in and nestle it in the bowl of ice. Cook the sauce over medium heat, whisking or stirring constantly with a wooden spatula until the mixture coats the spatula thickly. While stirring, be sure to scrape the bottom of the pan completely. To test the sauce for doneness, draw a line with your finger across the sauce coating the spatula; if it leaves a lasting trace, it is sufficiently thickened (it should read 185° to 187° on an instant-read thermometer at this point). Remove the pan from the heat immediately. (Do not allow the sauce to exceed this temperature or the yolks will begin to scramble. Should this occur, blend the sauce for a few seconds in a blender or with a handheld immersion blender and pass it through a sieve before continuing.) Pour the sauce through a fine-mesh sieve into the chilled bowl. Allow the sauce to cool completely, stirring occasionally. Store, covered, in the refrigerator until needed for up to 2 days, or freeze for up to 1 month. If frozen, after thawing, whisk well or blend with an immersion mixer or in a blender to restore the sauce's smooth texture.

One of the first things I learned about desserts at Restaurant Jacques Cagna, in Paris, where I apprenticed, is the distinction between pastry-shop or bakery desserts and restaurant desserts. Pastry-shop desserts are freestanding, commissioned, completed works of pastry chef art. They are often beautiful, edible sculptures that start out in a display case and can be boxed, transported, presented at the table, and carved into serving pieces for each lucky guest—cakes, tarts, pies, charlottes, Bavarian creams, flans, even individual pastries. Restaurant desserts, on the other hand, are fleeting assemblies by performance artists, rather than the objet d'art of an auteur-patissier. Not that you won't find pastry shop-style desserts in restaurants; an accomplished restaurant pastry chef should be talented in both media. But with the advent of nouvelle cuisine and open kitchens, restaurant desserts have come into a style all their own. They are popular because they tend to be less labor-intensive, they require less precious storage space, and they are less

(continued on page 171)

Jacques Cagna's Caramelized Apples
with Cinnamon Bark Ice Cream

Makes 6 servings

5 to 6 medium to large Sierra Beauty, Golden Delicious,
  or other apples that hold their shape when cooked
1 lemon, halved
½ cup unsalted butter, melted but not hot
½ to ⅔ cup sugar
¼ cup unsalted butter, cut into 24 pieces
½ recipe Cinnamon Bark Ice Cream (page 171)

Peel, core, and halve the apples, rubbing them with the lemon as you go. Lightly butter a 17 x 10-inch baking pan (jelly roll pan) with a little of the melted butter. Lay the apple halves out cut-side down in two rows, "head to tail," on a clean cutting board. With a thin, sharp knife, cut the apple halves crosswise into ⅛- to 3/16-inch-thick slices, leaving the apples in their original shape. (The thickness of the apple slices is important, since if they are too thin they will fall apart; measure the first couple of cuts with a ruler as a guide.)

When all of the apples are sliced, carefully lift them from underneath using the knife you used to slice them or a metal spatula, 2 halves at a time, and transfer them to the baking sheet. Line up the apple halves in 5 or 6 columns of 2 halves (flat-side down), still head to tail, so that the apples are facing the long side of the pan. Gently and evenly spread the apple slices flatly, overlapping like dominoes, so that the slices stand at a 45-degree angle to the bottom of the pan. The slices should fill up the whole pan snugly—this is important because if there is extra space the apples will slide around during baking. If there is more than ½ to 1 inch of empty space at one of the short ends of the pan, fill it with a folded piece of aluminum foil. If there is too much space along one of the long ends, flatten the apple slices a little more or fill the space with foil as well.

Preheat the oven to 475°. Brush the apple slices generously with the melted butter until well coated. Sprinkle the apples generously with the sugar (about 2 to 3 teaspoons per half), then dot the sugar with the butter pieces, using 2 pieces per apple half. Place the pan on the top rack of the oven and bake for 35 to 45 minutes, or until the tops of the apples are nicely caramelized, but not burnt. (If the apples look very soft but are showing no signs of browning, broil them briefly, but watch constantly that they don't burn.) Remove the pan from the oven and very carefully tilt the pan slightly over a bowl to pour off excess juices, which should be considerable. (These buttery, sweet apple juices aren't needed in this recipe, but they can be saved, refrigerated, to cook apples in later.) The recipe may be made to this point several hours in advance. If serving immediately, transfer the apples to their serving plates while still warm. The apples should be allowed to cool a bit before serving.

When ready to serve, preheat the oven to 300°. With a metal spatula, pick up clusters of apple slices, about 1½ inches long, and lay 3 or 4 clusters, spoke-like, on each of 6 dessert plates. Put the plates in the oven or under the broiler briefly to reheat apples. Place a scoop of Cinnamon Bark Ice Cream in the center of each warm plate just before serving.

Cinnamon Bark Ice Cream

Makes approximately 5 cups

2¼ cups half-and-half or whole milk

6 to 7 (2½-inch) cinnamon sticks, lightly crushed with
a heavy implement (to yield ⅓ cup crushed bark)

6 egg yolks

½ cup light brown sugar

½ cup granulated sugar

1 cup heavy whipping cream

To prepare the custard for the ice cream: Bring the half-and-half to a boil in a medium saucepan. Add the crushed cinnamon bark, cover, remove from heat, and set aside for 20 to 30 minutes to infuse (or longer for a very strong cinnamon flavor).

Meanwhile, beat the egg yolks, brown sugar, and granulated sugar with a handheld electric mixer in a medium bowl for 2 to 3 minutes, until pale and thick. Place the cream in a medium bowl. Fill a slightly larger bowl with ice water. Place the bowl of cream in the ice bath. Pour the cinnamon-infused half-and-half through a sieve into the yolk-sugar mixture, whisking to combine. Press down on the strained-out bark with the back of a spoon to extract as much liquid as possible, and then discard the cinnamon. Return the custard to the saucepan and cook over medium heat, whisking or stirring with a wooden spatula constantly, until the mixture coats the spatula thickly, about 5 to 7 minutes. While stirring, be sure to scrape the bottom of the pan completely. To test the custard for doneness, draw a line with your finger across the custard coating the spatula; if it leaves a lasting trace, it is sufficiently thickened (it should register 185° on an instant-read thermometer at this point). Remove from heat immediately and continue to stir briskly for 1 to 2 minutes more. (Do not allow the custard to exceed this temperature or the yolks will begin to scramble. Should this occur, blend the sauce for a few seconds in a blender or with a handheld immersion blender and pass it through a sieve before continuing.)

Pour the custard back through the sieve into the bowl of cream in the ice bath. Allow to cool completely, stirring occasionally, refrigerate for 2 hours (to 40°), and then freeze in ice cream maker according to manufacturer's directions.

wasteful—the simple truth is you don't have to worry about a dessert going bad if it is prepared to order. M. Cagna and his cooks were masters of this style of dessert—simple, elegant, and tasty.

It was in France, where they rarely spice apples with cinnamon, that I first tasted cinnamon ice cream served with an apple dessert. It was an inspired dish, one whose source of inspiration I attribute to American apple pie. It's nice to see the French, who have contributed so much to American cuisine, be on the receiving end for a change. I've had cinnamon ice cream made both from the infused bark and from the ground form, and definitely recommend the bark; it has a fresher flavor and doesn't create the granular texture that ground cinnamon can cause in the ice cream.

Pear, Vanilla, and Star Anise Soufflé

Makes 8 individual (4-ounce) soufflés, or 1 large (1-quart) soufflé; 6 to 8 servings

Vanilla Anise Syrup

½ large vanilla bean, split lengthwise and scraped clean (seeds reserved)

⅔ cup water

¼ cup granulated sugar

10 points star anise (2¼ pods)

Caramelized Pear

1 tablespoon clarified unsalted butter

1 medium Bartlett or Bosc pear, peeled, cored, quartered, and each quarter halved crosswise

Soufflé Base

6½ tablespoons milk

Reserved vanilla bean

Reserved star anise points

2½ tablespoons granulated sugar

1 tablespoon cake flour

Pinch of fine sea salt

1 tablespoon cornstarch

1½ teaspoons unsalted butter, at room temperature

3 egg yolks

2½ tablespoons pear eau-de-vie (brandy), preferably St. George Spirits's or other imported brand (see Glossary)

Pear Coulis Sauce

1 medium Bartlett or Bosc pear, peeled, cored, and cut into chunks

Reserved vanilla anise syrup

Reserved vanilla bean seeds

1½ teaspoons pear eau-de-vie (brandy), preferably St. George Spirits's or other imported brand (see Glossary)

Reserved star anise points (optional)

Unsalted butter and granulated sugar, for coating ramekins

⅔ cup egg whites

1½ teaspoons freshly squeezed lemon juice

1½ teaspoons sugar

Confectioners' sugar, for dusting

This is definitely a recipe to read through a few times before you start. It uses the three flavors of pear, vanilla, and star anise, and there are a number of different things going on at the same time, which makes it deliciously complex. The idea for this dessert comes from French chef Joël Robuchon, from *Simply French*, a cookbook he created with Patricia Wells, who interpreted his cuisine for an American audience. In the book, there are three desserts in which Robuchon combines the flavors of pear, vanilla, and star anise. Inspired, I made this composite dessert with the same three flavors. It's a hot soufflé in which the esters of the pear brandy—the volatile, brandied fruit aromas waft up to your nose as you are about to bite into and experience that quintessential soufflé texture. In the center of it you have a nugget of caramelized pear, and the accompanying sauce is a cool pear and star anise purée, so you have hot and cold, dense and light.

Margaret: It's a symphony.

To prepare the Vanilla Anise Syrup: Combine all of the ingredients for the syrup in a small saucepan oven medium heat, whisking to dissolve the sugar. Bring to a boil. When the sugar is completely dissolved, cover, remove the pan from heat, and set aside to infuse for 30 minutes. Strain out the bean and anise pieces, reserving them, and set the syrup aside.

Return the bean and anise to the saucepan and add the milk for the soufflé base. Bring the milk to a boil. Cover, remove from heat, and set aside to infuse for 15 to 30 minutes.

To caramelize the pears: Choose a skillet that will just hold all of the pears in a single layer. Heat the clarified butter until almost smoking, then add the pear pieces. Reduce the heat to medium-high and sauté, swirling the pan and gently stirring and turning the pears until they are an even, rich golden brown, about 5 minutes. Reduce the heat to medium. Deglaze the pan with $\frac{1}{4}$ cup of the reserved syrup and continue cooking over medium heat, stirring and spooning the juices over the pear pieces, until the liquid is thick and amber colored. (Try not to go beyond this point or the sugar will caramelize and separate out of its emulsion with the butter.) Pour the pears and syrup into a bowl and set aside.

To prepare the Soufflé Base: Strain the vanilla bean and anise pieces out of the milk, rinse them off, and reserve (the vanilla bean may be dried in a low (200°) oven and used to make vanilla sugar; the anise points may be reserved to increase the flavor of the coulis if desired). Meanwhile, in a bowl, whisk the sugar, flour, salt, and cornstarch together. Gradually pour the milk into the flour-sugar mixture, whisking to form a smooth paste. Return the mixture to the saucepan and bring it to a boil, whisking. Simmer for 1 minute, whisking constantly, until very thick. Whisk in the butter, then remove the pan from the heat and transfer the mixture to a bowl. Whisk in the egg yolks and then the eau-de-vie and cover with plastic wrap placed on the surface of the cream to keep a skin from forming. Allow to cool. The recipe may be prepared to this point up to 3 days in advance. If preparing ahead, refrigerate, and on the day of serving, allow the base to come to room temperature, and then whisk until completely smooth before using.

While the base is cooling, prepare the coulis. Combine the pear chunks, the remaining syrup, and the reserved vanilla seeds in a small saucepan. Cover and bring to a simmer over high heat. Reduce heat to low and simmer, covered, until the pear pieces are translucent and very soft, about 15 minutes. Transfer to a food processor and purée until fully blended. Pass through a fine-mesh sieve into a bowl to make sure the sauce is totally smooth, stir in the eau-de-vie, cover, and set aside. (If the star anise flavor is not strong enough at this point, return the reserved anise pieces to the coulis to infuse longer; strain out before serving.)

When ready to serve, butter and coat lightly with sugar 8 (4-ounce) ramekins or 1 (4-cup) mold. Preheat a convection oven to 375°. If you are preparing this recipe with a standard oven, preheat to 425° (see Note). In a copper bowl, whisk the egg whites and lemon juice together slowly over low heat until the whites reach the temperature of a hot bath (100° to 110°)—test the temperature on the inside of your wrist. Remove the bowl from the heat and continue whisking, at medium speed, until frothy. Transfer the mixture to the bowl of a heavy-duty electric mixer (or continue by hand) and whip at high speed until soft peaks form. Add the sugar and continue beating until the peaks are stiff and slightly shiny. Do not overbeat or they will become grainy. With a whisk, gently stir one third of the egg whites into the reserved, room-temperature base. Stir to homogenize and lighten, and then quickly and gently fold the mixture back into the whites, folding with a rubber spatula and turning the bowl until no streaks of white remain.

Place a small dollop of soufflé batter into each prepared ramekin (about 3 tablespoons for each ramekin, or slightly less than half the batter for the larger mold). Place a piece of caramelized pear in the center of each ramekin (1 piece per serving, whatever the mold size), then top with the batter, filling each ramekin. Tap the ramekins gently on the counter to eliminate air pockets and even out the tops. Put the ramekins on a baking sheet that will fit in the convection oven, warm the bottoms over a burner for 1 minute, then place the baking sheet on the lower rack of the convection oven for 6 minutes, until the tops are brown and the soufflés have risen well above the molds. Lower the heat to 325° (375° for a regular oven) and bake for another 3 minutes, or until the sides of the soufflés are golden brown and a toothpick inserted in the center comes out clean. (If using the larger mold, allow the soufflé to cook for slightly longer.) The soufflés are done when the sides as well as the tops are golden brown. Remove the pan from the oven, dust the tops of the soufflés with confectioners' sugar, and serve immediately. The soufflés must be presented within 1 minute of being removed from the oven to still be presentable. At tableside, poke a hole or make a 1-inch slit in the top of the soufflé(s) with a small fork or the tip of a sharp knife, and pour a tablespoon of coulis sauce in the center of each.

Note: Soufflés are much more successful when baked in a convection oven. Small countertop models work well and are relatively inexpensive.

Coconut Ice with Coconut Crisps and Passion Fruit Sauce

Makes 8 servings

Coconut Ice

3 (14-ounce) cans coconut milk (4½ cups)

1½ cups sugar

2½ tablespoons 80-proof white rum

Coconut Crisps

¾ cup unsweetened, dried coconut

¾ cup vanilla sugar (see Glossary) or regular granulated sugar mixed with ½ teaspoon vanilla extract

3 tablespoons cake flour (or substitute all-purpose flour)

3 egg whites

2½ tablespoons unsalted butter, melted

Passion Fruit Sauce

1 cup passion fruit juice, fresh or frozen (see Note)

Freshly squeezed lime juice to taste

Freshly squeezed orange juice or water to taste

¾ to 1 cup sugar, or to taste

Small fresh mint leaves, for garnish

This is a dish that we served as the second in a series of three dessert courses for our New Year's Eve dinner in 1991. The flavors are tropical and refreshing and the Deco presentation of bold colors in geometric curves and lines is striking and simple. It would make a perfect light summer dessert after a grilled meal because everything can be made in advance. The only tricky part is making the crisps, but with a little practice, you shouldn't have too much trouble—besides, with these crisps, eating the mistakes is half the fun!

To prepare the Coconut Ice: Combine the coconut milk and sugar in a saucepan and heat until sugar is dissolved and all lumps of coconut cream are melted. The mixture should be completely liquefied and smooth. Remove the pan from the heat and allow the mixture to cool to room temperature. Stir in the rum, and refrigerate, stirring occasionally, until cool to the touch. Remove from the refrigerator and freeze in an ice cream maker according to manufacturer's directions (usually for 20 to 30 minutes). Transfer the coconut ice to a container and freeze, covered, until ready to serve.

To prepare the crisps: Preheat the oven to 350°. Combine the coconut, sugar, and flour together in a small bowl, mixing to break up any lumps of coconut. Stir in the egg whites and then the melted butter, stirring until the mixture is well-blended. (The batter may be prepared in advance and stored in the refrigerator, covered, for up to 1 week.) Butter and chill several baking sheets.

Using 1 to 2 teaspoons of batter per cookie, spoon the batter onto the chilled baking sheets, spreading each portion into thin 3-inch rounds with the back of a spoon, leaving ½ inch of space or more between rounds.

Bake the rounds on the top rack of the oven for 4 to 6 minutes, or until golden brown. Without removing the baking sheets from the oven, using a wide metal pancake spatula, quickly remove the brownest crisps from the pan and transfer them to a work surface. Trim 2 sides with a large, sharp knife or metal scraper to make a fan shape. Set these aside to cool and harden and repeat with the remaining crisps. Work quickly while the crisps are warm and soft: as they cool, they become very brittle and will tend to shatter when you try to cut them. It is helpful to use two spatulas so you can scrape one spatula with the other spatula before picking up the next crisp. If the crisps harden too much on the baking sheet to be easily removed with the spatula, close the oven door briefly to soften them. If the crisps cannot be removed from the baking sheet without tearing them, put a bit more batter on them to thicken them slightly. Greasing and thoroughly chilling the baking sheets before you use them helps to prevent this. (Sometimes spraying the buttered, chilled pan with nonstick cooking spray helps, too.)

As soon as the crisps have cooled to room temperature, carefully put them in an airtight container to store until ready to use. They may be made up to 1 week in advance if you are meticulous about keeping them stored airtight, otherwise they will get soft.

To prepare the Passion Fruit Sauce: Combine the juices and sugar in a saucepan, heating just to dissolve the sugar. Taste and add more sugar or juice, if desired.

To assemble: Chill dessert plates. Place a round scoop of Coconut Ice in the center of each chilled plate and surround it with Passion Fruit Sauce. Cut a slit into the top center of each scoop with a small knife and poke the pointed tip of a Coconut Crisp into the slot so it stands upright. Garnish with a small mint leaf and serve.

Note: Puréed and sieved ripe mango pulp may be substituted for some or all of the passion fruit juice to make this sauce more affordable. With mango pulp, you will need to add less sugar and lime juice. Also, for a less intense and less expensive version of this sauce, dilute the passionfruit juice with orange juice or water to taste; an amount up to but no more than 1 cup will still allow the passion fruit flavor to come through. If the sauce becomes too thin, it may be thickened to taste by dissolving some cornstarch—about 1 teaspoon for 2 cups of sauce—in a little cold water, then adding it to the sauce and heating the sauce to a boil to thicken fully.

If you are using fresh passion fruits, you will need about 28 fruits to yield 1 cup of juice once all of the seeds have been strained out.

Huckleberry Pie

Makes one 9-inch pie; 8 servings

5 cups (1¾ pounds) huckleberries, fresh or frozen

⅓ to ½ cup sugar (depending on the tartness of
   the berries)

4 tablespoons quick-cooking tapioca

One 9-inch pie crust, prebaked and cooled
   to room temperature

Dough trimmings from 1 to 2 pie crusts (about 3
   ounces), balled up and refrigerated for at least
   10 minutes after rolling out

1 egg, lightly beaten with 1 teaspoon water

1 to 2 tablespoons unsalted butter, cut in small pieces
   (optional)

Suggested Accompaniments

Vanilla Bean Ice Cream (page 195) or whipped cream

Preheat the oven to 425°.

Put the berries in a bowl and toss with the sugar and tapioca. Let sit for 20 minutes. Put the berry mixture into the prebaked shell. On a cool, clean surface lightly dusted with cake flour, roll out the dough trimmings to a ⅛-inch-thick round sheet approximately 9 inches in diameter. Cut ½-inch-wide strips of dough. Moisten the edge of the crust with some of the beaten egg to allow the dough strips to stick to it. Weave them in a lattice pattern ½ inch apart on top of the berries. Brush the lattice all over with the egg and dot the berries visible between the lattice with the butter pieces, if using.

Set the pie on an aluminum foil–covered baking sheet. Gently wrap the foil over the pie rim to keep it from burning. Bake the pie on the top rack of the oven for 15 minutes. Reduce the heat to 375° and bake until the juices are bubbling and the lattice is golden brown, approximately 30 minutes.

Remove the pie from the oven and transfer it to a wire cooling rack for at least 30 minutes before cutting out pieces. Serve warm, accompanied by Vanilla Bean Ice Cream or topped with fresh whipped cream.

This is truly a product of Mendocino as much as it is mine. I had never tasted a huckleberry until I moved to Mendocino and Margaret converted me.

Margaret: Huckleberries are delicious. They are what every blueberry would really like to be.

Chris: They're like a cross between the really rich flavor of a blackberry and a blueberry.

Margaret: If you pick them yourself, you really develop a healthy appreciation for just how special they are. Picking huckleberries is very painstaking. The berries are very small. To acquire 5 cups or so for a pie means you're spending quite a bit of time, but oooh! Yummy!

Chris: We made this recipe as tartlets for the Beard Awards one year—1,200 individual huckleberry tartlets.

Margaret: That was the year after I'd purchased an astounding amount of huckleberries—to the point where Chris was actually yelling at me for being so foolish as to keep ordering more and more. "Are you crazy?" he said. "The freezer is overflowing with these." I said, "Yes, but in the depths of winter, you'll thank me." And then Chris had this idea to do the huckleberry tarts and thanks to moi, we had the huckleberries!

There is some history to the tastes in this dessert. The whiskey sauce is a traditional New Orleans complement to bread pudding. The combination of blueberries and maple syrup comes from a very simple dessert my dad offered in one of his early classes, which I think he told me was a James Beard combination.

Margaret: Some people have memories of bread pudding as real nursery food, very heavy and gluey and not anything worth fancifying. But this is really very elegant. It's got the pudding texture, but the top part is also a little crusty. So, you have the sweetness of the fruit, the mushiness of the pudding, the crustiness of the bread. This is one of those funny desserts that is quite rich, but somehow people perceive it as light. It's very, very nice.

Blueberry Brioche Pudding
with Maple Whiskey Sauce

Makes 6 to 8 servings

Maple Whiskey Sauce

1 cup half-and-half

3 egg yolks

2 tablespoons sugar

1/3 cup real maple syrup

3 to 4 tablespoons whiskey

1 teaspoon cornstarch

Pudding

1/2 vanilla bean, halved lengthwise, scraped clean and seeds reserved, or substitute 1 1/2 teaspoons pure vanilla extract

2 1/4 cups milk

2 3/4 cups (12 ounces) blueberries, fresh or frozen

12 ounces brioche (slightly stale is fine), trimmed of crust and cut into 1-inch cubes

3 large eggs plus 2 large egg yolks

10 tablespoons granulated sugar

1/2 cup fresh blueberries, for garnish

To prepare the sauce: Bring the half-and-half to a boil over medium heat in a small saucepan. Meanwhile, whisk the remaining ingredients together in a small bowl. Pour the hot half-and-half into the bowl, whisking constantly. Return the sauce to the saucepan and cook over medium heat, whisking or stirring constantly with a wooden spatula, until the mixture coats the spatula thickly. While stirring, be sure to scrape the bottom of the pan completely. To test the sauce for doneness, draw a line with your finger across the sauce coating the spatula; if it leaves a lasting trace, it is sufficiently thickened (it should register 175° on an instant-read thermometer at this point). Remove from heat immediately. (Do not allow the sauce to exceed this temperature or the yolks will begin to scramble. Should this occur, blend the sauce for a few seconds in a blender or with a handheld immersion blender and pass it through a sieve before continuing.) Pour the sauce through a fine-mesh sieve into a small bowl set over a medium bowl of ice water, or plunge the saucepan's bottom into an ice-water bath to stop the cooking process. Serve warm.

To prepare the Pudding: Preheat the oven to 325°. Butter an 8 x 8-inch coffee cake pan. Place the 1/2 vanilla bean with the seeds in a medium saucepan. Add the milk and bring to a boil. Remove the pan from the heat, cover, and set aside for 10 minutes to infuse. (If using vanilla extract, skip this step.)

Spread half of the blueberries on the bottom of the prepared pan, cover with the brioche cubes, and scatter the remaining berries over the top. In a bowl, whisk the eggs, yolks, and sugar together slightly, just to lighten the mixture, and pour in the warm milk, straining out the vanilla bean and stirring the yolk mixture while you pour. If using extract, add it now. Pour the custard batter evenly over the berries and bread. Place the pan inside a larger pan and put both on the top rack of the oven. Fill a pitcher with hot water and pour it into the larger pan to fill it halfway up the sides; this is a hot-water bath. Bake the pudding until the center is set and the top lightly browned, about 45 minutes. Carefully remove the pans from the oven. Lift the pan of pudding out of its water bath and allow it to cool for 10 to 15 minutes on a rack. Serve warm in individual bowls, and top each serving with Maple Whiskey Sauce and a few fresh blueberries.

Chocolate mousse is almost taken for granted these days. It preceded the croissant as most Americans' introduction to French cuisine, yet now it sadly risks relegation to mythic status—it is cited, referred to, revered in memory, but it is rarely appreciated as a dessert. In upscale restaurants, you will often find it playing a supporting role as a mere component of an elaborately assembled dessert. This is a shame, as a good chocolate mousse with a dollop of whipped cream is one of the easiest, most satisfying ends to a meal ever conceived. The fresh lemon and chocolate combination in this mousse was suggested to me by Robert Linxe, owner-chocolatier of La Maison du Chocolat, in Paris. "Everyone does orange with chocolate," he said, as he prepared to demonstrate a new truffle, "so I thought I'd try lemon." One taste and I knew he was definitely onto something. I think you'll agree.

Lemon-Chocolate Mousse

Makes 6 to 8 servings

8 ounces bittersweet chocolate, shaved or chopped (see Note)

2 tablespoons espresso or very strong coffee

2 tablespoons Stroh or Myers's or other dark rum, or Armagnac or Cognac

¼ cup water

Grated zest of 1 lemon (wash lemon in very hot water before zesting)

½ cup unsalted butter or heavy whipping cream (see Note)

4 large egg whites

1 teaspoon freshly squeezed lemon juice

3 tablespoons granulated sugar

Pinch of fine sea salt

Whipped cream, for topping

Put the chocolate, espresso, rum, water, lemon zest, and butter in a bowl over barely simmering water, stirring constantly to melt the butter and chocolate evenly. Remove the pan from the heat when the chocolate is about three quarters of the way melted, and continue to stir off-heat until the mixture is smooth. Allow the mixture to cool to lukewarm.

In a copper bowl over simmering water or directly over low heat, whisk the egg whites and lemon juice lightly for about 1 minute, until they are the temperature of a hot bath (110°); test the temperature on the inside of your wrist. Whisk off-heat at medium speed for another 1 to 2 minutes, until frothy. Transfer the mixture to the bowl of a heavy-duty electric mixer, or use a hand-held beater, and whip the whites at high speed until soft peaks form. Add the sugar and salt and continue to beat until the peaks are stiff and shiny.

Fold about one quarter of the whites into the lukewarm chocolate mixture to lighten it, then fold this back into the whites, folding until no streaks remain. Spoon into individual serving bowls and refrigerate to set for at least 2 hours or overnight, or chill to set in a larger container and scoop out with an oval ice cream scoop or two large spoons dipped in warm water, shaping oval quenelles of mousse on chilled dessert plates. Serve topped with whipped cream. The mousse may be refrigerated, covered, for up to 1 week, or frozen for up to 1 month.

Note: Whenever you cook with chocolate, buy a top-quality, imported bittersweet chocolate. This type has a high percentage of chocolate liquor and therefore has the richest flavor. If only semisweet chocolate is available, you can achieve a more intense chocolate flavor by substituting unsweetened chocolate for 1 or 2 ounces of the semisweet chocolate and adding 1 to 2 tablespoons sugar, or to taste, to the egg whites.

If using cream instead of butter, do not add it to the chocolate mixture for melting. Instead, whip the cream, using a handheld electric mixer, over a bowl of ice until soft peaks form, then fold it into the mousse after folding in the whites. The result will be a lighter mousse.

You may vary the amount of coffee and/or alcohol to taste, keeping the total amount of liquid—coffee, alcohol, and water—equal to $1/2$ cup total.

Chez Pauline's Ginger-Pumpkin Tourte

Makes two 9-inch tourtes; 16 servings

1 recipe Quick Puff Pastry (recipe follows)

6 cups diced Sugar Pie pumpkin or canned pumpkin

1½ cups sugar

6 tablespoons peeled and coarsely grated fresh ginger

¾ teaspoon freshly grated nutmeg

½ teaspoon ground cloves or allspice

3 large eggs, lightly beaten

¾ cup crème fraîche (or substitute heavy whipping cream)

½ cup heavy whipping cream

6 tablespoons peeled and diced fresh ginger (⅛-inch dice)

1 egg yolk beaten with 1 teaspoon water

Make the Quick Puff Pastry. One night or several hours before serving, divide the dough into 4 equal portions. Roll out one portion of the dough to ⅛-inch thick on a cool, smooth surface lightly dusted with cake flour. Place the dough in a 9-inch metal or glass pie pan and trim it so it is even with the edge of the pan. Repeat with a second portion of the dough and second pie pan. Roll out the third portion of dough to ⅛ inch and cut out a 10-inch disk. Repeat this procedure with the remaining portion of dough. Place both disks on a lightly buttered baking sheet. Cover the baking sheets and the 2 lined pie pans with plastic wrap and refrigerate.

To prepare the filling: Put the pumpkin in a medium-sized nonreactive saucepan with the sugar, grated ginger, and spices. Bring to a simmer over low heat and simmer, stirring often, until the pumpkin is very tender, about 15 minutes. If using canned pumpkin, cook gently for only 5 minutes, just to blend the flavors. Remove the mixture from the heat and purée in a food processor or blender until smooth. Strain the mixture through a fine-mesh sieve into a bowl to remove and discard any fibrous matter. Combine 3½ cups of the strained purée with the beaten eggs, crème fraîche, and cream in a bowl, whisking to blend. Taste for seasoning and adjust if desired. For a strong ginger flavor, stir in the diced ginger as is. If you prefer a more subtle version, put the diced ginger in a small pot of cold water, bring to a boil, drain, and then add the ginger to the filling.

Remove the pie shells from the refrigerator and pour the filling into them (it should come to within about ¼ inch from the top inside edge). Moisten the edge of one of the pastry shells with water and position one of the disks on top of it (there should be a slight overhang). Fold the overhanging edges of the top disk under the edge of the bottom shell. Press and flute the edges with a melon baller to seal. Brush the entire top crust with the egg yolk wash; do not let it run over the fluted edge. Refrigerate the tourte and repeat this process with the second tourte. Refrigerate both tourtes for another 30 minutes to set the egg wash and relax the dough. Cover them with plastic wrap and freeze for at least 30 minutes before baking. The tourtes may be prepared ahead to this point and stored in the freezer, wrapped, for up to several weeks. (To freeze for extended periods, cover with plastic wrap and aluminum foil to prevent freezer burn.)

To bake: Remove the tourtes from the freezer and preheat the oven to 425° for 10 to 15 minutes. Cut a ⅛-inch vent hole in the center of the crust with the tip of a small, sharp knife and fashion a small funnel-shaped chimney out of aluminum foil to place in the hole to keep it open. (The chimney allows steam to escape from the filling during baking.) Lightly scribe a decoration (such as spiraling lines from the center hole to the fluted points) on the top crust with the tip of a small, sharp knife. Put the tourtes directly on the floor of the oven (remove the lower rack if necessary to fit) and bake for 5 minutes. Check the bottom crust around the edges; if it still looks pale or raw, return it to the oven for another 5 minutes. If it is already browning, lower the heat to 350°. Bake for another 30 to 40 minutes, still directly on the floor of the oven, until the filling is set and the top crust is golden brown. (This is how we bake the tourte at the restaurant; baking directly on the oven floor is the only way to make sure the bottom crust gets cooked. However, I had one disastrous experience with this recipe at a friend's house. He had an oven with a large gas jet immediately below the bottom of the oven. After only 10 minutes baking at 425°, the bottom crust had burned. So, to be safe, check the tourtes after 5 minutes, and if the bottom is browning quickly, you may even want to move the tourtes off the oven floor and onto one of the racks.) The foil chimney can be removed as soon as the top crust is set. If the top isn't browning after 40 minutes, transfer the tourtes to the top rack of the oven for 5 minutes, until they turn a nice golden brown. Remove the tourtes from the oven and allow them to cool for 15 to 20 minutes on a wire rack before cutting. Serve slightly warm topped with whipped cream or vanilla ice cream.

Note: Because it is convenient to make puff pastry in batches of 1 pound or larger, because even small fresh pumpkins contain at least 6 cups of flesh, and because this tourte stores so well frozen, this recipe makes two tourtes. If you prefer to make only one tourte, use the following proportions for the filling:

3 cups fresh diced pumpkin or
   1 pound canned pumpkin

¾ cup sugar

3 tablespoons grated ginger plus
   3 tablespoons diced ginger

⅜ teaspoon grated nutmeg

¼ teaspoon ground cloves or allspice

1 large egg, lightly beaten

½ cup crème fraîche (or substitute heavy
   whipping cream)

¼ cup heavy whipping cream

Quick Puff Pastry

Makes about 1 pound

1½ cups plus 2 tablespoons Plugras (see Glossary) or
   other unsalted butter, cold
1½ cups unbleached all-purpose flour
½ cup cake flour
¾ teaspoon salt
½ cup cold water mixed with ¼ teaspoon freshly
   squeezed lemon juice

Cut the sticks of butter lengthwise in quarters, then cut the quarters crosswise into ½-inch dice and refrigerate.

Sift the all-purpose flour, cake flour, and salt together into a mixing bowl or into the bowl of a food processor fitted with the metal blade. Add the butter and blend together rapidly to make large flakes, about the size of lima beans. If using a food processor, cut the butter in with a few pulses. Do not overprocess.

Put the dough in a mixing bowl and blend in the water with your fingertips to form a very rough ball. On a floured work surface, push and pat the dough (which should be a shaggy mass at this point) into a rectangle. Lift the dough off the work surface and make a turn: Fold it in thirds like a business letter. Use a metal or stiff plastic pastry scraper to loosen dough sticking to the work surface. Turn the dough a quarter-turn (the end of the dough from the last fold is now at the side instead of at the bottom). Repeat this rolling and folding process 3 more times. With each turn, the dough should become more evenly textured. Use your knuckles to mark 4 dots to remind yourself how many turns you've made. (If at any time the dough feels difficult to roll out or becomes rubbery, dust off excess flour, wrap the dough in plastic wrap, and refrigerate it for 30 minutes.) Cover and refrigerate the dough for 40 minutes or longer before rolling it out to bake.

Remove the dough from the refrigerator, give it 2 more turns, make 6 dots to remind you it has now had 6 turns, and refrigerate the dough until firm. Use it within 24 hours, or freeze, well wrapped, for up to 2 months. Allow to thaw until soft enough to roll out without cracking around the sides, but not so soft that the butter oozes out and feels greasy.

Chocolate Profiteroles with Coconut Ice Cream and Warm Chocolate Sauce

Makes 6 servings

Coconut Ice Cream

1½ cups half-and-half

1 cup fresh grated or unsweetened dried coconut

1⅓ cups vanilla sugar or regular granulated sugar

6 large egg yolks

1 (14-ounce) can (1½ cups) coconut milk

1 cup heavy whipping cream

Chocolate Sauce

½ cup unsweetened cocoa

⅓ cup sugar

½ cup plus 2 tablespoons water

¼ cup heavy whipping cream

½ ounce unsweetened chocolate

1 tablespoon unsalted butter

1 recipe Chocolate Pâté à Choux (recipe follows)
  18 chocolate choux puffs; use a pastry bag fitted
  with a ½-inch (#10) round tip to shape the profiteroles

To prepare the Coconut Ice Cream: In a 2-quart saucepan, bring the half-and-half, coconut, and ⅓ cup of the sugar to a boil. Cover, remove from heat, and set aside for 15 minutes to infuse. In a medium bowl, beat the egg yolks with the remaining sugar for a couple of minutes until light and pale yellow. Return the half-and-half mixture to the stove and bring to a simmer, then pour through a fine-mesh sieve into the bowl, whisking to blend and scraping the sides to dissolve all of the egg-sugar mixture in the liquid. Press down on the strained-out coconut in the sieve to extract as much liquid as possible, then set the coconut aside. If the coconut milk is partially solidified, heat it in a small pan just enough to liquefy, then combine it with the cream and reserved coconut in a 2-quart bowl set over a larger bowl of ice.

Return the custard to the saucepan and cook over medium heat, whisking or stirring with a wooden spatula constantly, until the mixture coats the spatula thickly. While stirring, be sure to scrape the bottom of the pan completely. To test the sauce for doneness, draw a line with your finger across the custard coating the spatula; if it leaves a lasting trace, it is sufficiently thickened (it should register 185° on an instant-read thermometer at this point). Remove from the heat immediately and continue to stir briskly for 1 to 2 minutes more. (Do not allow the custard to exceed this temperature or the yolks will begin to scramble. Should this occur, blend the sauce for a few seconds in a blender or with a handheld immersion blender and pass it through a fine-mesh sieve before continuing.)

This variation on traditional profiteroles uses one of my favorite taste pairings—chocolate and coconut. I find that coconut is the best foil I've tasted for accentuating the intensity of good dark chocolate, but if you're not fond of coconut, you can make these with vanilla ice cream, a more traditional combination.

It takes some attention to certain points to succeed at pâte à choux, and it helps to have a pastry bag fitted with a ½-inch round tip to form even puffs. In a pinch, you can use a spoon instead of the pastry bag. After making and sampling many, many profiteroles, I've found that there is one secret to perfect puffs: Even if you bake them the day you serve them, always freeze them first, then briefly toast them just before cutting and filling. This procedure ensures that the profiteroles are exactly how they should be served—crisp yet tender on the outside and soft and moist inside.

Pour the custard through a sieve into the coconut milk-cream mixture. Discard any strained-out bits of coagulated egg. Allow to cool completely, stirring occasionally. Refrigerate for 2 hours (to 40°), then freeze in an ice cream maker according to manufacturer's instructions.

To make the Chocolate Sauce: Combine the cocoa, sugar, and water in a small saucepan. Bring to a boil and cook for 3 minutes. Whisk occasionally to prevent the mixture from boiling over. Add the cream and boil for 2 to 3 minutes more. Off-heat, whisk in the chocolate and butter. Return the pan to the heat and boil for 2 minutes more, whisking to prevent burning and boiling over, until thickened. (You can store this sauce in the refrigerator for up to 2 weeks, or in the freezer for up to 2 months.)

To assemble the profiteroles, warm the Chocolate Sauce gently in a small saucepan over low heat. Preheat the oven to 350° for 10 minutes (preferably a small convection or toaster oven). When the oven is warm, remove the puffs from the freezer, spread them out on a baking sheet and put them in the oven for about 2 minutes, just until they are warm and crisp to the touch. Remove them from the oven and, without allowing them to cool off too much, cut each puff in half horizontally about a quarter of the way up from the base.

Using a 1½-ounce (3-tablespoon) ice cream scoop dipped in warm water, scoop out the Coconut Ice Cream, placing the scoops on top of the pastry bases. Cover each ice cream scoop with a pastry top and place 3 profiteroles on each room-temperature (or slightly warm) dessert plate. Ladle or spoon the warm Chocolate Sauce over the profiteroles, using about a tablespoon per puff to coat the top of each and avoid pouring an excessive amount on the plate. Serve immediately.

EVENING FOOD

Chocolate Pâté à Choux

½ cup milk

½ cup water

½ cup unsalted butter

2 tablespoons granulated sugar

¼ teaspoon salt

⅔ cup unbleached all-purpose flour

⅓ cup cake flour or all-purpose flour

¼ cup unsweetened cocoa (not Dutch process)

2 pinches baking soda

4 to 5 large eggs, lightly beaten and at room
temperature (1 cup)

Preheat the oven to 425°. Combine the milk, water, butter, sugar, and salt in a small saucepan over medium heat and bring to a boil. Meanwhile, sift the all-purpose flour, cake flour, cocoa, and baking soda together through a sieve into a medium bowl. When the butter is completely melted and the liquid boils, remove the pan from the heat, add the flour-cocoa mixture all at once, and stir with a wooden spatula until it forms a unified sticky mass. Return the pan to medium heat and cook, beating with the spatula until the batter becomes oily when squeezed between the thumb and forefinger, about 3 to 5 minutes.

Meanwhile, warm the mixing bowl of a heavy-duty electric mixer. When the batter is oily, immediately transfer it to the warm mixing bowl and begin beating with the paddle attachment at medium speed. Beat in the eggs ¼ cup at a time, allowing each addition to become fully incorporated before adding the next. Do not overbeat after the last addition—the batter should be fairly stiff yet shiny. Allow the batter to cool to room temperature before using.

Butter and chill a baking sheet. (You may chill the batter at the same time to speed up its cooling.) Fit a pastry bag with a ³⁄₈-inch round tip and fill it with the paste. Pipe out small amounts of approximately 1½ tablespoons each onto the chilled, greased sheet until all the paste is used. Make mounds as even as possible and allow at least ½ inch in between them so they don't stick together when baking.

Bake on the top oven shelf for 12 minutes at 425°, then lower heat to 375° and bake another 15 to 20 minutes with the door held ajar with a wooden spoon to allow steam to escape. Puffs are done when no longer soft to the touch on the sides. Remove and allow to cool completely (puffs should stay light and crisp) and store airtight in the freezer until needed.

Jean-Louis's Persimmon Cake
with White Chocolate–Rum Sauce

Makes 8 to 10 servings

1 cup raisins (half yellow and half black, or all black) or currants

½ cup brandy

1 cup ripe persimmon pulp, puréed and sieved

1 cup plus 2 tablespoons sugar

2 teaspoons pure vanilla extract

¼ teaspoon ground cloves

¼ teaspoon freshly grated nutmeg

½ cup heavy whipping cream or milk

1 cup coarsely chopped toasted walnuts

1 cup cake flour or all-purpose flour

½ teaspoon fine sea salt

1 teaspoon baking soda

1 large egg white

¼ teaspoon freshly squeezed lemon juice

White Chocolate–Rum Sauce (recipe follows)

In a small saucepan, heat the raisins and brandy to a simmer, cover, and set aside to steep for at least 1 hour, or overnight.

Preheat the oven to 350° and butter and flour a 7- to 9-inch bundt pan or ten 4-ounce ramekins.

Combine the persimmon pulp, 1 cup of the sugar, the vanilla, cloves, nutmeg, and cream in a bowl. Add the nuts and raisin-brandy mixture and stir to blend. Sift the flour, salt, and baking soda together into a bowl, and add to the persimmon mixture. Set aside.

Whisk the egg white with the lemon juice in a copper bowl slowly over low heat to warm slightly (to 110°, the temperature of a hot bath; test on the inside of your wrist), then increase whisking speed off-heat as the mixture becomes frothy. Transfer to a heavy-duty electric mixer, or continue to beat by hand, and beat at high speed, adding the remaining 2 tablespoons sugar when the whites form soft peaks. Continue beating until stiff peaks form, then fold the whites gently into the batter.

Fill the prepared mold(s) and bake on the center rack of the oven, until a toothpick inserted in the center comes out clean and the surface is springy to the touch, about 60 to 75 minutes for a tube pan, less for ramekins. Allow to cool on a rack for an hour before unmolding. Serve warm with White Chocolate–Rum Sauce on the side.

White Chocolate–Rum Sauce

¼ cup (½ stick) unsalted butter, cut into chunks
2 ounces good-quality white chocolate, chopped
6 tablespoons confectioners' sugar
1 tablespoon light corn syrup
1 tablespoon heavy whipping cream (optional)
2 to 3 tablespoons Stroh or Myers's dark rum

Combine all of the ingredients in a saucepan over medium heat and whisk until the butter and chocolate are melted and the sauce is smooth and hot. Taste for rum flavor and add more if desired. Try to heat only what you plan to serve at one time because this sauce, like a beurre blanc, separates if it is allowed to cool to room temperature and then reheated. Once it is warm, try to keep it warm until you serve it. If it does start to separate, whisking in a tablespoon of cream will usually save it.

"Bananas Foxter" Ice Cream

Makes approximately 5 cups

¾ cups half-and-half

1 tablespoon crushed cinnamon bark (1 small stick)

¼ vanilla bean, split lengthwise, seeds scraped out and
    reserved, or ½ teaspoon pure vanilla extract

4 ripe bananas, cut into ¼-inch slices

½ cup packed dark brown sugar

⅔ cup Myers's dark rum mixed with ⅓ cup banana
    liqueur, or ¾ cup Myers's dark rum

4 egg yolks

9 tablespoons granulated sugar

¾ cup heavy whipping cream

Chocolate Sauce (page 185), optional

To prepare the custard for the ice cream: Put the half-and-half, cinnamon bark, and vanilla bean and seeds together in a small saucepan. Bring to a boil over medium heat and then cover and set aside to infuse. (If using vanilla extract, do not add it yet.)

Combine the bananas, brown sugar, and rum-liqueur mixture in a large skillet over medium heat and simmer for 5 to 10 minutes, until the bananas are softened and the alcohol has burned off. The rum may ignite on its own, but if it doesn't, carefully put a lit match near the simmering juices; the fumes should ignite. Continue to cook over medium heat, shaking the pan gently, until the flames are extinguished. Remove the pan from the heat and allow mixture to cool.

Meanwhile, beat the egg yolks and granulated sugar together in a bowl with a whisk or handheld electric beater for 2 to 3 minutes, until light and thick. Return the flavored half-and-half in the saucepan to a simmer. When it is hot, whisk the half-and-half into the yolk mixture. Rinse out the saucepan and pour the batter back into it through a sieve, straining out and discarding the cinnamon bark and vanilla bean.

Pour the banana mixture in a food processor and purée. Set a 6-cup mixing bowl inside a slightly larger bowl containing ice water. Pour the heavy cream into the mixing bowl and pour the banana purée through a sieve into the cream. Keep the sieve over the inner bowl. Return the custard to the saucepan and cook over medium heat, whisking or stirring with a wooden spatula constantly, until the mixture coats the spatula thickly. While stirring, be sure to scrape the bottom of the pan completely. To test for doneness, draw a line with your finger across the custard coating the spatula; if it leaves a lasting trace, it is sufficiently thickened (it should register 185° on an instant-read thermometer at this point). Remove from the heat immediately and continue to stir briskly for another 1 to 2 minutes. (Do not allow the custard to exceed this temperature or the yolks will begin to scramble. Should this occur, blend the sauce for a few seconds in a blender or with a handheld immersion blender and pass it through a sieve before continuing.)

Pour the mixture through a sieve into the bowl containing the chilled banana cream. Stir to blend. Add the vanilla extract, if using. Refrigerate the batter for 2 hours (to 40°), then freeze it in an ice cream maker according to manufacturer's directions. (Despite the flaming, the alcohol in this ice cream will cause it to remain on the softer side.) Transfer the ice cream to a container, cover, and freeze until ready to serve. Serve topped with warm Chocolate Sauce.

If you're a fan of rum raisin ice cream, you're in for a treat. A specialty of southwestern France, where the renowned prunes of Agen originate, this ice cream flavor is a standard in ice cream shops there much the way mint chip is here. Not only is the prune and Armagnac flavor marriage superb, but the alcohol in the unheated Armagnac keeps the texture a silken, freshly-made soft in the freezer—that is, if you can keep from finishing it the first day. This ice cream can be made with Cognac or even domestic brandy, but if you're unfamiliar with the special taste of Armagnac and are wondering what all the fuss is about, definitely try some in this recipe.

Prune and Armagnac Ice Cream

Makes approximately 6 cups

1 cup Brandied Prunes (page 129), coarsely chopped
6 tablespoons Armagnac, Cognac, or any good brandy
2 cups half-and-half or whole milk
6 large egg yolks
¾ cup granulated sugar
¼ cup packed dark brown sugar
1 cup heavy whipping cream

In a small saucepan, combine the prunes and 4 tablespoons (¼ cup) of the Armagnac. Over medium heat, bring to a bare simmer, cover, remove from heat, and set aside. In a medium saucepan, heat the half-and-half to a boil, cover, remove from heat, and set aside.

In a medium bowl, beat the egg yolks, granulated sugar, and brown sugar for about 2 to 3 minutes, until tripled in volume and thick. Whisk the hot half-and-half into the mixture gradually, scraping the sides of the bowl to dissolve all of the yolk-sugar in the liquid.

Return the custard to the medium saucepan and cook over medium heat, whisking or stirring constantly, until the mixture coats the spatula thickly. While stirring, be sure to scrape the bottom of the pan completely. To test the custard for doneness, draw a line with your finger across the custard coating the spatula; if it leaves a lasting trace, it is sufficiently thickened (it should register 185° on an instant-read thermometer at this point). Remove from the heat immediately and continue to stir briskly for 1 to 2 minutes more. (Do not allow the custard to exceed this temperature or the yolks will begin to scramble. Should this occur, blend the sauce for a few seconds in a blender or with a hand-held immersion blender and pass it through a sieve before continuing.)

Pour the custard through a sieve into the bowl with the cream and the remaining Armagnac. Add the reserved chopped prunes and Armagnac and stir to blend thoroughly. Allow to cool completely, refrigerate for 2 hours (to 40°), and then freeze in ice cream maker according to manufacturer's directions. Transfer the ice cream to a container, cover, and freeze until ready to serve. This ice cream is lovely by itself, but is also a nice accompaniment to any warm apple dessert, such as Pear and Apple Crisp (page 150) or Jacques Cagna's Caramelized Apples (page 170), in place of the cinnamon ice cream.

Nine Favorite Fruit Ices

Each makes approximately 5 cups

Blackberry, Strawberry, Raspberry, Mango, or Plum Ice

2 cups puréed, strained fruit pulp (3 cups blackberries, raspberries, or strawberries; 3 to 4 mangoes; 8 plums)
1½ cups sugar
1 cup water
¼ cup freshly squeezed lemon juice

Passion Fruit–Mango Ice

½ cup strained passion fruit pulp and juice (fresh or frozen; if using fresh, use approximately 14 passion fruits)
1 cup puréed and strained mango pulp
1¼ cups sugar
1 cup water
2 tablespoons freshly squeezed lime juice

Melon Ice

2 cups puréed and strained ripe melon
1½ cups sugar
1 cup water
¼ cup freshly squeezed lime juice

Peach or Nectarine Ice

1¼ cups water
1 cup vanilla sugar
2 tablespoons peach liqueur or Grand Marnier
3 to 4 tablespoons fresh lemon juice
3 to 4 freestone peaches or nectarines (18 to 20 ounces), ripe and juicy but not bruised

Pear and Star Anise Ice

1¼ cups water
1 cup vanilla sugar (see Glossary)
2 tablespoons pear eau-de-vie (brandy), preferably St. George Spirits's or other imported brand
1 star anise pod
3 to 4 (18 to 20 ounces) fresh Bartlett or Bosc pears, ripe and juicy but still firm
3 to 4 tablespoons freshly squeezed lemon juice (1 cut lemon half reserved)

Food science writer Harold McGee came into the restaurant while he was working on his book, *The Curious Cook*. It features a wonderful chapter called "Fruit Ices, Cold and Calculated." We got to talking about fruit ices, or sorbets. He had developed a computer program that calculated the amount of sugar, water, and fruit purée that would make differently textured ices for 35 common fruits. I thought it was a brilliant idea! A lot of these proportions definitely owe him a nod for that revolutionary work.

To make Blackberry, Strawberry, Raspberry, Mango, Plum, Melon, or Passion Fruit–Mango Ice: In a medium bowl, whisk together all of the ingredients thoroughly to dissolve the sugar and freeze in an ice cream maker according to manufacturer's instructions. Transfer to a container, cover, and freeze until ready to serve.

To make Peach or Nectarine Ice: Combine all of the ingredients except the fruit in a medium saucepan. Bring to a simmer to dissolve the sugar, and then set aside. Boil 4 to 6 cups of water in a medium pot. Fill a small bowl with ice water. Cut a crisscross pattern just through the skin opposite the stem end of each peach or nectarine, and plunge the fruit into the boiling water for 15 to 45 seconds, just until the skins are loosened. Drain and refresh in the ice water.

Remove the loosened skins, cut the fruit into quarters, discard the stones, and measure 2 cups (16 ounces). Add the fruit to the saucepan of syrup. Bring the syrup to a simmer and poach the fruit gently for 10 to 15 minutes, until the fruit is easily pierced with the tip of a knife. Remove from heat and allow to cool completely. Purée in a food processor, then pass through a sieve into a medium bowl, cover, and refrigerate for 2 hours (to 40°). Freeze in an ice cream maker according to manufacturer's instructions.

To make Pear and Star Anise Ice: Combine all of the ingredients except the pears and lemon half in a medium saucepan and bring to a simmer to dissolve the sugar. Meanwhile, peel, quarter, and core the pears, rubbing them with the cut lemon as you go. Measure 2 cups of trimmed pears and add them to the syrup. Cover the surface directly with plastic wrap or parchment paper and simmer gently for 10 to 15 minutes, until the pears are easily pierced with the tip of a knife. Remove from heat and allow to cool completely.

Remove and discard the star anise pod. Purée the pears with the syrup in a food processor until smooth. Pass through a sieve into a medium bowl, cover, and refrigerate for 2 hours (to 40°). Freeze in an ice cream maker according to manufacturer's instructions.

Five Great Fruit Ice Creams

Each makes approximately 4 cups

Blackberry, Strawberry, or Raspberry

3 cups blackberry, strawberry, or raspberry purée (4¾ cups blackberries or raspberries, puréed and strained through a fine-mesh sieve to remove seeds; 6 cups strawberries, washed and puréed)

1 cup plus 6 tablespoons sugar

Mango

5 to 6 ripe mangoes, peeled, stoned, and strained to remove fibers (3 cups purée)

1 cup plus 2 tablespoons granulated sugar

¼ cup freshly squeezed lime juice

Plum

8 ripe plums, washed, pitted, puréed, and strained to remove larger bits of skin, if desired (3 cups purée)

1¼ cups granulated sugar

¼ cup freshly squeezed lemon juice

To prepare any ice cream: In a medium bowl, whisk together all of the ingredients thoroughly to dissolve the sugar. Stir in 2 cups of Vanilla Bean Ice Cream batter (recipe follows) and refrigerate the mixture for 2 hours (to 40°). Freeze in an ice cream maker according to manufacturer's instructions.

Vanilla Bean Ice Cream

Makes approximately 6 cups

2 cups half-and-half or whole milk

½ vanilla bean, split and seeds scraped out and reserved

8 large egg yolks

1⅓ cups granulated sugar

2 cups heavy whipping cream

1 teaspoon vanilla extract (optional)

To make the custard for the vanilla ice cream: In a medium saucepan, bring the half-and-half to a boil with the vanilla bean and seeds. Remove from heat, cover, and set aside to infuse for 15 minutes.

This recipe was inspired by my desire for a fruit ice cream with the perfect texture. I had often found that fruit ice creams didn't have the texture I wanted. So I experimented, figuring if you were to take a good fruit sorbet recipe, so you knew you had the fruit and sugar in the right balance, and mixed that with a good ice cream recipe, you would have a wonderful ice cream. Sure enough, it is true. You just take a quart of the fruit ice mix, add 2 cups of Vanilla Bean Ice Cream batter, and freeze. The procedure for the five ices that can be made into ice cream is the same.

Meanwhile, beat the egg yolks and sugar together in a bowl until very pale yellow in color and doubled in volume, about 5 minutes. Return the infused half-and-half to a boil, remove from heat, and immediately whisk it into the yolk-sugar mixture. Scrape the sides of the bowl to make sure all of the mixture is dissolved in the liquid, then pour the custard back into the saucepan through a fine-mesh sieve, straining out the vanilla bean.

Put the cream and vanilla extract in a medium bowl set over a large bowl of ice water. Cook the custard on medium heat, stirring constantly with a wooden spatula and being careful to scrape the bottom of the pan completely, until the batter has thickened noticeably. To test custard for doneness, draw a line with your finger across the custard coating the spatula; if it leaves a lasting trace, it is sufficiently thickened (it should read 185° on an instant-read thermometer). Remove from the heat and continue to stir briskly and thoroughly for 2 more minutes. (Do not allow the custard to exceed this temperature or the eggs will begin to scramble. Should this occur, blend the sauce for a few seconds in a blender or with a handheld immersion blender and pass it through a sieve before continuing.)

Pour the thickened custard through a fine-mesh sieve into the bowl of chilled cream, stirring to blend. Allow this batter to cool completely, stirring from time to time. Keep the batter over ice water or refrigerate until it is 45°. Then freeze the custard in an ice cream maker according to manufacturer's instructions.

Fresh Tarragon Sorbet

Makes 1 quart

1½ cups sugar

3¼ cups water

1 cup loosely packed fresh tarragon leaves

1 tablespoon freshly squeezed lemon juice

1 tablespoon vodka

Combine the sugar, water, and tarragon in a saucepan over medium heat, stirring to dissolve the sugar. Bring to a simmer, cover, remove from heat, and allow to steep for at least 30 minutes. Allow to cool completely, then strain out and discard the herbs. Transfer the mixture to a small bowl, add the lemon juice and vodka, cover, and refrigerate for 2 hours (to 40°). Freeze in an ice cream maker according to manufacturer's instructions. If making ahead of the day it is to be served, transfer the sorbet from the freezer to the refrigerator 30 minutes before serving to soften it.

Fresh herb sorbets are an idea born of the nouvelle cuisine movement in France in the seventies. I took this one with me from Restaurant Jacques Cagna, where I apprenticed, and used it as a palate cleanser course in the trial meal that landed me the dinner chef position at Cafe Beaujolais. Although the structure of our menu these days doesn't have a place for such an intermezzo, I still enjoy the palate cleansing course when I go out to dine in fancy restaurants. If you have an elegant dinner party planned, perhaps to impress a prospective employer or potential spouse, you may want to include this frill course for a minimum of extra work. It would also go nicely with fresh fruit as a light summer dessert. (Basil, chervil, and mint also work well in place of the tarragon.)

Basic Recipes and Glossary of Ingredients

Beaujolais Basics

Bittersweet Chocolate

Bittersweet chocolate is the sweetened chocolate with the highest percentage of chocolate liquor and, thus, the richest flavor. At the restaurant we use San Francisco's Ghirardelli bittersweet chocolate (Callebaut and Cacao Barry are also good) or, for a pricier splurge, the French brand Valrhona. Try tasting several of these brands to find your own favorite. If only semisweet chocolate is available, you can achieve a more intense chocolate flavor by substituting up to 25 percent of the semisweet chocolate called for in a recipe with unsweetened chocolate, and by adding a little more sugar to taste to the dessert you're making.

Butter

At Cafe Beaujolais, we use exclusively unsalted butter and, indeed, professional chefs and serious home cooks customarily prefer the flavor of unsalted butter over salted, as it usually has a fresher, cleaner flavor. Since salt acts as a preservative, it often is used to mask off flavors of older butter and to extend its shelf life. Evidence of this is the typically bright yellow color of salted butter: it yellows as it oxidizes, so paleness is indicative of a fresher, better tasting product. In addition to flavor, water content is another factor to consider when shopping for butter, especially for sauce and dessert recipes. European butter tends to have a fat content of around 82 percent, the rest being water and milk solids (the curds and whey that rise to the surface and settle to the bottom when butter is melted to clarify it). European pastry dough and butter cream recipes were created using this butter and, not surprisingly, produce good results with it.

American butter, and Californian butter in particular, tends to have a higher water content, and I used to be quite frustrated at how poorly our pastry would come out and how often our butter creams would break when using American butter. Fortunately, in the past ten years, a new European-style butter called Plugras (*plus gras* means "more fat" in French) has been produced and distributed in this country. It has the 82 percent fat content of premium European butter as well as excellent flavor. It won our in-house taste test hands down and produces wonderfully flaky pastry and silken butter creams. We use it in all our recipes calling for butter, and encourage you to use it also, especially in the sauce and dessert recipes. Plugras is becoming more widely available in specialty retail markets; look for it in 8-ounce blocks with a gold wrapper.

Chiles

Dried chiles

Anchos, cascabels, chipotles, and guajillos are among the dried chiles used frequently in Mexican cuisine. They can be purchased at many Mexican markets and by mail from specialty food suppliers (see Sources).

Fresh chiles

At the restaurant, we use primarily poblanos (for stuffing and for cutting into strips for soups) and jalapeños and serranos (for slicing into rings or mincing).

Edible Flowers

Edible flowers are a regular addition to our salads at the restaurant. The blossoms we pick from our garden include borage, calendula, chervil, chives, cilantro, dill, fennel, garlic chives, geraniums, johnny jump-ups, lavatura, nasturtiums, pansies, roses, salvias, and wild radishes. While not an integral flavor component, they add a subtle flavor accent to our greens mix, and their vibrant colors make a pretty garnish.

Fish Stock

Fish stock is an essential ingredient in several recipes in this book, and good a thing to know how to make. While you can often substitute bottled clam juice, the juice is often saltier and lacking in flavor, and this stock only takes about a half an hour to make. There are two things to pay attention to in making a good fish stock: selecting fresh bones and using finely chopped vegetables. Get your fish bones right at the fishmonger's or, if you're cleaning the fish yourself, throw the heads and bones into fresh water until the excess blood leaches out. As for the vegetables, they need to be finely chopped because the stock doesn't cook that long, and you want to be sure to get the maximum flavor out of them. I've found that pulsing them in a food processor works well.

Fish Stock:

Makes 3¹/₃ cups

2 pounds fish heads and bones (preferably from non-oily whitefish, such as sole, halibut, or rockfish)

3 tablespoons light olive oil or peanut oil

¹/₃ cup peeled and finely chopped shallots (about 2)

1¹/₂ cups washed and chopped mushrooms (about 3 ounces)

¹/₂ cup washed and chopped celery, leaves included (about 1 rib)

³/₄ cup washed and chopped leek, white and green parts (1 small or ¹/₂ medium leek)

¹/₂ teaspoon sea salt

¹/₂ teaspoon whole white peppercorns

4 flat-leaf parsley sprigs

2 thyme sprigs

¹/₂ cup dry white wine

6¹/₂ cups water

Split fish heads, chop carcasses, and soak bones in several changes of water to leach out blood.

Heat the oil in a stockpot, add the vegetables, and cook over medium-high heat until soft, about 5 to 7 minutes. Add the fish heads and bones and cook another 5 minutes, stirring occasionally (do not let the vegetables brown). Add salt, peppercorns, herbs, and wine.

Bring to a boil and allow to simmer for 1 minute, then add water. Return to a boil, then reduce heat and simmer for 20 minutes, skimming frequently. Remove from heat, let sit 10 minutes, then strain through a fine sieve or cheesecloth. Measure liquid. If there is more than 3¹/₂ cups, return to heat and simmer until reduced to that amount. Keep 2 to 3 days in the refrigerator; if planning to store longer, keep frozen.

Flour

We use exclusively organic, unbleached flours (all-purpose and pastry). We buy Giusto's organic flour, milled in South San Francisco. Their all-purpose flour is 12 percent protein; the pastry flour is 10 percent protein.

Goat Cheese

Thanks to Laura Chenel and a steadily increasing number of small producers, excellent quality domestic goat cheeses, both fresh and dried, are now commonly available. At the restaurant, we use Laura Chenel's cheeses. When I first started cooking at the Beaujolais, Laura was truly a pioneer in the field, creating the only domestic goat cheese I knew of that compared to the cheeses I learned to adore in France. Although she now is surrounded by worthy competition in the market, we continue to choose her cheeses because her commitment to quality remains a benchmark in the industry.

Pear Vinegar

Pear vinegar is a simple flavored vinegar that we make at the restaurant when our home pear crop arrives in the late summer and early fall. To make your own, take a few ripe, preferably organic pears with a strong aroma (I prefer Bartlett), wash them, and coarsely chop them by hand or pulse them a few times in a food processor to roughly chop them up. Transfer the pears to a large, clean glass or plastic container with a lid and add enough white wine vinegar to cover the pears generously (by at least 2 inches). Stir the mixture once or twice, then cover and set aside in a cool, dark place for at least a couple of days—preferably a week or longer—to infuse. To use, either pour or ladle the vinegar off the top (the pear pieces should be settled in the lower part of the mixture), or pour what you need through a fine-mesh sieve to strain out the solids. Top off with enough white wine vinegar to keep the pears covered and return to storage. This vinegar will keep (as long as the vinegar level remains above the pear pieces) for a full year, when you can make a new batch with fresh fall pears.

Recado de Toda Clase

Recado de todo classe is a ground spice mixture. Here's my version, adapted from Diana Kennedy's *The Art of Mexican Cooking*:

1/4 cup black peppercorns

1/2 teaspoon, rounded, whole cloves

1 teaspoon, rounded, allspice berries

1 tablespoon crushed cinnamon bark (approximately one thick 2-inch stick)

3/4 teaspoon cumin seeds, lightly toasted in a dry skillet

1/4 cup dry oregano, preferably Mexican, lightly toasted in a dry skillet

Water to form a paste

Grind all the spices to a powder in an electric spice mill (or with a mortar and pestle). Mix in just enough water to form a paste.

Vegetable Oil

We use canola oil in dishes where a neutral flavor and/or a high smoking point is desired.

Vanilla Sugar

Vanilla sugar is made from ordinary white granulated sugar and used vanilla beans. It is easy to prepare, useful in many desserts, and a great way to get more true vanilla flavor out of expensive beans. It is the vanilla flavoring of choice, along with the beans themselves, of frugal European cooks. Once you have split a fresh vanilla bean, scraped out its seeds, and used the seeds and bean to flavor a liquid (such as milk for a custard) simply rinse off the bean under hot water to remove any milk residue, then dry

it in a low (200°) oven (set a timer so you don't forget it's in there and burn it!). Once it is no longer damp to the touch (it doesn't have to be brittle and desiccated), bury it in an airtight container of sugar, wait a few days, and voilà! The more beans you store in a given volume of sugar, the stronger your vanilla sugar will be. They can be left in the sugar indefinitely. When you use some of the sugar, merely replace what you take with fresh sugar. (You may want to have two containers going so one has a chance to gain flavor while you take from the other.)

Glossary

Achiote seeds: The seeds of the annatto tree, which grows in the Caribbean and on the Yucatán Peninsula of Mexico. They are a brick-red color and have a number of culinary applications. Their most economically significant use is as a coloring agent, for which they are widely used to turn foods, such as cheddar cheese and margarine, yellow or orange. In the cuisine of their native Yucatán, they are commonly ground to a paste that is diluted with Seville orange juice and used in marinades. This achiote paste is available in small packages (which often contain salt, garlic, and other spices) in Mexican and Latin American markets. It is sometimes called *recado rojo*.

Basmati rice: A long-grain white rice originally grown in India, basmati has an appealing flavor and texture. We use organically grown basmati rice in all our recipes calling for white rice, such as Mexican Rice (page 98) and Coconut Rice (page 99). Thai jasmine rice is another long grain white rice whose flavor and texture I enjoy. It has an intriguing, delicate floral aroma which, not surprisingly, goes well with Thai and other Asian food. Unfortunately, we have yet to find it available organically grown.

Chipotle chiles: The smoked form of the spicy jalapeño chile. They are available both dried and canned in adobo sauce. The canned version are available in many supermarkets; both the dried and canned forms are available in Mexican markets.

Coconut milk: Used extensively in Southeast Asian cuisines, much as dairy products are used in northern European–derived cuisines. It is created by soaking the shredded flesh of fresh, ripe coconuts in water and then squeezing the coconut pulp dry, saving the thick, white liquid that is rich in coconut flavor (and fat). It is possible to make fresh coconut milk yourself from either shredded, fresh coconut meat or the dried, shredded coconut (the unsweetened variety) available in health food stores. However, it is a lot of work and this is actually an instance where the canned product, in my experience, is truly superior. (After several years of making my own coconut milk from recipe books, wondering why my Thai dishes didn't taste like those I had in restaurants, and wondering why I always saw cases and cases of the canned product in Thai markets, I finally put it all together. I tried canned coconut milk once, immediately tasted the difference, and have never made it from scratch since!) Canned coconut milk is most commonly sold in 14-ounce cans, which hold a generous 1³/₄ cups liquid measure, and they are widely sold in supermarkets and Asian markets. Our brand of choice is Thai Kitchen because of its consistent quality and because it is processed without preservatives.

Dried shrimp: An ingredient used in tropical cuisines around the globe. In this country, they are sold in small plastic bags (usually weighing 2 or 4 ounces) in some supermarkets and most Mexican and Thai or Southeast Asian markets. The Asian shrimp tend to be smaller than their Mexican counterpart. They have a strong flavor and chewy texture that can be an acquired taste to palates not familiar with them. At the restaurant, in dishes such as Dried Shrimp Pozole (page 64) and Zanzibar Fish Soup (page 68), we grind half of the shrimp to a powder. The dish benefits from their full flavor, which is fabulous with the chiles and tomatoes in those soups, but the texture is more balanced with fewer whole shrimp to chew on.

Epazote: A pungent annual herb used frequently in authentic Mexican dishes. It is sometimes available in Mexican markets in this country. If you are unfamiliar with its flavor, don't be put off by your initial reaction. Although it smells and tastes somewhat of kerosene by itself, it is a wonderful flavor catalyst when used in small quantities with bean and corn dishes. If you have trouble finding it, you might choose to grow your own. It grows like a weed in warm weather and reseeds readily. Seeds can be purchased from specialty garden stores or by mail from Nichols Garden Nursery, Inc., 1190 North Pacific Hwy., Albany, OR 97321; phone (541) 928-9280. If not available fresh, omit.

Fish sauce: Made from fermented anchovies and salt, this sauce is used throughout Southeast Asia as a principal seasoning. It is available in most supermarkets and all Asian markets. In a pinch, soy sauce may be substituted, but it does not have quite the same flavor.

Foie gras: The fattened liver of large Muscovy or Moulard ducks and geese has been consumed as a great delicacy in western Europe, especially in France, for centuries. Traditionally, both goose and duck livers were marinated and cooked whole in a terrine, then served chilled and sliced, with the classic rendition, *pâté de foie gras*, becoming so renowned that to this day foie gras and pâté are synonymous in many people's minds. In the past twenty years, however, there has been a growing trend to treat foie gras as they traditionally have in southwestern France: to use duck foie gras to the exclusion of goose, and to slice it raw, sauté the slices, and serve them warm. Before the early 1980s, fresh foie gras was not available in the United States: it could only be imported in canned form from Europe, as it was illegal here to force-feed poultry in the manner required to produce it. Fortunately for American chefs and connoisseurs, in the past fifteen years, duck farmers—first in upstate New York and then in Northern California—have learned to produce foie gras that met with USDA approval.

Galangal: Related to ginger, this rhizome is available fresh in many Asian markets, as well as many upscale produce departments and markets. It is used frequently in Thai cuisine, especially with seafood. It is also often available in Asian markets (especially Thai markets) dried in small packages, both sliced and powdered. If it is available fresh, buy it that way, even if the recipe you are preparing calls for dried. It is easy to dry yourself and will have a much fresher flavor that way. To dry fresh galangal, slice it across the grain as thinly as you can by hand or using a mandoline, then lay the slices in one layer on a baking sheet. If you own an electric dehydrator, follow its directions to dry the slices. If you have a gas oven, set the galangal slices in the oven with the pilot light on overnight. If you have an electric oven, set it at its lowest setting, put the pan of slices in the oven, and check on them every hour until they are ready. The slices should be completely dry to the touch or they will mold in storage. Once dried, they may be stored in a clean, dry jar with a lid, in a cool dark place, until needed. If galangal is unavailable either fresh or dried, substitute fresh or dried ginger.

Hominy: The product of tough feed, or field corn. In contrast to sweet corn that is tender and best eaten fresh, field corn is palatable to humans only once it has been dried, soaked with lime (calcium oxide, also know as quicklime—not the citrus fruit!), and cooked. Once this has been done, it can be consumed in a variety of ways. Coarsely ground into hominy grits, it is the basis of a popular porridge in the South, with a texture similar to polenta. Ground into masa in Mexican cuisine, it is used to make corn tortillas and the filling for chile rellenos. Left whole, hominy is a wonderful, toothsome component of the popular Mexican brothy stews known as *pozoles* (in fact, the Mexican word *pozole* means both the whole corn kernels we call hominy and the stew containing them). Although whole, cooked hominy is available canned in most supermarkets and all Mexican markets, you will create the most delicious pozole by preparing your own from the dried product. Dried hominy and powdered lime, known as *mais para pozole* and *cal* respectively, are available in bulk in most Mexican markets and some tortillerias.

To prepare dried hominy for cooking, place 1 cup of hominy in a small pot with 2 cups of cold water. Dissolve 2 teaspoons of powdered lime in a little water and add it to the pot. Bring to a simmer and simmer strongly, until the skins have turned bright yellow and can be easily rubbed off the kernels, about 20 to 30 minutes. Allow the hominy to cool slightly, then drain it in a colander and transfer it to a bowl of cold water. Rub the kernels between your hands until the skins have been removed. Change the water several times during this process to wash away the skin residue. Rinse the hominy again and, with the tip of a paring knife or with your thumbnail, remove the pedicels (the small, hard tip of the kernel where it was attached to the cob). One cup of dried hominy will yield 1 cup of prepared hominy, which will expand to about 2 cups when cooked.

Huitlacoche (pronounced "wheat-la-koh-chay," and sometimes spelled *cuitlacoche*): A fungus (or, to be botanically precise, a smut) that attacks corn, swelling the kernels and turning them a silvery gray-black color. It is unappealing to look at, but unusual and delicious to eat. Considered a great delicacy in Mexico for centuries, huitlacoche is finally catching on in this country. Look for it during corn season at farmers' markets or specialty produce stores. Or, try asking a corn farmer about it after a summer rain or an especially foggy or humid period, because, like wild mushrooms, it usually appears in moist conditions.

Kaffir lime leaves: The leaves of a variety of lime tree (*citrus hystrix*) indigenous to Southeast Asia. Both the leaves and peel of the fruit (but, surprisingly, not the juice) are used extensively in the cuisines of the region. Their distinctly floral lime flavor is one of the distinguishing characteristics of Thai food in particular, and the leaves are available in American Thai markets. If you don't know what to look for, ask for *bai makrut*. The leaves are sold in small bags dried, frozen, and, recently, sometimes fresh. If only dried are available, substitute grated lime zest instead. The fresh leaves will be the most fragrant, but frozen leaves also work well.

Lemongrass: A reed with a distinctive lemony flavor and a very tough, fibrous, grass-like texture. Only the inner core, finely sliced or chopped, is tender enough to eat, though the outer leaves can be used to infuse soups and stocks. It is increasingly available, even organically grown, in supermarket produce departments and most Asian markets. There is no substitute.

Orange flower water: Sometimes called orange blossom water, this fragrant flavoring can be found in the spice department and/or the liquor department of many supermarkets. It tastes much as you would expect it to—floral and orangey. At the restaurant, we use it primarily in dishes with a North African flavor, such as Seafood Couscous (page 138), but it can also be added to apple desserts, such as Pear and Apple Crisp (page 150), for a subtle and unusual accent. Just be careful not to add so much that its floral component is overpowering!

Pancetta: Pork belly that is cured in an Italian manner, by skinning and rubbing with salt, sugar, and spices, and rolled into a log shape to cure. Unlike most bacon, it is not smoked; rather, it has its own distinctive flavor from the spice rub, which can be delicious. It is available in many meat departments and delicatessens. Try out several brands to find your favorite. Pancetta can vary considerably in saltiness; if the brand you buy tastes too salty, blanch it briefly in plain water before cooking it as directed.

Parmesan cheese: A product we use with gusto at the restaurant because of my fondness for pasta and risotto. We use imported Parmigiano-Reggiano. You may wish to substitute sharp, aged grating cheeses, such as Romano, Asiago, dry Jack, and aged goat cheeses, which can also be delicious. Whatever grating cheese you choose, grate it fresh yourself whenever possible.

Prosciutto: An Italian-style air-cured ham that is so popular these days it scarcely needs an explanation here. I mention it, though, because the flavor and texture variation between true, imported Italian prosciutto, which has only been allowed into this country relatively recently, and some domestic versions is extreme. Not that all domestic-cured prosciuttos are bad, but because so many are somewhat to significantly inferior, I encourage you either to splurge on authentic imported prosciutto, or to be highly selective when shopping among domestic brands.

Pickled garlic: Available in small jars in most Thai markets.

Shao-hsing: A type of aged, fortified rice wine used frequently in Chinese cuisine, it looks and tastes more like dry sherry than like the other common rice wine, sake. Shao-hsing is used in Chinese cooking much as fortified wines (sherry, port, Madeira, and Marsala) are used in European-based cuisines. If unavailable, substitute dry sherry.

Soybean oil with chili: Sold in jars in Thai markets, it blends the ingredients of soy, sesame, and chiles in a flavor amalgam that will be recognized by fans of Thai soups and sauces.

Star anise pods: Can be found in the spice departments of many Asian markets and some health food stores and supermarkets. The mellow, appealing licorice flavor of these small, brown seed pods appears regularly in Chinese seasoning. They also taste superb with pears and vanilla.

Sticky rice: Also called glutinous rice, this especially starchy variety of rice is popular in northeastern Thailand. It can be found in Thai markets in both short- and long-grain versions. In Thai restaurants, it is most often served for dessert with sweetened coconut milk and fresh mango slices, although if you ask, you can often get it unsweetened to accompany your meal. It is soaked and then steamed, resulting in a pleasantly chewy texture that is very different from that of regular "steamed" rice, which is actually boiled. Since first tasting sticky rice in Thailand, I have grown increasingly fond of it, and we usually serve it with our Thai-style curries at the restaurant.

Stroh rum: An Austrian rum made from beet sugar (Caribbean rums are distilled from cane sugar), which gives it a wonderfully distinctive butterscotch-like flavor, perfect in many desserts. It is available in this country in specialty liquor stores. Unfortunately, it costs much more here than in Austria, but because it is very strong (80 percent alcohol) with a concentrated flavor, a little goes a long way.

Thai curry pastes: Can be found in a variety of flavors and packages in Thai markets. When we use commercial curry pastes, we purchase the type that come in resealable plastic tubs: they have good flavor and are convenient: My favorite is panang curry paste. However, if you have the time to prepare your own pastes from scratch, you will be rewarded by the flavor difference. Thai curry paste recipes can be found in virtually all Thai cookbooks; I especially recommend those in Bruce Cost's excellent book, *Asian Ingredients*.

Tomatillos: Also called *tomates verdes*, these fruits are a staple of Mexican cuisine and are quickly establishing a widespread popularity and availability in this country. They can now be found in many farmers' markets, greengrocers, and upscale supermarket produce departments. They resemble small tomatoes in shape, although they grow within a papery husk, and their color ranges from dark green to a paler, whitish green and even yellow as they ripen. (There is also a purple variety that is striking, but bear in mind that the fruit will turn green when cooked.) Tomatillos are quite tart, but, as they ripen, develop a nice sweetness to balance their acidity. When shopping for tomatillos, look for those that are firm and fill their paper casings to the point of bursting out—that is when they are at their ripest and sweetest.

Truffles and truffle products: Can be purchased from some specialty food stores and by mail directly from some importers (see Sources). Fresh truffles are imported only in the European winter season, usually from mid to late November through the end of February. If fresh truffles aren't available, ask for flash-frozen, which are available year-round. They are almost as expensive as fresh and have very good truffle flavor; however, they won't perfume their surroundings with their flavor in the way a fresh truffle will. They are also usually only sold in 7-ounce packages, so you may want to organize some friends for a communal purchase. Canned truffles are the least expensive type and the biggest gamble. If they are very high quality, or home-canned, they can be good, but sadly they often prove to be virtually tasteless.

Truffle butter is usually available from the same specialty food sources as fresh and flash-frozen truffles. Truffle butter is the most economical, consistently flavorful, convenient-to-use-and-store truffle product that I know of; I recommend it highly. Other truffle products include juice, sauce, and oil. Truffle juice is a product of the canning process and seems to be of similarly inconsistent quality. If the juice was made from the first cooking of fresh truffles it can be sensational; unfortunately, like whole canned truffles, it often ranges from mediocre to worthless. The sauce and oil are comparable in flavor quality and consistency to the butter, but are much more expensive. If you are splurging on fresh truffles, don't bother purchasing any of these other products. Instead, wash your fresh truffle(s) and allow to marinate for a few days, refrigerated, in olive oil and you will have your own truffle oil! (If you are preparing Joël Robuchon's Truffled Herb Salad (page 78) use this oil in the dressing.)

Verjus: The French name for the tart juice of underripe wine grapes, *verjus* literally means "green juice." It was widely used in the Middle Ages in marinades and sauces, when it was readily available to vineyard tending families and safer to have around than vinegar, since the bacteria responsible for turning wine into vinegar can easily spread to wine not intended for vinegar. It is still used commercially in France, most significantly in authentic Dijon mustard (the white "wine" in those jars labeled "made from white wine" is actually verjus). In the past ten years, it has undergone a renaissance of popularity both in France and the U.S. Our friends at Navarro Vineyards in Mendocino County's Anderson Valley have been producing verjus for us from their Chardonnay grapes for nearly eight years. We have developed a number of recipes for it that we use in-house, some of which are compiled in an attractive booklet accompanying bottles of Navarro Verjus. Navarro Vineyards sells these bottles at the winery and from their mail order catalog; we also have it available through the Cafe Beaujolais Bakery mail order catalog (see Sources) and at the restaurant. I've heard that someone in the Napa Valley is also producing it now in much larger quantities, so I suspect it will become increasingly available at the retail level through wineries and fancy food shops.

Sources

Mexican Ingredients

Casa Lucas Market

2934 24th Street
San Francisco, CA 94110
(415) 826-4334

A good selection of dried chiles, spices, and hominy, as well as canned and frozen produce.

La Palma

2884 24th Street
San Francisco, CA 94110
(415) 618-5500

A few doors down from Casa Lucas and a source of prepared *masa* and *cal* (lime) for preparing your own hominy.

Southeast Asian Ingredients

Erawan Market

1463 University Ave.
Berkeley, CA 94702
(510) 849-9707

The best source we've found in the Bay Area for Thai ingredients, especially Kaffir lime leaves and galangal.

Bangkok Grocery

3226 Geary Blvd.
San Francisco, CA 95404
(415) 221-5863

Phnom Penh

9234 Petaluma Hill Road
Santa Rosa, CA 95404
(707) 545-7426

Duck, Game, Foie Gras, and Veal

Western Foie Gras Distributing Co.

P.O. Box 5184
Santa Rosa, CA 95402
(707) 573-0728

Muscovy duck foie gras, legs, breasts, and fat

D'Artagnan, Inc.

399–419 Saint Paul Ave.
Jersey City, NJ 07306
(800) DARTAGN
(201) 792-0748
Fax: (201) 792-0113

Moulard duck foie gras, legs, breasts, and fat

Summerfield Farms

SR4 Box 195A
Brightwood, VA 22715
(703) 948-3100

Humanely raised free-range veal (or baby beef to purists, since the calves are allowed to graze in addition to feeding on their mother's milk). Also a source for glace de veau, lamb, pheasant, and seasonal fresh morels.

Epazote Seeds

Nichols Garden Nursery

1190 North Pacific Highway
Albany, OR 97321-4580
(503) 928-9280

Shepherd's Garden Seeds

Order Dept.
30 Irene St.
Torrington, CT 06790
(408) 335-6910 (California)
Fax: (408) 335-2080
(203) 482-3638 (Connecticut)
Fax: (203) 482-0532

The Redwood City Seed Company

P.O. Box 361
Redwood City, CA 94064

Huitlacoche

Glenn Burns

16158 Hillside Circle
Montverde, FL 34756
(407) 469-4490

Bags of huitlacoche (off the cob) sold frozen by the pound and shipped overnight packed in dry ice. Since the word is spreading around this country about huitlacoche, you might try asking organic corn farmers at farmer's markets about it; tell them that if they ever get any smut on their crop you'd love to buy some. However, if local sources don't pan out, Glenn has considerable experience farming huitlacoche and maintains consistent, excellent quality. As with any of the perishable products listed here, since they must be sent overnight or second day, a large portion of the cost is the shipping, so it behooves you to buy as much as you can at a time. Products such as this and truffle butter keep well in the freezer and are easy to thaw and use in small quantities. Or consider placing a collective order with some foodie friends.

Truffles and Truffle Products

Urbani West

5849 W. Washington Blvd.
Culver City, CA 90018
(800) 5URBANI (587-2264)
(213) 933-8202
Urbani Truffles U.S.A.
Long Island City, NY
(718) 392-5050

Seasonal fresh black and white truffles, and a year-round source of flash-frozen truffles, truffle butter, and truffle oil, as well as a large line of other preserved truffle and wild mushroom products.

Index

• DAUGHTER OF EVENING FOOD •

So here's the situation. In the course of preparing this book (a process that took over five years) more than 200 recipes were developed, modified, tested, tested again, and written up for publication. And when we were all done, the folks at Ten Speed Press said, in effect, "Hey, wait a minute, this book is going to be three inches thick, and have to sell for forty bucks. You've got to cut the number of recipes by half."

Sadly, we did.

But those other recipes, the ones that didn't get in the book, are no less interesting, ("In fact, some of our favorites!," Margaret says), and we'd like to make them available to you, directly from our kitchen to yours.

Here's the deal:

I've taken those 100 or so recipes, together with several new ones from the current season, and had them bound together into a modest book. It's unpretentious in design, it doesn't have as many stories and anecdotes (those are mostly in *this* book), but I think it is safe to say that if you like *Evening Food*, you'll also like *Daughter of Evening Food*.

The only place on earth to get *Daughter of Evening Food* is right from us. The price is $20 postpaid. Send a check or money order to the address listed below and we'll get your copy out as soon as possible.

Thank you,
Chris

P.S. For those of you smitten by computer technology, we're also offering these recipes on a floppy disk, economical in both space and price. Please contact me for up-to-the-minute details.

Christopher Kump, P.O. Box 1130, Mendocino, CA 95460. *Call or fax:* (707) 937-0618. *E-mail:* mfox@mcn.org

The Recipes Include:

• Soft-shell Crab with Toasted Hazelnuts and Pineapple Sage • Chestnut and Wild Mushroom Ragout • Mussel and Celery Root Chowder • Wood Fire–Roasted Corn and Vegetable Soup • Smoked Salmon Salad with Ginger, Chervil, and Lime • Rabbit Rillettes Salad with Toasted Walnuts, Brandied Prunes, and Creamy Blue Cheese Croutons • Duck Leg Braised with Boletus, Tomatoes, and Savory • Pan-Roasted Sturgeon Filet with Truffle Emulsion • Caramelized Apple Clafoutis with Calvados • Austrian-Style Plum Gratin with Rum Sabayon and Poppy Seed Ice Cream • and much, much more.

• SCHLOSS MATZEN •

Have we tantalized you with tales of Austria and our castle bed and breakfast? We've hinted at the wonders of our authentic 12th-century Austrian castle, located in the dramatically beautiful Tyrolean Alps, 30 miles east of Innsbruck and just 40 minutes from the Italian border. In this magnificent spot, which has been our family vacation home for the past forty years, we've hosted such friends and cooking greats as James Beard, Simca Beck and Marion Cunningham. Now we invite you to join us at our castle bed and breakfast inn and share in its myriad treasures. To receive a color brochure of Schloss Matzen, call or fax us at (707) 937-0618, or send us an e-mail at mfox@mcn.org.

• CAFE BEAUJOLAIS MAIL ORDER BAKERY •

Since 1983, the Cafe Beaujolais Bakery has offered distinctive delectables by mail order. These include our popular dark chocolate-covered graham crackers, Pear Barbecue Sauce, and Wild Mendocino Blackberry Jam. Interestingly, though, we're best known for our panforte, an Italian confection dating from the Middle Ages. Panforte di Mendocino is a rich blend of flavor and texture, filled with nuts, spices, honey, and lemon. Call us at (800) 930-0443 or drop us a line at P.O. Box 730-E, Mendocino, CA 95460 for an entertaining catalog.

• BOOKS •

You can order the first two Beaujolais books, *Cafe Beaujolais* and *Morning Food* from us at the address above, or from our publisher. Their address is Ten Speed Press, P.O. Box 7123, Berkeley, CA 94707, (800) 841-BOOK. Call for current mail-order prices.